A HANDBOOK FOR DEVELOPING MULTICULTURAL AWARENESS

THIRD EDITION

Paul Pedersen

5999 Stevenson Avenue
Alexandria, VA 22304

A HANDBOOK FOR DEVELOPING MULTICULTURAL AWARENESS
Third Edition

10 9 8 7 6 5 4 3

American Counseling Association
5999 Stevenson Avenue
Alexandria, VA 22304

Director of Publications
Carolyn C. Baker

Copyeditor
Elaine Dunn

Cover design by Brian Gallagher

Library of Congress Cataloging-in Publication Data

Pedersen, Paul, 1936-
  A handbook for developing multicultural awareness/by Paul Pedersen—3rd ed.
    p. cm.
  Includes bibliographical references and index.
  ISBN 1-55620-177-X (alk.)
    1. Cross-cultural counseling. 2. Minorities—Counseling of. 3. Ethnopsychology.
I. American Counseling Association.   II. Title.
  BF637.C6 P336   2000
  158'.3—dc21   99-055851

I would like to dedicate this book to my colleagues in Taiwan
who greatly increased my own multicultural awareness:
Dr. Jing Jyi Wu, Fulbright Foundation;
Dr. Kwang Kuo Hwang, National Taiwan University;
and Dr. Ping Hua Chen, National Taiwan Normal University.

—Paul Pedersen

TABLE OF CONTENTS

PREFACE

No matter how highly skilled, well trained, or intelligent one is as a counselor, if the counselor is making wrong or culturally inappropriate assumptions, he or she will not be accurate in assessment, understanding, or interventions. The inaccuracy or misattribution resulting from wrong assumptions translates into defensive disengagement by both the provider and consumer of counseling, each trying to protect the truth as he or she perceives it. Developing multicultural awareness is too often classified as a secondary or tertiary prevention strategy. This book examines multicultural awareness training through a three-stage developmental sequence as a primary prevention strategy in counseling.

It is difficult to know the culture of others until and unless one has an awareness of one's own culturally learned assumptions as they control one's life. Counselors dare not assume that they or their colleagues have already achieved a high level of cultural self-awareness. Counselor education frequently minimizes multicultural awareness as a primary foundation of self-awareness. The importance of unexamined, underlying culturally learned assumptions is frequently underestimated by failing to recognize that one's assumptions reflect one's own cultural context.

All behaviors are learned in a cultural context and displayed in a cultural context. Counselors who disregard a client's cultural context are unlikely to interpret a client's behavior accurately. The same behavior across cultures might have a very different interpretation just as different behaviors might have the same interpretation. Therefore, developing multicultural awareness is a primary prevention strategy for counselors who must accurately interpret the meanings of cultural similarities and differences.

The counselor has only two choices: to ignore the influence of culture or to attend to it. In either case, however, culture will continue to influence a client's and a counselor's behavior with or without the counselor's intentional awareness. It seems likely, therefore, that the current trend toward increased multicultural awareness among counselors will become a "fourth force" in the helping professions of the next decade with as profound an impact on counseling as the third force of humanism had on the prevailing psychodynamic and behavioral systems of that time (P. Pedersen, 1998). The multicultural dimension is not competing with other counseling theories. By making culture central to humanism, psychodynamism, and behavioral psychology, those perspectives are strengthened, not weakened.

The importance of culture has been most evident in minority groups' political struggle for equity. Multicultural awareness provides a safe and accurate approach to managing differences across groups in the multicultural populations of the United States. Culture has provided the rationale and "roots" for unifying and defining ethnic populations of Blacks, Asian Americans, Hispanics, Native Americans, and, more recently, White ethnics. The same model has also coalesced support among the elderly, gender groups, physically disabled, gay men, lesbians, and many other special populations. The importance of culture is broader than indicated by any one or two of these special interest groups. Culture provides a metaphor to better understand how people are similar and how they are different across boundaries. Perhaps, more importantly, multicultural awareness provides a metaphor for understanding different perspectives within each person as the thousands of different culturally learned social roles compete, complement, and cooperate with one another in one's internal dialogue (P. Pedersen, 1997b, 1997d).

I make several assumptions as I write this book, some of which are more controversial than others. Let me state these assumptions directly and explicitly.

1. *Culture* is broadly and inclusively defined in the tradition of Geertz (1973), who described culture as "thick description" and "webs of significance." *Thick description* indicates the complexity of culture as a multidimensional construct that could not be captured in simplistic or "thin" descriptive categories. *Webs of significance* indicates the network of cultures attached to other cultures through relationships in a network or "web" that gives each participating cultural strand meaning beyond its isolated independent existence.

2. All counseling takes place in a multicultural context, given the complexity of ethnographic, demographic, status, and affiliation variables in every counseling interview.

3. Culture includes both the more obvious objective and verifiable symbols and the more subjective perspectives hidden within each of us waiting their turn to become salient.

4. Both cultural similarities and differences are equally important in the multicultural perspective to protect against exclusionary stereotyping from a particularist emphasis, on the one hand, or power exploitation through a universalist perspective, on the other hand.

5. The most important elements of multicultural awareness can be learned but cannot be taught. Good teaching can, however, create the favorable conditions for multicultural awareness to occur.

There are many sources of multicultural awareness, knowledge, and skill. Some of those have been identified in this book, and the reader is urged to seek them out for a deeper understanding of specific aspects. Multicultural awareness is too complex a topic for any one book to cover completely. This handbook is intended to guide the reader toward specific publications and resources already available on developing multicultural awareness. However, the reader is given enough information to determine where to go next in the search for multicultural awareness.

This third edition of the handbook is shorter and more streamlined than its previous editions, recognizing the high cost of books and the many different demands on the time of professional counselors reading it. The book does not try to duplicate other excellent and more comprehensive books about multicultural counseling already published. Rather, this handbook is a guide for readers to fill in the gaps of their own "multicultural awareness" about counseling.

The three-stage model of Awareness–Knowledge–Skill is highlighted in chapter 1 to help the reader or the student plan his or her own five-step training plan from a comprehensive needs assessment to an evaluation of what he or she has learned. Some of the rules required to follow in a multicultural perspective are described in detail in chapter 2 to stimulate discussion and in some cases disagreement both among the readers and perhaps with the book author. In any case, this chapter makes the author's assumptions about multiculturalism explicit so that the reader will be able to agree or disagree from the beginning.

The increasingly important field of alternative and complementary therapies is discussed in chapter 3 with regard to underlying assumptions that are different from conventional therapies. Here again, by looking at underlying assumptions, it becomes more possible for the reader to take a clear and unambiguous position on what aspects of alternative therapies can be incorporated into conventional therapy.

The process of developing a cultural identity is covered in chapter 4 with special attention to relational identities, orthogonal models, and some of the more recent developments about identity theory. Some of the previous models for describing cultural systems are presented so that the reader can be informed in discussing those models as well as know where to go to learn more about each model.

Chapter 5 presents culture as a pattern, narrative, or story about who we are and where we came from. Some of these stories involve dispositional values and others learned beliefs about ourselves and the world around us. A personal–cultural orientation is provided in a cultural grid to help us connect the relationships that define us to the individual we are.

Rather than attempt to review the extensive literature on research about multiculturalism, chapter 6 is focused on what we do not know. These unanswered questions submitted by the leading authors in the multicultural literature should stimulate discussion in class, generate research and training projects, suggest dissertation titles, and explore the possibilities in this rich and exciting field.

Chapter 7 looks at ethical bias, particularly in the American Counseling Association Code of Ethics but also in other professional ethical guidelines for counselors. The arguments against simplistic "rule following" and for "ethical thinking" are presented.

Counseling is increasingly focused on constructive conflict management. Chapter 8 looks at how reframing conflict into cultural categories makes conflict easier to manage constructively. Chapter 9 reviews the Triad Training Model as a promising training approach. This chapter presents enough about the model so that the reader can try it out on his or her own in safety, but the reader is referred to P. Pedersen (2000) for more extensive discussion of the Triad Training Model.

Finally, chapter 10 looks at multiculturalism as a "fourth force." It is clear that multiculturalism has had a powerful impact on the field of counseling and that this impact is increasing in importance. Some of the controversies surrounding the role of multiculturalism are presented for discussion.

Many persons have contributed to this handbook. First of all, the sources cited in the volume deserve credit for their extensive publications. No doubt other valuable authors have been inadvertently omitted from this rapidly growing literature on multicultural counseling as our awareness of resources grows and develops. My hope is that this book will lead readers to find examples of how multicultural awareness can make their counseling task easier rather than harder and can increase their satisfaction in working with clients from other cultures.

Parts of chapter 6 were taken from "The Cultural Context of Psychology: Questions for Accurate Research and Appropriate Practice," by P. Pedersen, R. T. Carter, and J. G. Ponterotto, 1996, *Cultural Diversity and Mental Health, 2,* 205–216.

Parts of chapter 7 are from "The Cultural Context of the American Counseling Association Code of Ethics," by P. Pedersen, 1997a, *Journal of Counseling and Development, 76,* 23–29.

Parts of chapter 8 were taken from "Intercultural Understanding: Finding Common Ground Without Losing Integrity," by P. Pedersen, 1999b, in D. Christie, D. Wagner, and D. Winter (Eds.), *Peace, Conflict and Violence: Peace Psychology for the 21st Century,* Englewood Cliffs, NJ: Prentice Hall.

Parts of chapter 10 were published in *Multiculturalism as a Fourth Force,* by P. Pedersen, 1998, Philadelphia, PA: Bruner/Mazel.

ABOUT THE AUTHOR

Paul Pedersen is a professor in the School of Education, Department of Human Studies, Counseling Program, The University of Alabama at Birmingham. He has been on the faculty at Syracuse University, University of Hawaii, University of Minnesota, University of Malaya, and Nommensen University in Indonesia. He taught at Harvard Summer School for 5 years and was director of the National Institute of Mental Health project "Developing Interculturally Skilled Counselors" at the University of Hawaii for 4 years. He was also a Senior Fellow at the East West Center for 5 years and a Fulbright Scholar teaching at National Taiwan University for 1 year. He has written 33 books, 62 chapters, and 92 articles on various aspects of multicultural counseling. More information is available on his Web site: *www.dpo.uab.edu/~pedersen.*

CHAPTER 1

Developing Multicultural Awareness, Knowledge, and Skill

Major objective:

1. To describe a three-stage developmental progression from awareness to knowledge to skill.

Secondary objectives:

1. To describe the five stages of developing a training design.
2. To describe examples of multicultural awareness training.
3. To describe examples of multicultural knowledge training.
4. To describe examples of multicultural skill training.

Developing multicultural awareness is not an end in itself, but rather a means toward increasing a person's power, energy, and freedom of intentional choice in a multicultural world. Multicultural awareness increases a person's intentional and purposive decision-making ability by accounting for the many ways that culture influences different perceptions of the same solution.

Multicultural awareness occurs in a global context. In the 10th Annual United Nations Human Development Report, Jahan (1999) described how globalized technology is a double-edged sword that links and divides. While the Internet now allows 130,000 artisans in 14 Asian, African, and Latin American countries to sell their wares, 75% of schools and many hospitals in South Africa—usually considered the most modernized African country—do not even have a telephone line. Those who are getting most benefits are typically men below 30 years old who have higher incomes. Per capita income has tripled in the last 50 years and child death rates have been cut in half since 1965 while the percentage of children in primary and secondary schools has doubled. On the negative side, globalization has weakened the family and traditional community resources for mutual assistance, especially in the areas of health and mental health. While globalization has increased wealth, it has also contributed to job instability and increased the visibility of organized crime, with illegal drug trade estimated to be $400 billion in 1995. We need to develop multicultural awareness on a globalized scale to respond appropriately to the problems and opportunities of globalization.

Culture is not only external but also "within the person," and it is not separate from other learned competencies. Developing multicultural awareness is therefore a professional obligation as well as an opportunity for the adequately trained counselor. Millions of people today live and work in a culture other than their own. People who live in an unfamiliar culture are likely to become more multicultural in their awareness of alternative values, habits, customs, and lifestyles that were initially strange and unfamiliar. Sometimes they have learned to adjust even more profoundly and effectively than they themselves realize. They have learned to respond in unique ways to previously unfamiliar situations and come up with the right answers without always being aware of their own adjustment process.

In this chapter, a culture-centered approach is described in a three-stage developmental sequence, from multicultural awareness to knowledge and comprehension to skills and applications. First, auditing the assumptions being made by counselors and increasing the level of cultural self-awareness by both the provider and the consumer of counseling services challenge the culturally encapsulated conventions about health and illness. Second, documenting facts and knowledge for increased comprehension is essential to meaningful understanding of a presenting problem in its cultural context and will provide or construct a receptive site for research, training, and direct intervention. Third, generating appropriate intervention skills for bringing about appropriate and effective change will match the skill to the cultural context. The same shared positive values and expectations—common ground—may be expressed differently in each cultural context. By developing multicultural awareness, the counselor is able to interpret the client's behavior in the cultural context in which that behavior was learned and is displayed.

The three-stage developmental sequence of awareness, knowledge, and skills is based on the work of D. W. Sue et al. (1982). The National Institute of Mental Health project titled "Developing Interculturally Skilled Counselors (DISC)" from 1978 to 1981 brought Derald Sue as evaluator, Tony Marsella as director of training, and Paul Pedersen as principal investigator together at the University of Hawaii to review and develop multicultural training programs (P. Pedersen, 1981, 1986). Prior to beginning the grant, Sue, Marsella, and Pedersen examined other multicultural training programs that had failed.

Programs seemed to fail for three reasons. The first reason for failure was when the program overemphasized "awareness" to the point that participants were sick and tired of being made "aware" of cultural bias in an effort that, isolated from knowledge and skill, seemed nonproductive as an end in itself. The second reason for failure was when the program overemphasized knowledge, facts, and information to the point that participants, lacking awareness and skill, could not see how all that information was relevant. The third reason for failure was when the program jumped directly to teaching skills, but the participants, lacking awareness and knowledge, could not tell if their skills were making things better or worse! For that reason, this three-stage developmental sequence from awareness to knowledge to skill was developed as an evaluation framework for all classes, workshops, and training done through the DISC program from 1979 to 1981 (P. Pedersen, 1981).

It is difficult to know the culture of others until and unless you have an awareness of your own culturally learned assumptions as they control your life. Much training and most counselor education programs skip over the primary stage of developing multicultural awareness about a person's underlying assumptions. We dare not assume that we or our colleagues have already achieved a high level of cultural self-awareness because this is an ongoing, incomplete developmental process. The importance of these unexamined underlying assumptions is frequently underestimated. Once you have achieved some degree of self-awareness, both as you perceive yourself and as you are perceived by others, it is appropriate to move to the second level.

The second level involves accumulating information that will result in comprehension. Increased awareness will help you ask the right questions about the facts and information you will need. Increased awareness will also help you, as the counselor, find the similarities and differences between and among the populations being served. Once you have accomplished both cultural self-awareness and accumulated the facts, information, and knowledge necessary to that comprehension, you are ready to identify the appropriate skills you will need.

The third level involves developing culturally appropriate skills. The same skill that is appropriate in one culture may be completely inappropriate in another culture. Because every test and theory was developed in a specific cultural context, it is likely to reflect assumptions implicit in that context and, to a greater or lesser extent, be biased. Culture-centered skill is the ability to use data from culturally biased tests or theories and still apply them appropriately, meaningfully, and helpfully in a variety of other different cultural contexts.

This handbook is an attempt to review the development of multicultural awareness. Readers should benefit from this awareness in two ways. First, reviewing the influence of their own multicultural identity will help readers already living in another culture to better understand their own constantly changing viewpoint. Second, they will be able to anticipate the right questions to ask as they adapt their lifestyle to multicultural alternatives. Increased awareness will provide more freedom of choice to persons as they become more aware of their own multiculturalism.

Multicultural development, as presented in this handbook, is a continuous learning process based on three stages of development. The *awareness* stage emphasizes assumptions about cultural differences and similarities of behavior, attitudes, and values. The *knowledge* stage expands the amount of facts and information about culturally learned assumptions. The *skills* stage applies effective and efficient action with people of different cultures on the basis of the participants' clarified assumptions and accurate knowledge. Multicultural counselors need to be trained in awareness, knowledge, and skill to develop multicultural competency. The five-step training program—needs assessment, objectives, design techniques, training, and evaluation—suggests guidelines for organizing multicultural awareness training (Center for Applied Linguistics, 1982; P. Pedersen, 1983b).

1. Needs Assessment

The first step in structuring an orientation or training program is a needs assessment of awareness, knowledge, and skill. Assessing the level of a trainee's awareness is an important first step. Otherwise the trainer is likely to "scratch where it doesn't itch." Awareness is the ability to accurately judge a cultural situation from both one's own and the other's cultural viewpoint. The trainee should be able to describe a situation in each culture so that a member of that culture will agree with the trainee's perception. Such an awareness will require a trainee to have

- ability to recognize direct and indirect communication styles;
- sensitivity to nonverbal cues;
- awareness of cultural and linguistic differences;
- interest in the culture;
- sensitivity to the myths and stereotypes of the culture;
- concern for the welfare of persons from another culture;
- ability to articulate elements of his or her own culture;
- appreciation of the importance of multicultural teaching;
- awareness of the relationships between cultural groups; and
- accurate criteria for objectively judging "goodness" and "badness" in the other culture.

Assessing the level of a trainee's knowledge becomes important once the trainee's awareness has been corrected and judged to be adequate. If awareness helps the student to ask the "right questions," then knowledge provides access to the "right answers." The increased knowledge and information should clarify the alternatives and reduce the ambiguity in a trainee's understanding about a culture. Learning the language of another culture is an effective way to increase one's information. Anticipating preconceptions and stereotypes from another culture's viewpoint requires knowledge about the myths and widely "understood" perceptions from that culture's viewpoint. It is also important to know the right way to get more information about the culture in question so that the teaching and learning resources will be appropriate.

In a needs assessment to determine the trainee's level of knowledge about a culture, the following questions provide guidelines for measuring knowledge awareness.

1. Does the student have specific knowledge about the culturally defined group members' diverse historical experiences, adjustment styles, roles of education, socioeconomic backgrounds, preferred values, typical attitudes, honored behaviors, inherited customs, slang, learning styles, and ways of thinking?
2. Does the trainee have information about the resources for teaching and learning available to persons in the other culture?
3. Does the trainee know about his or her own culture in relation to the other culture?
4. Does the trainee have professional expertise in an area valued by persons in the other culture?
5. Does the trainee have information about teaching and learning resources regarding the other culture and know where those resources are available?

A great deal of information is necessary before the trainee can be expected to know about another culture. Some assessment of the trainee's level of knowledge prior to training is essential so that the teacher can fill in any gaps with accurate factual information that will allow the trainee to proceed with an accurate and comprehensive understanding of the other culture.

Assessing the level of a trainee's skill becomes important once the trainee's informed awareness is supplemented with factual data about the other culture. Skill becomes the most important stage of all and therefore requires a great deal of preparation in teaching about awareness and knowledge. By teaching a skill, the teacher is enabling the trainee to "do" something that he or she could not do before. It is possible to measure the things a trainee now can do effectively that he or she could not do before training. Skill requires the trainee to do the right thing at the right time in the right way and provides the final test of whether the training has been effective after all.

Skills are difficult to evaluate. Sometimes the suggested solution is not credible to all persons in the other culture. Skill requires the ability to present a solution in the other culture's language and cultural framework. Skill requires the trainee to test stereotypes against real and present situations and to modify them accordingly. Skill requires the trainee to seek agreement on evaluation criteria and to implement change that will cause an improvement.

In a needs assessment to determine the trainee's level of skill development, a trainer might examine several of the following aspects:

1. Does the trainee have appropriate teaching and learning techniques for work in the other culture?
2. Does the trainee have a teaching and learning style that will be appropriate in the other culture?
3. Does the trainee have the ability to establish empathic rapport with persons from the other culture?
4. Is the trainee able to receive and accurately analyze feedback from persons of the other culture?
5. Does the trainee have the creative ability to develop new methods for work in the other culture that will go beyond what the trainee has already learned?

2. Objectives

Once the needs of trainees have been analyzed, the second step is to design appropriate objectives for a training plan. The relative emphasis on awareness, knowledge, or skills will depend on the results of the needs assessment. An awareness objective will change the person's attitudes, opinions, and personal perspectives about a topic. The primary need may be to help groups discover their own stereotypical attitudes and opinions. Usually the awareness objectives focus on a person's unstated assumptions about another culture or about the person in relation to the other culture.

Once clearly stated training objectives are identified, it is useful to look at the awareness aspect, the knowledge aspect, and the skill aspect of each objective. One may, therefore, imagine a matrix in which the same objective will have an awareness aspect, a knowledge aspect, and a skill aspect.

The awareness objectives for multicultural training focuses on changing the trainees' attitudes, opinions, and personal perspectives about themselves and the other culture so that these elements will be in harmony with one another. Specific objectives for multicultural training might be based on several important elements of awareness:

1. Is the trainee aware of differences in cultural institutions and systems?

2. Is the trainee aware of the stress resulting from functioning in a multicultural situation?
3. Does the trainee know how rights or responsibilities are defined differently in different cultures?
4. Is the trainee aware of differences in verbal and nonverbal communication styles?
5. Is the trainee aware of significant differences and similarities of practices across different cultures?

In identifying the training objectives for a particular group, one should proceed from an analysis of the group members' awareness needs to their knowledge or information needs and finally to their skill needs. It is important to identify the needs from the group's viewpoint rather than that of outsiders.

The knowledge component for developing multicultural objectives focuses on increasing the amount of accurate information available to the trainee. Having developed a correct and accurate awareness of the other culture, trainees enrich that awareness by testing attitudes, opinions, and assumptions against the body of factual information they now control. The trainees' level of awareness is certain to increase in direct proportion to the extent of their knowledge about the other culture. Specific objectives for multicultural teaching might be based on several knowledge perspectives:

1. Does the trainee know the other culture's historical background?
2. Does the trainee know about social services and how they are delivered to needy and deserving members of the culture?
3. Does the trainee know about the theory of culture shock and stages of cultural adaptation as they relate to the other culture?
4. Does the trainee know how the other culture interprets its own rules, customs, and laws?
5. Does the trainee know patterns of nonverbal communication and language usage within the other culture?
6. Does the trainee know how differences and similarities are patterned in the other culture and how priorities are set in different critical situations?

The skill objective for developing multicultural objectives focuses on what the trainees can now do. If any of the previous training about awareness and knowledge is missing or inadequate, the trainees will have difficulty making right decisions in multicultural communication. If awareness has been neglected, they will build their plan on wrong assumptions. If knowledge has been neglected, they will describe the cultural situation inaccurately. If skill has been neglected, they may well change a situation in counterproductive directions. Specific objectives for developing multicultural objectives for skills might be based on several important perspectives:

1. Is the trainee able to gain access to social services and resources in the community that will satisfy the trainee's basic needs?
2. Is the trainee able to cope with stress and manage difficulties in the new culture?
3. Is the trainee able to understand consequences of behavior and choose wisely among several options that the other culture presents?
4. Is the trainee able to use the culture's language to react appropriately to others from that culture?
5. Is the trainee able to function comfortably in the new environment without losing her or his own cultural identity in the home culture?

These are a few examples of skills objectives that must be assessed to ensure that the trainee has been taught to communicate in the other culture. Many additional skills will be developed for each specific situation.

3. Design Techniques

The third step in developing a training program is to design a plan that shows how the identified objectives will be carried out in such a way that the identified needs will be met. There are many different ways to match techniques with awareness, knowledge, or skill objectives. Some examples follow.

Techniques to Stimulate Awareness

- Experiential exercises such as
  Role plays
  Role reversals
  Simulations
- Field trips to other cultures in the community
- Critical incidents about the problems that come up across cultures
- Observation of the experiences culturally different people have
- Questions/answers/discussion with resource persons from the community

Teaching increased awareness frequently relies on experiential exercises such as role plays, role reversals, or simulations of multicultural interaction. Other approaches include field trips to areas where the culture exists normally on a day-to-day basis. Sometimes critical incidents or brief case studies from the culture can be analyzed to increase a trainee's awareness of the culture. A resource person or informant from the culture enables effective bicultural observation whereby both individuals and groups may exchange questions and answers in a thorough discussion. Almost any approach that challenges the trainee's basic assumptions, tests the trainee's prevailing attitudes, and elicits the trainee's implicit opinions about the culture will serve to increase the trainee's awareness.

Techniques to Impart Knowledge

- Guided self-study with reading list
- Lecture and discussion
- Panel discussion
- Audiovisual presentations
- Interviews with consultants and experts
- Observations

The increase of multicultural knowledge frequently relies on books, lectures, and classroom techniques. Guided self-study with a reading list also is an effective way to help trainees increase their knowledge. Panel discussions about the other cultures help trainees absorb more information relevant to their particular situation. Audiovisual presentations, when available, provide valuable knowledge. Interviews with consultants or resource persons and experts knowledgeable about the other culture help trainees fill in gaps where accurate information might otherwise be impossible to secure. Simply observing persons from the other culture in their daily activities is an important means for learning about the culture, provided the trainee knows what to look for.

Increasing knowledge about multicultural skills takes many forms. Modeling and demonstrating a skill is an effective means of developing the skill in trainees. When available, audiovisual resources provide important feedback to trainees both about how the skill is performed in the other culture and about how they are doing in modeling that skill. Supervising trainees' work in the other culture provides a valuable ongoing means of assessing developing levels of skill. The opportunity to practice new skills and behaviors enables trainees to improve their skill in a variety of situations.

Techniques to Develop Skills

- Modeling and demonstration of counseling microskills
- Using video and media resources for feedback to and from other cultures
- Supervising and/or being supervised by someone from another culture
- Practicing a new behavior pattern to target intentional change
- Practicing writing skills to describe other cultures as they see themselves

The increase of multicultural skills is often premature before the trainee has acquired competence in awareness and knowledge. The standard counseling skills are very relevant when they are based on a foundation of multicultural awareness and knowledge in sequence. It is important to realize that "one size does not fit all" and that each skill must be adapted and adjusted to each cultural context.

4. Training Approaches

The fourth step in developing a training package is the actual implementation of a training design. After determining the date, time, place, and cost of the training, the trainer needs to draft an agenda, check supplies, and locate physical facilities for training. Trainers need to select resource participants or guest speakers and gather relevant resource materials. Preparation should include assembling packets or workbooks so that all the information conveyed to trainees verbally is also available in writing for later clarification. Finally, the trainer needs to develop evaluations of the training.

Most training workshops begin in more or less the same way. There is an introduction with some attempt to break the ice. This might include a formal welcome from an official host or an informal welcome by the workshop leader. A discussion of the group's objectives and expectations as well as sharing of the trainer's objectives and expectations ensues. Then the agenda is reviewed so that all of the participants know what is likely to happen in sequence; this helps them to review the materials in their workshop packet for any necessary clarification. The better trainees are prepared to work with one another, the more positively they are likely to view the training experience.

Once these general group-building tasks have been completed, the workshop may begin by emphasizing a balance of appropriate objectives focused on awareness and planning data. Each of these three alternative components (awareness, knowledge, and skill) will suggest a different training format.

In training for awareness, you should help trainees to become aware of the contrast and conflict between their background and that of the target population. In training for knowledge, you should help trainees to have knowledge of the target population, including institutions at national, regional, and local levels. In training for skill, you should help trainees to bring about appropriate change by working with interpreters and cultural informants.

5. Evaluation

The fifth and last step of a training sequence is evaluating whether the persons you trained have met your objectives in awareness, knowledge, and skill. This is called *formative* evaluation. Another kind of evaluation is a long-term and much more complicated evaluation to verify whether or not your objectives were appropriate and met the long-term needs of your target group. This second type of evaluation is called *summative* evaluation.

Evaluation methods range from informal discussions over wine and cheese to formal written evaluations of long-term changes in productivity determined by random work samples. However you proceed, you should allow room for evaluation in your training activities. These data will be valuable to your trainees in giving them feedback on their accomplishment, valuable to you in demonstrating the strength or weakness of your design, and valuable to those sponsoring the training activity as a basis for making decisions. The following are some of the criteria for evaluating.

Trainees are trained to increase their *awareness* so they will:

1. Appropriately recognize the valued priority they give to basic attitudes, opinions, and assumptions.
2. Accurately compare their own cultural perspective with that of a person from the other culture.
3. Sensitively articulate their own professional role in relation to the other culture.
4. Appropriately estimate constraints of time, setting, and resources in the other culture.
5. Realistically estimate the limit of their own resources in the other culture.

Trainees are trained to increase their *knowledge* so they will:

1. Understand the process of institutional change in the other culture at local, national, and regional levels.
2. Cite the relevant literature of the other culture.
3. Identify similarities and differences of their own home culture and the other cultures.
4. Identify referral resources in the other culture.
5. Select key resource persons from the other culture for more information.

Trainees are trained to increase their *skill* so they will:

1. Efficiently plan, conduct, and evaluate training about the other culture.
2. Accurately assess the needs of a person from the other culture.
3. Utilize the talents of interpreters and cultural informants from the other culture.
4. Observe, understand, and accurately report about culturally learned behaviors in the other culture.
5. Interact, advise, and appropriately manage their assigned task in the setting of the other culture.

Multicultural development is presumed to proceed from an awareness of attitudes, opinions, and assumptions to a knowledge of facts and information to skill in taking the appropriate action. Most persons being trained, however, are at different stages of development. Some trainees will require more emphasis on awareness, some more emphasis on knowledge, and others can proceed directly to skill development.

6. Examples of Multicultural Awareness Training

Training is an attempt to increase a person's alternatives for being accurately understood in a wide variety of cultures. Multicultural training of counselors must be responsive to the variety of cultures within both the client and the counselor. The benefits of multicultural training are measured by their relevance to real-life situations. The more culturally defined alternatives or strategies a counselor possesses, the more likely that the counselor will identify the right choice in culturally different settings (P. Pedersen & Ivey, 1993). A variety of multicultural training approaches have been used to prepare counselors to work in other cultures. These various approaches can be classified according to their emphasis on awareness, knowledge, or skill as the primary focus. An examination of examples for training will help clarify the specific emphasis at each developmental level.

Awareness requires the ability to accurately see a situation from one's own and the other person's perspective. Several multicultural counselor training approaches emphasize awareness through experiential learning, cultural awareness, and specific cultural values clarification.

Experiential learning allows participants to "experience" the effect of cultural similarities and differences through their own involvement with others. The assumption is that increased involvement in the lifestyle of culturally different people through field trips and direct or simulated contact will increase the trainee's accuracy of judgments, attitudes, and assumptions about other cultures. A counselor educator facilitates this involvement by providing a "safe" setting in which the trainee can and will take risks. Having a significant intercultural experience through immersion, field trips, or role-playing is not, by itself, enough. The trainee needs to analyze the effect of that experience to "capture" the resulting insights for future reference.

Cultural immersion requires the trainee to live and work in another culture and learn by experience alongside culturally different persons. Any contact with culturally different persons or groups can provide the opportunity for learning through immersion. Some counselors have become highly skilled without any formal training by learning through their own mistakes and triumphs. Unguided immersion is an effective training approach, although learning from experience without any preparation tends to be expensive in time, money, and emotional stress for the client as well as the counselor.

Field trips provide a less traumatic example of experiential training through brief visits to other cultures on their home turf. Many aspects of a host culture can be learned by observation but cannot be "taught" through abstract principles. Trainees visiting a host culture can become participant observers in that host culture in its own home context. By observing people from the host culture cope with problems and make decisions, the trainee is able to recognize culturally distinctive patterns of activity. To be effective, field trips require skilled debriefing to help the trainee articulate what was learned. There are two types of field trips possible. The first type is organized around a specific agenda. These field trips need to be organized around a specific focus to illustrate or challenge specific attitudes, opinions, and assumptions from one or both cultures. The second type is to deliberately avoid any agenda preconception or expectation before the experience and let the insights grow out of the interaction itself.

Role-playing is another frequently used experiential training approach in which an individual learns about other cultures by taking on the role of a person from that culture. The experience of becoming someone from the other culture, to the extent that is possible, often changes a participant's level of awareness. This approach usually relies on articulate and authentic resource persons from the host culture to guide the trainee. It is easy to find resource persons who are authentic but not articulate or articulate but not authentic. It is more difficult to find resource persons who are both articulate and authentic. When asked how they manage to do such a good job, skilled but untrained resource persons frequently respond: "I can't tell you or teach you how to do it but I can demonstrate for you what I would do if you give me a problem situation." In any case, the trainer must provide careful structures to guide the learning through role-playing, both to provide a safe context in which the role player might take risks and to generate insights about the other culture.

Experiential approaches to awareness training are expensive and require highly skilled trainers as well as cooperative host culture resource persons. Experiential training works when participants feel safe enough to take risks. If the experience becomes unsafe, the trainee will experience high levels of stress that might be counterproductive to training and potentially dangerous to the participants. If the trainee feels "unsafe," he or she will not take risks, and without taking risks little learning will occur. Sometimes the awareness is focused on cultural processes, and at other times it is focused on a specific cultural content.

Culture-general approaches help people articulate their own implicit cultural attitudes, opinions, and assumptions about themselves. Self-awareness emphasizes the values of a person's home culture as contrasted with the values of many other cultures. The emphasis is usually on areas of general similarity and difference. Our own cultural values are frequently so familiar that we are not explicitly aware of them. In some cultures, for example, the importance of individualism is not seen as "cultural" but simply "the way things naturally are." Brislin, Cushner, Cherrie, and Young (1998) described 18 culture-general themes for training, illustrating how each person believes that his or her perspective is assumed to be the normal and universal perspective: culture-general experiences (1–5), knowledge areas (6–13), and ways of organizing information (14–18). These themes include (1) anxiety, (2) disconfirmed expectancies, (3) belonging, (4) ambiguity, (5) confrontation with one's prejudices, (6) work, (7) time and space, (8) language, (9) roles, (10) importance of the group and importance of the individual, (11) rituals and superstitions, (12) hierarchies of class and status, (13) values, (14) categorization, (15) differentiation, (16) ingroup–outgroup distinction, (17) learning style, and (18) attribution. This culture-general approach has gained considerable popularity.

Culture-specific approaches require training in the specific values of a particular target culture. Culture-specific training is usually limited in focus to the particular target group and has a very specific focus. Learning the language of a host culture, for example, is an important culture-specific way of learning about the attitudes, opinions, and assumptions in that particular culture. Other examples include learning the behaviors, expectations, and values of that particular culture. Most professional counseling associations have indicated that counselors who work with specific other cultures without culture-specific awareness about that culture are behaving in an unethical manner.

A variety of other awareness training approaches focus on the trainee's self-awareness and awareness of the trainee's home culture. This awareness will emphasize both similarities and differences by contrasting the home culture with one or more other cultures. The emphasis of awareness training is always on reevaluating the trainee's attitudes, opinions, and assumptions about his or her own culture and other cultures.

7. Examples of Multicultural Knowledge Training

Increasing the counselor's knowledge about other cultures is another popular focus for multicultural training. Knowledge training means having correct and sufficient information about one's own as well as target cultures. The most frequently used knowledge training approaches are through publications, reading materials, audio and visual media, and presenting the other cultures to the trainee in terms of facts and information.

Classroom training emphasizes lectures, group discussions, written materials, and media presentations to help trainees increase their information about other cultures. Trainees are provided with factual information about the host culture to understand their own role as outsiders. These facts might relate to socioeconomic, political, or social structures; the climate and physical setting; the decision-making styles and habits; or the values underlying daily behavior. Classroom training provides models and structures for organizing, classifying, and analyzing other cultures.

The facts themselves will be most useful if trainees are highly motivated to learn the new information and see an immediate relevancy of these facts for their own situation. It is essential that the factual data be based on an awareness of why the data are important to trainees. Unless the trainees have adequate awareness, they are unmotivated to learn information about the other cultures. Trainees who have achieved awareness of the target culture in relation to themselves will be prepared to document that awareness in the facts and information describing similarities and differences. With appropriate preparation, trainees can become highly motivated to increase their knowledge through learning facts and information-oriented training.

Attribution training is a second form of knowledge-based training that has proved to be successful. Attribution training methods guide the trainee to explain behavior from the host culture's viewpoint rather than from their own self-reference. Presented with a critical incident or paragraph-length description of an event, the trainee chooses between several alternative explanations "attributed" to the incident. One of the attributed explanations offered to the trainee is more accurate than the others for specific reasons. Trainees are coached to select the most accurate and appropriate attribution through practice in analyzing a series of critical incidents. This method assumes that trainees will learn a culture's implicit patterns of decision making through attribution training, in which they can generalize from the critical incidents to unfamiliar cultures and situations. Brislin et al. (1998) provided 100 critical incidents using attribution training methods in a culture-general approach.

The best-known application of attribution training is the *culture assimilator* developed by Harry Triandis and others (Triandis, 1975). Many different culture assimilators have been designed for specific cultures and social groups, resulting in a great deal of research and evaluation data. There are probably more data on the culture assimilator than any other cross-cultural training approach. Culture assimilators provide a structured series of incidents and alternative responses in a specific cultural context with a series of explanations or attributions. One of the alternative attributions is more accurate and appropriate than the others. Each alternative is matched with explanations to explain the rightness, wrongness, and consequences of each choice. To the extent that culturally accurate and appropriate attributions can be determined for each situation, the culture-specific culture assimilator has been generally successful.

In addition to the formal knowledge-training approaches, there is also an informal alternative in which the individual, who has achieved a high level of awareness, looks for her or his own answers. One sign of having achieved awareness is increased sensitivity to the implicit culture perspective in all reported facts and information. We are accumulating cultural facts and information whether we are aware or not as we are socialized by the media and other public sources of facts or information. Self-guided training will provide purpose to the accumulation of facts and information through reading, observation, and reflective experiences. These facts may be accumulated about a specific other culture, one's self, or cultures that generally contrast with one's own understanding. A purposive program for self-guided learning about other cultures can be an inexpensive and very effective approach. If "awareness" training articulates the questions we ought to be asking, then "knowledge" training guides us toward comprehensive answers to those questions. Students in my cross-cultural course will frequently come to me and exclaim: "Have you noticed how the news recently has put so much emphasis on culture!"

8. Examples of Multicultural Skill Training

Multicultural skill goes beyond *knowing* what needs to be done to being able to actually do it. Skill training provides the multicultural counselor with the strategies to match the right method to the right situation in the right way at the right time. Because multicultural skills are based on awareness and knowledge, they require cognitive comprehension and affective sensitivity as well as behavioral facility to interact with the trainee's complex and dynamic cultural context. There are many different examples of these more comprehensive and "general" multicultural skill training approaches.

Cognitive or behavioral modification training depends on identifying rewards or goals in the trainee's cultural context from the client's viewpoint. Once you find out what the trainee wants, it is easier to teach the trainee acceptable ways of getting it. When the trainee moves to an unfamiliar culture, the more familiar strategies that worked before might not work as well, and new or unfamiliar ways of thinking or acting need to be learned to reach the goal of respect, friendship, trust, or success. If the new ways of thinking and acting can be matched with the trainee's agenda and can be shown to work better than the old ways, the trainee can be persuaded to try them on. For this training to work, the trainer needs to know the trainee's agenda as well as the problems and opportunities in the trainee's cultural context and ways of thinking or acting that would be appropriate and effective.

Training approaches focused on affective or "feeling" goals also depend on structured interaction among the trainee, the culture, and the method. This training can occur in either a real-life or simulated setting in which skills can be practiced and rehearsed with feedback. In the safety of a simulated encounter, the trainee can learn to deal with risky or dangerous feelings but avoid the consequences of hurting people. As the trainees become more skilled in dealing with dangerous feelings in the new cultural context, they become more confident in trying their skills out in real-world settings.

Microskills training has also proved effective in multicultural settings (Ivey, 1988; P. Pedersen & Ivey, 1993). By dividing the more general skill areas into smaller "micro" units, the trainee learns step by step how to increase his or her skill. These skills build on attending behaviors through influencing skills toward integrative skills. The trainee builds or constructs a hierarchy of skills toward the ultimate goal of becoming a skilled counselor. As the microskills become progressively more difficult and complicated, the trainee builds on basic foundation skills toward more advanced skills. There is more empirical research data supporting the effectiveness of microskills training than any other skill-building method in the literature.

Structured learning is another social–behavioral method used in building multicultural skills (Goldstein, 1981). This method focuses on practical skills and abilities to do a necessary function or achieve a valued goal in the trainee's cultural context. Structured learning proceeds through a sequence of steps. First, the skill is presented and discussed; second, the skill is demonstrated with an opportunity for clarification; third, the skill is rehearsed and practiced in role-playing with feedback; and fourth, the skill is transferred to the real-world setting.

Culture-general skill training assumes a foundation of international or multicultural attitudes, opinions, and assumptions that apply to different cultures. The previously mentioned and other popular methods of counselor training can be applied to the multicultural setting providing they are based on appropriate multicultural awareness and accurate multicultural knowledge. These culture-general methods document the ways in which different groups share some of the same values and expectations even though they display very different behaviors.

Culture-specific skill training also provides strategies that target a specific group, problem, identity, or role. Large amounts of specific factual knowledge and information help document the ways in which each group's behavior is different and distinct even though the groups share some of the same values and expectations. There are many examples in the literature of culture-specific skill training for groups defined by nationality, ethnicity, religion, language, age, gender, region, socioeconomic status, educational background, and an almost unlimited number of other formal or informal affiliations. The culture-specific focus may be on the group's identity, a specific problem, or any other carefully defined context. Culture-general and culture-specific skill training approaches complement one another. In any multicultural setting, there are both cultural similarities and cultural differences on which to focus.

9. The Developmental Sequence

The three-stage developmental sequence described in this chapter and demonstrated in this book provides a convenient structure to organize the necessary elements of multicultural training. This three-step approach is best known through the definition of multicultural counseling competencies (D. W Sue et al., 1982).

Other more recent reinterpretations of what has come to be known as "the multicultural counseling competencies" have included the Association for Multicultural Counseling and Development monograph by Arredondo et al. (1996), D. W. Sue et al. (1998), and Pope-Davis and Coleman (1997). The multicultural competencies of awareness, knowledge, and skill have been endorsed by both the American Counseling Association (ACA) and the American Psychological Association as the most articulate examples of assessing counseling competencies across cultures.

Awareness provides the basis for accurate opinions, attitudes, and assumptions. It is essential to first become aware of implicit priorities given to selected attitudes, opinions, and values. Awareness presumes an ability to accurately compare and contrast alternative viewpoints, relate or translate priorities in a variety of cultural settings, identify constraints and opportunities in each cultural context, and have a clear understanding of one's own limitations. A well-defined awareness becomes essential for teaching, research, training, direct service, and consultation. If the awareness stage is overlooked in multicultural training, then the knowledge and skills, however accurate and effective, may be based on false assumptions. If, however, training does not go beyond awareness objectives, the clients will be frustrated by seeing the problems but not being able to do anything to change things.

Knowledge provides the documentation and factual information necessary to move beyond awareness toward effective and appropriate change in multicultural settings. Through accumulated facts and information based on appropriate assumptions, it is possible to understand or comprehend other cultures from their own viewpoint. The facts and information about other cultures are available in the people, the literature, and the products of each culture at the local, national, and regional levels. The second stage of gaining knowledge helps people access those facts and information, directs people to where the knowledge can be found, and identifies reliable sources of information to better understand the unfamiliar culture. If the knowledge stage is overlooked in training, then the cultural awareness and skill, however appropriate and effective, will lack grounding in essential facts and information about the multicultural context, and the resulting changes may be inappropriate. If, however, training does not go beyond the collection of facts and information about other cultures, the clients will be overwhelmed by abstractions that may be true but will be impossible to apply in practice.

Skill provides the ability to build on awareness and apply knowledge toward effective change in multicultural settings. Trained people will become skilled in planning, conducting, and evaluating the multicultural contexts in which they work. They will assess needs of other cultures accurately. They will work with interpreters and cultural informants from the other culture. They will observe and understand behaviors of culturally different people. They will interact, counsel, interview, advise, and manage their tasks effectively in multicultural settings.

The ACA has proposed a revised set of these competencies based on (a) counselor awareness of own assumptions, values, and biases; (b) understanding the worldview of the culturally different client; and (c) developing appropriate intervention strategies and techniques. These competencies are described in the D. W. Sue, Arredondo, and McDavis's (1992) publication on multicultural counseling competencies. I discuss these competencies in the order in which they are presented as the most promising competency guidelines available for developing multiculturally skilled counselors.

10. Awareness Competencies

The first level of developing multiculturally skilled counselors requires developing an awareness of the culturally learned starting points in the counselor's thinking. This foundation of multicultural awareness is important because it controls the counselor's interpretation of all knowledge and utilization of all skills. The need for multicultural awareness is seldom addressed in the generic training of counselors, and counseling skills are generally assumed to be universally uniform in the literature about counseling and counselor education. The multiculturally skilled counselor does not take awareness for granted. The following competencies are provided for attitudes, beliefs, knowledge, and skill (see D. W. Sue et al., 1992, p. 484).

Attitudes and Beliefs

Culturally skilled counselors have moved from being culturally unaware to being aware of and sensitive to their own cultural heritage and to valuing and respecting differences. Culturally skilled counselors are aware of how their own cultural backgrounds, experiences, attitudes, values, and biases influence psychological processes. These counselors are able to recognize the limits of their competencies and expertise. They are comfortable with differences that exist between themselves and clients in terms of race, ethnicity, culture, and beliefs.

Knowledge

Culturally skilled counselors have specific knowledge about their own racial and cultural heritage and how it personally and professionally affects their definitions of normality–abnormality and the process of counseling. These counselors possess knowledge and understanding about how oppression, racism, discrimination, and stereotyping affect them personally and in their work. This allows them to acknowledge their own racist attitudes, beliefs, and feelings. Although this standard applies to all groups, for White counselors it may mean that they understand how they may have directly or indirectly benefited from individual, institutional, and cultural racism (White identity development models). Culturally skilled counselors possess knowledge about their social impact on others. They are knowledgeable about communication style differences, how their style may clash or foster the counseling process with minority clients, and how to anticipate the impact it may have on others.

Skills

Culturally skilled counselors seek out educational, consultative, and training experiences to improve their understanding and effectiveness in working with culturally different populations. Being able to recognize the limits of the competencies, they (a) seek consultation, (b) seek further training or education, (c) make referrals to more qualified individuals or resources, or (d) engage in a combination of these. Culturally skilled counselors are constantly seeking to understand themselves as racial and cultural beings and are actively seeking a nonracist identity.

Pope-Davis and Dings (1995) provided the best discussion of the research attempting to measure and validate the multicultural competencies. Four different measures have been developed to assess multicultural awareness, knowledge, and skill. The Cross-Cultural Counseling Inventory–Revised (CCCI-R) by LaFromboise, Coleman, and Hernandez (1991) directs a supervisor to rate the counselor on 20 Likert-scale items. Ponterotto, Rieger, Barrett, and Sparks (1994) suggested that it measures one unidimensional factor but that the CCCI-R is more a measure of knowledge than awareness. The Multicultural Awareness–Knowledge–Skill Survey (D'Andrea, Daniels, & Heck, 1991) includes three 20-item scales to measure awareness, knowledge, and skills useful for examining student performance in relation to coursework for multicultural courses organized around the awareness–knowledge–skill structure. The Multicultural Counseling Awareness Scale–B described by Ponterotto et al. (1994) includes two subscales: a 14-item awareness scale and a 28-item knowledge/skills scale with some evidence that the subscales measure different factors. The Multicultural Counseling Inventory (MCI) by Sodowsky, Taffe, Gutkin, and Wise (1994) contains four factors: Skills (11 items), Awareness (10 items), Knowledge (11 items), and Counseling Relationship (8 items). The advantage of the MCI is that it includes the relationship factor and the items describe behaviors rather than attitudes (W. M. I. Lee, 1999). Ponterotto et al. (1994) and S. Sue (1998) suggested that more study is needed and that the awareness–knowledge–skill measure of competency has not yet been satisfactorily validated.

For a discussion in greater depth of multicultural counseling, the reader should consult Ponterotto, Casas, Suzuki, and Alexander (1995), which is being revised into an even better reference volume. P. Pedersen, Draguns, Lonner, and Trimble's (1996) book is also being revised into a new and even better volume. D. W. Sue and Sue (1999) also provided an excellent and comprehensive volume as a standard reference. Multicultural counseling is becoming increasingly complicated as it is infused into counseling as a generic "fourth-force" perspective (P. Pedersen, 1998) so that no single volume can now cover the topic comprehensively.

11. Conclusion

Just as culture is complex but not chaotic, so should multicultural training also be guided by a sequence of learning objectives that reflect the needs of both the student and the multicultural context. Teaching multicultural counseling and communication should include any and all methods relevant to the multicultural context from that culture's viewpoint. Training designs need to be comprehensive enough to include both culture-general and culture-specific perspectives. The developmental sequence from awareness to knowledge to skill provides an eclectic framework for organizing the content of multicultural training and a rationale for educational development in multicultural settings.

EXERCISE: The Truth Statement

We often focus on the process of training without looking at the basic assumptions that are implicit in the training content. Generate a "truth statement" related to an obvious and widely accepted truth that most or all of the group members are likely to accept, and modify it through discussion until everyone agrees to its truthfulness.

When everyone has written down the statement, ask them all to write a second statement explaining why their first statement is true.

When everyone has completed the second statement, ask them to write a third statement explaining why the second statement is true.

When everyone has completed the third statement, ask them to write a fourth statement explaining why the third statement is true.

You may choose to go on to a fifth and sixth statement, but probably by this time most participants have reached the point at which they're saying, "I don't know or even care why it is true. It's just true!" Most in the group are probably frustrated and irritated, and some may be even hostile toward the trainer.

Discuss (a) how hard it is to follow the chain of implicit assumptions underlying statements we accept as truthful; (b) how we get angry when pushed back to those assumptions in an argument or discussion on, for example, topics of religion and politics; and (c) how frequently the implicit underlying assumptions go unexamined. Often participants will say something like: "Why are we wasting our time talking about something so obviously true? Now, let's get on with the training and stop wasting time!" You may want to discuss how group members believed in the same beginning truth statement for entirely different reasons.

THE TRUTH STATEMENT EXERCISE

Participant Objectives:
1. To identify a statement believed to be true.
2. To identify the chain of evidence proving the statement true.
3. To identify the basic assumption behind the evidence.

Learning Objective:
1. Truth is based on culturally learned assumptions.

CHAPTER 2

The Rules of Multiculturalism

Major objective:

1. To demonstrate the utility of defining culture inclusively.

Secondary objectives:

1. To demonstrate the importance of both similarities and differences.
2. To demonstrate the necessity of accepting cultural complexity.
3. To demonstrate the ever-changing dynamic characteristics of culture.
4. To demonstrate the cultural salience of ethnographic, demographic, status, and affiliation variables.

Before we were born, cultural patterns of thought and action were already being prepared to guide our lives, influence our decisions, and help us take control of our lives. We inherited these cultural patterns from our parents and teachers, who taught us the "rules of the game." As we developed awareness of other people and cultures, we learned that "our" culture was one of the many possible patterns of thinking and acting from which we could choose. By that time, most of us had already come to believe that our culture was the best of all possible worlds. Even when we recognized that some new ways were better, it was not always possible to replace our cultural habits with new alternatives. The primary enemy of multiculturalism therefore is our exclusive reliance on the "self-reference criterion" by which we measure the goodness or badness of others exclusively according to ourselves and our own "natural" perspective. George Bernard Shaw (1919) in his script for *Man and Superman: A Comedy and a Philosophy* pointed out: "Do not do unto others as you would that they should do unto you. Their tastes may not be the same" (p. 227).

D. W. Sue and Sue (1999) described the implications of rapid increases in the racial/ethnic minority populations as the diversification of the United States or the changing complexion of society. Recent migrations are different from earlier White European migrations that were more oriented toward assimilation. The current immigrants consist primarily of Asians (34%), Latin Americans (34%), and other groups who are not White Europeans (Atkinson, Morten, & Sue, 1998). About 75% of those entering the labor force are visible racial/ethnic minorities and women. By the year 2000, 45% of the students in public schools will be racial/ethnic minorities. The representation of these racial/ethnic minorities in graduate-level training as counselors and therapists, however, is less prominent.

> It is our contention that although multicultural coverage is increasing, the reports of its increase are inflated. Most graduate programs continue to give inadequate treatment to mental health issues of ethnic minorities. Cultural influences affecting personality formation, career choice, educational development, and the manifestation of behavioral disorders are too often omitted from the mental health training or treated in a tangential manner. (D. W. Sue & Sue, 1999, p. 12)

1. Cultural Similarities and Differences Are Both Important

Multiculturalism presents us with a paradox because it requires us to look at how we are the same and how we are different at the very same time. The multicultural perspective is one of the most important ideas in this century because it emphasizes both the ways that we are each unique *and* the ways that we share parts of our identity with others. Alternative views of culture have made three serious mistakes.

1. The "melting pot" metaphor made the mistake of overemphasizing the ways we are the same and ignoring differences. This has usually resulted in the more powerful groups imposing their perspective on everybody else.
2. The overemphasis of differences has resulted in stereotyped and disconnected "special interest" cultural groups in a typical hostile exclusionary perspective while ignoring the common ground of shared interests that makes the welfare of each group important to each other group.
3. The assumption that you must select *either* the universalist *or* the particularist viewpoint has resulted in a false choice because both are important to define the cultural context accurately and comprehensively. Each cultural perspective is unique, but each perspective also shares overlapping features with each other group like overlapping fish scales. We can best understand the cultural perspective by focusing one eye clearly on the part that is shared and the other eye on the part that is unique in a "cross-eyed" but accurate perspective.

2. Cultural Opposites Can Both Be Reasonable

We are moving toward a culture of the future that promises to be so different from our present lives that we hardly can imagine what it will be like. Furthermore, those who cannot adapt to that future culture will not survive. We are left with the alternative of learning adaptive skills through contact with cultures whose assumptions are different from our own. The means for learning those adaptive skills are through having contact with different cultures, developing new ways of thinking, and challenging our unexamined assumptions.

Rothenberg's (1983) creativity research on the "janusian process" of cognition involves actively conceiving two or more opposites or antitheses at the same time. The Greek god Janus had two faces, one half smiling and the other half crying. In the janusian process, ideas or images are clarified and defined by opposite or antithetical concepts coexisting simultaneously (Watts, 1963). Janusian thinking is not illogical but a conscious and adaptive cognitive process. Carl Jung emphasized the reconciliation of opposites in self in much the same mode as Asian followers of Zen or the Tao tried to capture truth in a dialectical process. In science, the janusian process has been documented as important to the creative achievements of Einstein, Bohr, Watson, Darwin, Pasteur, and Fermi (Rothenberg, 1983, p. 938). Albert Einstein, for example, described as his happiest thought and the key idea leading to his general theory of relativity that a man falling from the roof of a house is both in motion and at rest simultaneously (Rothenberg, 1979).

Most of our educational emphasis is spent examining the rational and reasonable process of a single culturally learned viewpoint. I suggest we reexamine the starting-point assumptions that determine the trajectory of those viewpoints. Two rockets may both fly straight but be pointed in different directions. Many viewpoints, however similar, disagree because they have different starting points that lead them toward divergent assumptions. Looking at reasonable opposites will enlarge our repertoire of adaptive skills. A "test of reasonable opposites" provides a means of testing those basic assumptions that frequently escape examination in our educational system.

First, the application of this test begins by identifying a basic but unexamined truth and the assumption(s) behind those truth statements. Second, it asks what the alternative policy positions are that would reverse those assumptions and provide a policy based on opposite or contrary assumptions. Finally, it compares the two statements and their assumptions to determine which alternative is more reasonable. In a surprisingly large number of instances, the opposite assumption seems at least as reasonable and sometimes even more so than the original assumption. In applying the test of reasonable opposites, I have found (a) that my thinking is usually so ambiguous that it is difficult to identify the opposite of what I assume to be true, (b) that once an opposite truth statement has been generated, it is often as reasonable as what I originally assumed, and (c) that the generation of reasonable opposites results in new and creative alternatives that otherwise might not have been discovered! Some examples of opposites are the following: (first) Differences are important versus similarities are important; (second) Counseling decreases pain versus counseling increases pain; (third) You are right versus you are wrong.

The reasonable opposite provides a stimulating alternative to unexamined assumptions. There is an urgency for us to distinguish between multicultural disagreements (e.g., where the assumptions are different) and interpersonal conflict (e.g., where the assumptions are similar). By challenging our assumptions, we can develop adaptive skills for working with a wider range of different perspectives, and we can learn more about our own environment from other viewpoints. In the course of our social and professional evolution, these adaptive skills are likely to be very important. As an example, let us consider the assumption that a more complete "understanding" between two individuals will contribute to their communication whereas "misunderstanding" is likely to damage the relationship. The reasonable opposite would be that a more complete understanding will be damaging whereas misunderstanding might contribute to a more healthy relationship.

Pearce (1983) contended that a complete understanding is not only irrelevant and unexciting in a relationship but may even be dangerous. The alternative is a kind of creative ambiguity that can *deepen* friendships, *save* marriages, *improve* businesses, and *prevent* wars! The theory of "coordinated management of meaning" has 35 supporting studies to its credit and boils down to this: How a listener interprets a speaker's remarks and acts upon the interpretation is more important than whether the two understand each other. In short, good things *can* happen when there is misunderstanding among people, businesses, or nations. Pearce favored interpretation over understanding. People are getting along well despite and sometimes because of misunderstandings. If nations really understood one another accurately, there might be more war and turmoil than there is now! Relationships can *sometimes* thrive on misunderstandings, and more understanding will not *necessarily* result in more harmony. For example, the separation of Asian and Western cultures sometimes obscures more than it illuminates.

3. One Size Does Not Fit All

Some views of multiculturalism proceed from the assumption of radical cultural relativism: that each culture is unique and different and that all cultures are equal in value. Others evaluate all cultures according to a single absolute measure of truth. Just as cultural relativism defines each culture on its own terms, customs, symbols, norms, and beliefs, cultural absolutism assumes a universal measure of normal psychological functions and the ways those functions relate to behavior. The universalist position assumes that the same psychological processes are operating in all humans, independent of culture. Patterson (1978, 1996) took a universalist position in criticizing counselors for modifying counseling to fit different cultures. Although counseling needs to be modified for clients of different ages, sexes, experiences, and social backgrounds to fit the different expectations of clients, Patterson disputed the need for different sets of skills, emphases, and insights for use in each culture, emphasizing that the *context,* not the *process,* is multicultural. As Draguns (1989) pointed out, this criticism constructively raises questions about the limits of cultural accommodation and the universal versus the particular perspective of counseling.

The rhetoric in support of cultural differences and multicultural counseling has been written into documents of counselor accreditation, certification, licensure, and professional identity for many years. According to the exclusionary definition of culture, these statements have been perceived as political favors to the special interests of one group or another. According to the inclusionary definition of culture, however, multiculturalism goes beyond the self-interests of any particular group to redefine the very basis of identity for both the counselor and the client, regardless of her or his skin color, age, gender, socioeconomic status, sexual preference, or membership in any of the many other formal or informal affiliations to which any of us may belong. The argument on which much of the previous rhetoric has been based has been largely humanitarian or ethical in its basis. The argument from an inclusionary definition of culture is based on the functional accuracy necessary to good counseling, without at the same time diminishing the ethical or humanitarian imperative.

Miles (1989) pointed out that it is a mistake to limit the parameters of racism by reference to skin color. The extensive evidence of racism and related exclusionary practices requires that we define racism broadly to include sexism, ageism, and nationalism as well as the exclusionary practices associated with these ideologies. Miles rejected J. H. Katz's (1978) definition of racism as a "White person's problem" for being simplistic in its disregard for the differential definitions of power across situations. At the same time, he supported Katz's contention that Whites have been socialized into a perspective that presumes White superiority. Every attempt to reduce cultural differences according to skin color alone has resulted in simplistic, stereotyped, or polarized alternatives that disregard the necessary complexity of multiculturalism.

Miles (1989) gave a concise history of racism as an idea. He also provided a critical analysis of the controversies surrounding the topic of racism. Miles's book makes a strong case for the usefulness of racism as a political concept. Miles acknowledged that the term *racism* is discredited as a scientific/ biological term and is negatively loaded as a term of political abuse. It is this political implication of the term *racism* that gives the construct of *race* a meaning. Miles first of all took a historical view of the concept going back to the 15th and 16th centuries, when it applied primarily to differences between European Christians and Middle Eastern Muslims. Second, Miles also linked the concept to the capitalist mode of production, bringing in the close relationship between racism and socioeconomic factors. Third, Miles brought in the Western world context of racism as a philosophical construct of cultural beliefs. These three factors provide the context in which racism is best understood.

The concept of racism is frequently used as an ideology to categorize people and for the attribution of meaning. There is a similarity among racism, nationalism, and sexism in this regard as negative forces in modern society. Racism brutalizes and dehumanizes both its object and those who articulate it. It is therefore a problem for the total social context where it is articulated and where it promotes exclusionary practices. Racism has come to represent a pervasive force of exploitation by one group against another group in which the protection of self-interest becomes more important than fairness, equity, justice, and truth.

There are several factors that are important to a historical understanding of racism toward the less powerful outsiders by the more powerful insiders, according to Miles (1989). First, representations of the outsiders implies both *including* those who are like us and *excluding* those who are not like us, in which there is an implied superiority–inferiority relationship. Exclusion and inclusion are the two sides of racism. Second, racism has not been limited to Black–White relationships or even the colonial context but has been widely applied elsewhere. Third, racist representations of the outsider change along with the changing social, economic, or political conditions, with attention to class differences. Fourth, physical features such as skin color or other somatic characteristics are often used to characterize the outsider, although racism does not require these characteristics. Fifth, scientific discourse, if based on the assumptions of representational inclusion–exclusion, may be used to legitimize those earlier representations.

The concept of racism has broadened as we have become more aware of its complexity in recent years. C. Ridley (1989) pointed out some underlying assumptions about modern racism that demonstrate its pervasiveness. First, racism is reflected in behavior, in what the person does rather than how that person feels or thinks, although attitudes are important in motivating people to behave differently. Second, racist acts can be performed by prejudiced as well as nonprejudiced persons. There is no causal relationship in which racism depends on prejudice as its antecedent. Well-intentioned but misinformed persons can still behave in racist ways. Third, no single ethnic group is responsible for racism. Anyone can be racist. Fourth, the criteria for judging an act as racist lies in the consequences rather than the causes of the behavior. Consciousness raising is not enough to eliminate racism and will not by itself prevent racist acts. Fifth, racism is perpetuated by the power or powerlessness of groups with respect to one another.

Miles (1989) linked racism to the process of seeing history in racial terms, where the powerful are separated from the powerless and where those in power are presumed to have the right or even the responsibility to exclude the powerless from consideration. As an ideology, it is necessary to acknowledge the complexity of racism, avoiding simplistic applications to historical events. As a political and economic force, it is always essential to view racism with regard to its consequences through including some and excluding others' access to power. Racism may often include contradictory and multidimensional ideas in an unthinking and unexamined justification for action.

4. The Multicultural Perspective Has an Upside

Culture is emerging as one of the most important and perhaps one of the most misunderstood constructs in the contemporary counseling literature. Culture may be defined narrowly as limited to ethnicity and nationality or defined broadly to include any and all potentially salient ethnographic, demographic, status, or affiliation variables. Given the broader definition of culture in this handbook, it is possible to identify at least a dozen assets that are exclusively available through developing multicultural awareness (Kiselica, 1999; P. Pedersen, 1999).

1. *Accuracy*: Because all behaviors are learned and displayed in a cultural context, accurate assessment, meaningful understanding, and appropriate interventions are culturally contextual constructs. When I encounter colleagues opposed to multiculturalism, I ask them if they consider accuracy to be important, which they always do. Then I suggest that we are on the same side, in our search for accuracy.

2. *Conflict management*: The common ground of shared values or expectations can be expressed by contrasting culturally learned behaviors so that reframing conflict in a culture-centered perspective will allow two people or groups to "apparently" disagree in their behaviors without disagreeing on their shared values. Not everyone who smiles is your friend, and not everyone who shouts at you is your enemy. If we prematurely judge others' behaviors out of context, we are likely to turn potential

friends into enemies. If we begin by increasing our awareness of shared positive values and expectations, we can both teach and learn about which behavior is best in each cultural context.

3. *Identity*: The visual image I have of culture is the picture of a thousand people sitting with me and following me around day and night. An articulate awareness of these thousand culture teachers, accumulated from relatives, friends, enemies, and fantasies, whisper advice, reward, and censure as they celebrate our accomplishments and mourn our failures. Our internal dialogue with these culture teachers is a frequently underutilized resource in our decision-making and hypotheses-forming processes. These culture teachers construct our identity.

4. *A healthy society*: A healthy socioecosystem requires a diversity of cultural perspectives just as a healthy biosystem requires a diverse gene pool. Utopian or cult groups that have cut themselves off from outside society have failed throughout history. Superpowers that have failed to recognize and acknowledge their interactive dependence on smaller nations have inevitably fallen. Culture is a growing, changing, and always emerging force that resists capture and incarceration by language, military power, or political influence.

5. *Encapsulation–protection*: A culture-centered perspective protects us from inappropriately imposing our own culturally encapsulated self-reference criteria in the evaluation of others. Culturally encapsulated counselors define everyone's reality according to their own cultural assumptions, minimize cultural differences, impose self-reference criteria in judging the behavior of others, ignore proof that disconfirms their perspective, depend on techniques and strategies to solve their problems, and disregard their own cultural biases in a culturally encapsulated perspective (Wrenn, 1962).

6. *Survival*: Contact with culturally different groups provides an opportunity to rehearse adaptive functioning for our own future survival in the global village. We know the future is so different that it is beyond our imagination, and we know that some of us will not survive because we will not be ready. By seeking out people and groups who do *not* think, dress, eat, play, work, or talk like ourselves and by learning to interact with those people or groups who are different, we will learn the facility for our own survival in that beyond-imagination future.

7. *Social justice*: Understanding social justice and moral development in a multicultural context helps us differentiate necessary absolutes from culturally relative principles. Social justice typically requires an inclusive rather than an exclusive perspective, and moral exclusion has consistently resulted in classifying society according to the oppressed and the oppres-

sors (Opotow, 1990). Cultural relativism has failed because it prevents discussion of social justice across cultures. Cultural absolutism has also failed because those who are in power are not always right. Multicultural awareness offers a more interactive and relational perspective.

8. *Right-thinking*: A culture-centered perspective reflects the complementarity of the quantum metaphor of Niels Bohr (1950) that light is both a particle and a wave at the same time by emphasizing both the similarities and differences between and among people in a balance of opposites. Overemphasizing differences will erect barriers and lead to hostile disengagement. Overemphasizing similarities will result in a melting pot in which the person or group that is in power will make the rules.

9. *Personalized learning*: All learning and change involves some degree of culture shock to the degree that it influences one's basic perspectives. Much can be learned through the culture shock of active learning that could not be learned in any other way. The really important things we have learned are not abstractions but are profoundly personal internalized changes in our lifestyle. Culture shock provides a metaphorical model for education and the personalized learning process generally, recognizing and accepting the pain or discomfort and reframing the experience in a positive and lasting perspective.

10. *Spirituality*: A culture-centered perspective enhances our spiritual completeness by linking culturally different spiritual perspectives to the same shared reality. The mystery of our being cannot be comprehended by any religion in isolation. In many cultures, the only really important questions are the questions about where humans came from before birth and where we are going after death.

11. *Political stability*: A culture-centered perspective builds pluralism as an alternative to authoritarianism or anarchy in our social organization. However, pluralism has never really been tried successfully. We have not developed the skill, or perhaps the ultimate necessity, to survive with one another. However, with population growth, pollution, and rapid utilization of limited global resources, we will be forced to one of these three choices, and learning to live together will be much preferred to the alternatives.

12. *Strengthening psychological theory*: A culture-centered perspective will strengthen contemporary theories of humanism, behaviorism, and psychodynamism rather than weaken or displace them. The only reality we have is the one we learn to perceive through our senses, and the rules for perception are themselves culturally learned. By making culture central rather than marginal to our psychological theory of choice, that theory will function more effectively in a variety of different cultural contexts.

5. Culture Is Complex and Not Simple

Complexity is our friend and not our enemy because it protects us from accepting easy answers to hard questions. This process is most apparent in our use of scientific theories. In attempting to understand complexity, we develop simplified models that can be explained and understood but that reflect only selected aspects of reality. Our embedded rationality requires that we construct simplified models of complex reality to explain things. If we behave rationally with regard to the model, we assume the behavior is appropriately explained in the real world. The danger is that we confuse simple explanations and labels with a more complex reality. There is a natural tendency to "keep things simple." We normally have little tolerance for the confusion of aggregate, mixed-up, unsorted, undifferentiated, unpredictable, and random data. We naturally move quickly to sort, order, and predict simplified patterns from the chaos (Triandis, 1975). This preference for simplicity is dangerous.

By perceiving the world from a narrow or rigid frame of reference, we ignore the complex reality around us in the illusion of simplicity. Theories of cognitive complexity suggest that people who are more cognitively complex are more capable than others of seeing these multiple perspectives. Research in adult development likewise suggests that cognitive complexity is related to broader and more advanced levels of development. Quantum physics uses the principle of complementarity to prove that sometimes light may be regarded as a particle and sometimes as a wave, so that both quantum and wave theories are necessary to explain the "real" nature of light (Bohr, 1950). The principle has likewise proved itself useful in gastroenterology, ecclesiology, literary criticism, the philosophy of science, organizational behavior, economics, and political science (P. Pedersen, 1984).

Science has long accepted genetic diversity as essential to the survival of a species. However, some persons are able to tolerate complexity better than others. These people are better at either differentiating and perceiving several dimensions in a range of alternatives or integrating and seeing complex connections between different sources. People who are more complex are able to see many different dimensions, classifications, theories, or alternatives to explain a situation. Because reality tends to be complex, those who are able to identify more alternatives are more likely to see correctly and make more appropriate decisions, although this process requires a high tolerance for ambiguity.

Culture's complexity is illustrated by the hundreds or perhaps even thousands of culturally learned identities, affiliations, and roles each person assumes at one time or another. The dynamic nature of culture is demonstrated as one of those alternative cultural identities replaces another in salience. A counselor must keep track of the client's *salient* cultural identity as it changes even within the context of a single interview. Counselors develop their competence through stages of progressively more complex and adaptive facility in making decisions and processing information. *Complexity* involves the identification of multiple perspectives within and between individuals. For example: Can the counselor perceive a problem from the multiple viewpoints of a culturally different client in the many different and changing culturally learned roles that the client fills from time to time and place to place (Draguns, 1989)?

The following are 10 examples of how a complicated culture-centered perspective of counseling can be more useful:

1. Identify multiple but conflicting culturally learned viewpoints in the client's context.
2. Identify multiple but conflicting culturally learned viewpoints within the individual client.
3. Explain the actions of clients from their own cultural perspectives.
4. Listen for information about cultural patterns in the interview that can later be shared at an appropriate time with the client.
5. Learn to shift topics in culturally appropriate ways.
6. Reflect culturally appropriate feelings in specific and accurate feedback.
7. Identify culturally defined multiple support systems for the client.
8. Identify alternative solutions and anticipate the consequences for each cultural context.
9. Identify culturally learned criteria being used by the client to evaluate alternative solutions.
10. Generate accurate explanations for the client's behavior from the client's cultural context.

These 10 examples of cultural complexity discussed as counseling skills are already familiar features of the counseling literature, but not as they apply to multicultural counseling. Rather than separate the multicultural perspective as a special branch of counseling, one must see it as a viewpoint and perspective applicable to all areas of counseling.

6. Culture Balance Is Dynamic and Not Static

Cognitive balance is a search for consistency in an otherwise volatile situation and has traditionally been achieved by changing, ignoring, differentiating, or transcending inconsistencies to avoid dissonance (Triandis, 1977). However, there are more complicated and even dissonant definitions of balance demonstrated through a tolerance for inconsistency and dissonance in which differences are not resolved but are managed in a dynamic, ever-changing balance (P. Pedersen, 1988).

In a more complicated and asymmetrical definition of dynamic balance, the task of counseling may be to find meaning in both pleasure and pain rather than to resolve conflict in favor of increased pleasure. Social change in this context is perceived as a continuous and not an episodic process. Balance as a construct seeks to reflect the complex and sometimes asymmetrical metaphors of organic systems in holistic health. Problems, pain, and otherwise negative aspects of our experience may also provide necessary resources for the dark side of healthy functioning, in an ecological analysis of psychological process (Berry, 1980).

Watt (1961) compared counseling to a social game based on conventional rules that define boundaries between the individual and the cultural context. It is then the duty of a counselor to involve participants in a "counter game," which restores a unifying perspective of ego and environment so that the person can be liberated and a balanced context restored. In some cases, balance has been restored through counseling by bringing in a "mediator" as a third person in addition to the counselor and client. Bolman (1968) advocated the approach of using two professionals, one from each culture collaborating in cross-cultural counseling, with traditional healers as co-counselors. Weidman (1975) introduced the concept of a "culture broker" as an intermediary for working with culturally different clients.

In many non-Westernized systems, there is less emphasis on separating the person from the presenting problem than in Western cultures. There is less tendency to locate the problem inside the isolated individual but rather to relate that individual's difficulty to other persons or even to the cosmos. Balance describes a condition of order and dynamic design in a context in which all elements, pain *as well as* pleasure, serve a useful and necessary function. The non-Western emphasis is typically more holistic in acknowledging the reciprocal interaction of persons and environments in both their positive and negative aspects.

Success is achieved indirectly as a by-product of harmonious two-directional balance rather than directly through a more simplistic one-directional alternative. In a one-directional approach, the goal is to make people feel more pleasure and less pain, more happiness and less sadness, more positive and less negative. In the two-directional alternative, the goal is to help people find meaning in *both* pleasure and pain, *both* happiness and sadness, *both* negative and positive experience. In the Judeo-Christian tradition, God not only tolerates the devil's presence but actually created demonic as well as angelic forces in a balance of alternatives.

The restoration of value balance provides an alternative goal to the more individualized goal of *solving* social problems. In the context of value balance, social change is perceived as a continuous and not episodic process, taking place independently both because of and despite our attempts to control that change. Value balance is a process rather than a conclusive event or events. In a similar mode, the problems, pain, and other negative aspects of education provide necessary resources for creating a dynamic value balance.

Balance as a construct for multicultural counseling involves the identification of different or even conflicting culturally learned perspectives without necessarily resolving that difference or dissonance in favor of either viewpoint. Healthy functioning in a multicultural or pluralistic context may require a person to simultaneously maintain multiple, conflicting, and culturally learned roles without the opportunity to resolve the resulting dissonance.

Ten examples of observable and potentially measurable counseling behaviors demonstrate the elusive construct of dynamic and asymmetrical balance:

1. Identifying positive implications in a negative experience.
2. Anticipating potentially negative implications from an otherwise positive experience.
3. Integrating positive and negative events as part of a holistic perspective.
4. Avoiding simplistic solutions to complex problems.
5. Recognizing both the collectivistic and individualistic perspective across clients.
6. Adjusting for the client's changing level of empowerment across topics and time.
7. Avoiding stereotyping of clients.
8. Recognizing how the same person can change identity across his or her life roles.
9. Adjusting the influence of the counselor to match the strengths and weaknesses of the client.
10. Maintaining harmony within the interview.

Although the construct of dynamic balance is elusive, the preceding 10 examples of observable counselor behaviors describe some of the essential aspects as applied to multicultural counseling. These examples are rooted in the traditional counseling research literature and are not, by themselves, controversial. Because these examples are familiar, they may provide a conceptual bridge for counselors to develop multicultural counseling skills with culturally different clients.

7. Multiculturalism Is Inclusive and Broadly Defined

The multicultural perspective seeks to provide a conceptual framework that recognizes the complex diversity of a pluralistic society while at the same time suggesting bridges of shared concern that bind culturally different persons to one another. The ultimate outcome may be a multicultural theory, as Segall, Dasen, Berry, and Poortinga (1990) suggested:

> There may well come a time when we will no longer speak of cross cultural psychology as such. The basic premise of this field—that to understand human behavior, we must study it in its sociocultural context—may become so widely accepted that all psychology will be inherently cultural. (p. 352)

During the last 20 years, multiculturalism has become recognized as a powerful force, not just for understanding exotic groups but also for understanding ourselves and those with whom we work.

By defining culture broadly, to include within-group demographic variables (e.g., age, sex, and place of residence), status variables (e.g., social, educational, and economic), and affiliations (formal and informal), as well as ethnographic variables such as nationality, ethnicity, language, and religion, the construct *multicultural* becomes generic to all counseling relationships. The narrow definition of *culture* has limited multiculturalism to what might more appropriately be called a *multiethnic* or *multinational* relationship between groups with a shared sociocultural heritage that includes similarities of religion, history, and common ancestry. Ethnicity and nationality are important to individual and familial identity as one subset of culture, but the construct of culture, broadly defined, goes beyond national and ethnic boundaries. Persons from the same ethnic or nationality group may still experience cultural differences. Not all Blacks have the same experience, nor do all Asians, nor all American Indians, nor all Hispanics, nor all women, nor all old people, nor all disabled persons. No particular group is unimodal in its perspective. Therefore, the broad and inclusive definition of culture is particularly important in preparing counselors to deal with the complex differences among and between clients from every cultural group.

Just as differentiation and integration are complementary processes, so are the emic (culture-specific) and etic (culture-general) perspectives necessarily interrelated. The terms *emic* and *etic* were borrowed from "phonemic" and "phonetic" analysis in linguistics describing the rules of language to imply a separation of general from specific aspects. Even Pike (1966), in his original conceptualization of this dichotomy, suggested that the two elements not be treated as a rigid dichotomy but as a way of presenting the same data from two viewpoints. Although research on the usefulness of emic and etic categories has been extensive, the notion of a "culture-free" (universal) etic has been just as elusive as the notion of a "culture-pure" (totally isolated) emic.

The basic problem facing counselors is how to describe behavior in terms that are true to a particular culture while at the same time comparing those behaviors with a similar pattern in one or more other cultures (P. Pedersen,

1984). Combining the specific and general viewpoints provides a multicultural perspective. This larger perspective is an essential starting point for mental health professionals seeking to avoid cultural encapsulation by their own culture-specific assumptions (Sartorius, Pedersen, & Marsella, 1984).

There is a strong argument against the broad definition of culture. Triandis, Bontempo, Leung, and Hui (1990) distinguished among cultural, demographic, and personal constructs. Cultural constructs are those shared by persons speaking a particular dialect; living in the same geographical location during the same time; and sharing norms, roles, values, associations, and ways of categorizing experience described as a "subjective culture" (Triandis, 1972). This view contends that demographic-level constructs deal with these same topics but are shared only by particular demographic groups within a culture, such as men and women or the elderly and young adults. Personal-level constructs belong to still another category of individual differences and cannot be meaningfully interpreted with reference to demographic or cultural membership. The problem with this perspective is that it tends to be arbitrary in defining the point at which shared constructs constitute cultural similarity, because, as Triandis et al. (1990) pointed out:

> We cannot expect that 100% of a sample agrees with a position. We decided arbitrarily, that if 85% of a sample shares the construct, it is cultural. Similarly, if 85% of the men share it, we consider it gender linked. If less than 85% share the construct we might examine if it is shared by the majority of a sample but if less than 50% of a sample share the construct, we definitely do not consider it shared. (p. 304)

Likewise, C. C. Lee (1997) made a persuasive argument against the broad definition of culture. Lee argued that the term *multicultural* is in imminent danger of becoming so inclusive as to be almost meaningless. The broad definition includes all constituent groups that perceive themselves as being disenfranchised in some fashion. This has resulted in diffusing the coherent conceptual framework of multiculturalism in training, teaching, and research. "As the term has been increasingly stretched to include virtually any group of people who consider themselves 'different' the intent of multicultural counseling theory and practice has become unclear" (Locke, 1990, p. 6). In responding to Fukuyama's (1990) argument for a more universalist emphasis of culture for understanding the complex interacting systems of society, Locke (1990) suggested that the broad view of multicultural at best serves as a prologue for a narrow or "focused" perspective:

> A view of multicultural counseling that does not direct attention toward the racial/ethnic minority groups within that culture is but an attempt to eliminate any focus on the pluralistic nature of that culture. Such a system views cultural differences as no more than individual differences. (Locke, 1990, p. 24)

The distinction between individual differences and cultural differences is real and important. The cultural identities to which we belong are no more or less important than is our individual identity. Skin color at birth is an individual difference, but what that skin color has come to mean since birth is cultural. Although culture has traditionally been defined as a multigenerational phenomenon, the broad definition of culture suggests that cultural identities and culturally significant shared beliefs may develop in a contemporary horizontal as well as vertical historical time frame and still be distinguished from individual differences.

Another application of the broad inclusive definition of culture is *cultural psychology*, which presumes that every sociocultural environment depends for its existence and identity on the way human beings give it meaning and are in turn changed in response to that sociocultural environment. Cultural psychology studies the ways cultural traditions and social practices regulate, express, and transform people in patterned ways. "Cultural psychology is the study of the ways subject and object, self and other, psyche and culture, person and context, figure and ground, practitioner and practice live together, require each other, and dynamically, dialectically and jointly make each other up" (Shweder, Mahapatra, & Miller, 1990, p. 130).

8. It's Dangerous to Ignore Culture

The tendency to depend on one authority, one theory, and one truth has been demonstrated to be extremely dangerous in the political setting. It is no less dangerous in a counseling context. The encapsulated counselor is trapped in one way of thinking that resists adaptation and rejects alternatives. By contrast, a broader definition leads counselors toward a more comprehensive understanding of alternatives and a more complete perspective of one's own beliefs. The broader inclusive perspective offers liberation to the culturally encapsulated counselor. By ignoring cultural differences, counselors are placed in danger of being inconsistent.

Although counseling has traditionally emphasized the importance of freedom, rational thought, tolerance, equality, and justice, it has also been used as an oppressive instrument by those in power to maintain the status quo (D. W. Sue & Sue, 1999). Whenever counseling is used to restrict rather than foster the well-being and development of culturally different persons, then counselors are participating in overt or covert forms of prejudice and discrimination. The culturally different client approaches counseling with caution, asking, "What makes you, a counselor/therapist, any different from all the others out there who have oppressed and discriminated against me?" (D. W. Sue & Sue, 1990, p. 6).

Multiculturalism, the power of cultural bias, and the recognized importance of cultural awareness have been widely recognized for a long time, especially among authors from a minority background such as DuBois (1908/1982). Ponterotto and Casas (1991) documented the perception that "the majority of traditionally trained counselors operate from a culturally biased and encapsulated framework which results in the provision of culturally conflicting and even oppressive counseling treatments" (pp. 7–8). Counseling training programs are often presumed to be defenders of the status quo, stimulating considerable criticism regarding counseling research by racial and ethnic minority groups.

There is a history of moral exclusion, when individuals or groups are perceived as nonentities, expendable, or undeserving (Opotow, 1990). This exclusionary perspective has been described as a form of encapsulation. Wrenn (1962, 1985) first introduced the concept of *cultural encapsulation* for counseling. This perspective assumes five basic identifying features. First, we define reality according to one set of cultural assumptions and stereotypes, which becomes more important than the real world. Second, we become insensitive to cultural variations among individuals and assume that our view is the only real or legitimate one. Third, each of us has unreasoned assumptions, which we accept without proof and which we protect without regard to rationality. Fourth, a technique-oriented job definition further contributes toward and preserves the encapsulation. Fifth, when there is no evaluation of other viewpoints, then there is no responsibility to accommodate or interpret the behavior of others except from the viewpoint of a self-reference criterion.

Even multicultural counselors have been culturally encapsulated. Ponterotto (1988) summarized many of the criticisms leveled at cross-cultural research on counseling regarding methodology in its disregard for cultural complexity.

1. There is no conceptual theoretical framework.
2. There is an overemphasis on simplistic counselor–client process variables while important psychosocial variables are disregarded.
3. There is overreliance on experimental analogue research outside the "real-world" setting.
4. There is disregard for intracultural within-group differences.
5. There is overdependence on student samples of convenience.
6. There is continued reliance on culturally encapsulated measures.
7. There is a failure to adequately describe the sample according to cultural backgrounds.
8. There is a failure to describe the limits of *generalizability*.
9. There is a lack of minority cultural input.
10. There is a failure of responsibility by researchers toward minority subject pools.

Many, if not all, of these weaknesses have resulted from a narrow definition of culture and disregard for the broad definition.

Defining culture broadly rather than narrowly helps avoid the problems of encapsulation. First, the broad definition allows and forces counselors to be more accurate in matching a client's intended and culturally learned expectation with the client's behavior. Second, a broad definition helps counselors become more aware of how their own culturally learned perspective predisposes them toward a particular decision outcome. Third, a broad perspective helps counselors become more aware of the complexity in cultural identity patterns, which may or may not include the obvious indicators of ethnicity and nationality. Fourth, the broad definition encourages counselors to track the ever-changing salience of a client's different interchangeable cultural identities within a counseling interview.

9. White Privilege Is Real

It is sometimes difficult for the dominant culture to recognize the privileges that come with dominant culture membership. It is easy to assume that everyone is on the same "level playing field" from the perspective of advantage. Many of the opponents of affirmative action take this perspective, saying affirmative action is at best unnecessary and at worst a racist policy. The Multi-City Study of Urban Inequality recently completed a 5-year study of Boston, Atlanta, Detroit, and Los Angeles sponsored by the Russell Sage Foundation and the Harvard University Multidisciplinary Program in Inequality and Social Policy (O'Connor, 1999). In this 5-year study, 50 researchers interviewed 9,000 households and 3,500 employers. They found that race is deeply entrenched in the cultural landscape of the United States and that racial stereotypes and attitudes heavily influence the labor market in its attempts to understand the specific basis of racial and cultural inequality.

D. W. Sue and Sue (1999) pointed out:

> Euro-American mental health professionals need to realize that they have directly or indirectly benefited from individual, institutional, and cultural racism. While many Whites may acknowledge that minorities and women are placed at a disadvantage in the current system, few realize or recognize "White privilege." (p. 219)

White privilege refers to the invisible systems that confer dominance on Whites (McIntosh, 1989), even though none of them may have chosen to be racist or biased or prejudiced, through being socialized in a racist society. There is a need to accept responsibility for the consequences of White privilege, however unintentional it may be, and understand the anger that might well be a consequence of that privilege. Peggy McIntosh (see Cruz & Cooley,

1994) has developed specific examples illustrating White privilege in a list of 27 statements about ordinary decisions of daily life, which can be routinely done by a member of the dominant culture but not as easily done by a member of a minority culture. Considerable research has been done on White awareness (Axelson, 1999; Helms & Cook, 1999; D. W. Sue & Sue, 1999) in the attempt to get beyond guilt toward developing a positive cultural identity among White cultural groups.

10. Conclusion

The development of multicultural awareness begins with an awareness of culturally learned assumptions. The assumptions highlighted in this chapter are as follows:

1. Multicultural perspectives emphasize each group's similarities and differences at the same time.
2. Multicultural perspectives are necessarily complex.
3. Multicultural perspectives are dynamic for each person, place, and time.
4. Multiculturalism is broadly inclusive and not narrow.

The inclusive multicultural perspective of emphasizing both similarities and differences has inhibited research on multicultural aspects of counseling because the measures of culture are inadequate. It is easier to ignore culture or to limit the cultural perspective to either similarities or differences. Breaking this first rule of multiculturalism has resulted in false, inadequate, and incomplete choices. The controversy over "political correctness" reflects the inadequacy of this false dichotomy in which both sides of the argument are wrong. The argument supporting an objectively "correct" view of each culture rightly protects the unique and different perspectives of each cultural group against insult but wrongly presumes that culture is defined by these objective guidelines. The argument against political correctness rightly emphasizes the need to find common ground across cultures but wrongly presumes that cultural differences are unimportant.

To escape from what Wrenn (1985) called *cultural encapsulation*, counselors need to challenge the cultural bias of their own untested criteria. To leave our assumptions untested or, worse yet, to be unaware of our culturally learned assumptions is not consistent with the standards of good and appropriate counseling.

EXERCISE: Label Awareness

How do you discover when another person's perception of you may differ from your own perception of yourself? Organize participants into small groups of five to eight persons. Attach a gummed label of positive adjectives or nouns to the forehead or back of each group member and ask the group to discuss any topic relevant to the program. Interact with each participant *as though* the adjectives or nouns on their forehead or back label were true for each of the other participants, with all participants considering each other's label as real and truthful for a 5-'to 10-minute interaction.

Each participant will know which labels are on the foreheads of the *others* in the group but *will not* know his or her *own* label. The labels may be typed up beforehand, or you may ask each participant to write an appropriate label, making sure that no participant gets his or her own label for the discussion. When the participants have successfully identified the label on their foreheads or back, they can remove the label. The objective is to provide clues to others about the label on their forehead through behavior toward that person without directly giving away his or her identity. Can you accurately interpret how others perceive you based on what they say or do to you?

Can participants successfully guess their labels or accurately interpret cues from others in the group? When all participants have guessed their labels, discuss the function of actual labels by which others perceive and evaluate us. If some participants have not guessed their labels within 5 to 10 minutes, ask them to remove their labels anyway and begin the discussion. The emphasis is on the wide diversity of perceived identity labels we attach to one another.

THE LABEL AWARENESS EXERCISE

Participant Objectives:
1. To provide feedback to others appropriate to their assigned label.
2. To analyze feedback from others appropriate to one's own label.
3. To identify one's own label accurately based on feedback.

Learning Objective:
1. Each of us wears a culturally assigned label in the perception of others.

CHAPTER 3

Alternative and Complementary Therapies

Major objective:

1. To demonstrate cultural biases in counseling and what can be done to change them.

Secondary objectives:

1. To identify 10 examples of frequently encountered cultural biases in counseling.
2. To identify non-Western alternative perspectives and assumptions about counseling.
3. To describe the construct of individualism and its consequences.
4. To examine unintentional racism.

Conventional counseling methods typically refer to methods derived from research in Europe and the United States and disseminated elsewhere in what Berry, Poortinga, Segall, and Dasen (1992) called *scientific acculturation*. The importance of indigenous psychologies has been increasingly apparent throughout the field of psychology (U. Kim & Berry, 1993). Western cultures are described as more idiocentric, emphasizing competition, self-confidence, and freedom, whereas non-Western cultures are more allocentric, emphasizing communal responsibility, social usefulness, and acceptance of authority. Approximately one third of the people in the United States, half of those in Europe, and more than three quarters of people worldwide regularly use some kind of complementary or alternative health treatment, frequently originating in non-Western cultures (Micozzi, 1996).

Western and non-Western approaches are becoming more complementary to one another as counseling and psychology increasingly include attention to non-Western therapies. There are several assumptions that distinguish non-Western therapies (Nakamura, 1964).

1. In non-Western cultures, self—the substance of individuality—and the reality of belonging to an absolute cosmic self are intimately related. Illness is related to a lack of spiritual balance in the cosmos as much as to physical ailments.
2. Asian theories of personality generally deemphasize individualism and emphasize social relationships. Collectivism more than individualism typically describes the majority of world cultures.
3. Interdependence or even dependency relationships in Hindu and Chinese cultures are valued as healthy. Independence is much more dysfunctional in a collectivist culture.
4. Experience rather than logic can serve as the basis for interpreting psychological phenomena. Subjectivity and objectivity are perceived as psychologically valid approaches to data.

Sheikh and Sheikh (1989, 1996) provided a good review of non-Western therapies with specific examples.

1. Conventional Assumptions

Counseling has been characterized by conventional assumptions from the Euro-American cultural context in which counseling originated as a professional activity. Ten examples of these assumptions demonstrate their pervasive influence on counseling.

1. Counselors all share the same single measure of what is normal behavior. There is a frequent assumption that describing a person's behavior as normal reflects a judgment both meaningful and representative of a desired pattern of culture-specific behaviors across social, economic, political, and cultural contexts.
2. Individuals are the basic building blocks of society. The presumption is that counseling is primarily directed toward the development of individuals rather than collectivities or groups such as the family, the organization, or society itself.
3. Only problems defined within a framework of the counselor's expertise or academic discipline boundaries are of concern to the counselor. There is a tendency to isolate the professional identity of the counselor from that of other professionals even though multicultural problems wander across these boundaries freely.
4. There is a superior quality judgment attached to abstractions. In our use of professional jargon, we all attach the same meaning to the same words across contexts. While this assumption is typical of a "low-context culture" in which the context is less relevant, it would not apply to cultures in which all meaning is contextually mediated.

5. Independence is desirable and dependence is not desirable. As part of the Western emphasis on individualism, there is a belief that individuals should not be dependent on others or allow others to become dependent on them. This is not the case in a more collectivistic culture.

6. Clients are helped more by formal and professional counseling than by their natural support systems. Family and peer support are the primary resources in many cultures in which counseling is a last resort, only when everything else has failed. The long-term positive effect of counseling may require family and peer support.

7. Everyone thinks the same way, moving linearly from cause to effect. It is not just the content of our thinking that is culturally mediated but the very process of thinking itself. Nonlinear thinking, typical of many non-Western cultural groups, will seem illogical to linear thinkers.

8. Counselors need to change clients to fit the system and not change the system to fit the client. Advocacy by counselors is frequently considered unethical. Much of counseling relates to client adjustment, sometimes even when the system is wrong and the client is right.

9. History is not relevant for a proper understanding of contemporary events. Counselors are more likely to focus on the immediate here-and-now events that created a crisis and consider historical background a distraction at best and a defensive evasion at worst.

10. We already know all of our culturally learned assumptions. Each time we discover something new about ourselves, we disprove this assumption. As we increase our contact with persons and groups from other cultures, this process of self-discovery is accelerated.

All counseling is, to a greater or lesser extent, multicultural. As we increase our contact with other countries and cultures, we can expect to learn a great deal about ourselves. We can expect to challenge more of our unexamined assumptions about ourselves as we learn to know and comprehend the world around us. We can expect to move beyond the parochial concerns of our culturally limited perspective to see the world around us in a new and more comprehensive perspective. The primary argument for increasing our multicultural knowledge and comprehension is to enhance our accuracy and effectiveness as counselors across the great variety of cultural contexts.

2. Alternative and Complementary Assumptions

Alternative therapies (ATs) do not rely primarily on drugs, medical technology, or other conventional therapeutic approaches. There are many reasons why ATs have become more popular recently and why there are so many anecdotal examples of success using AT: AT is typically less expensive; insurance companies are increasing their recognition of AT for third-party payments; reverse technology transfer has become popular; the AT patient is more involved as a participant in healing; AT is considered less invasive, more low tech, and more gentle and natural; AT relies on self-healing capabilities; and AT values subjective relationship aspects (Tart, 1975).

There are many different kinds of ATs. One type has an intellectual foundation and time-tested methods, such as homeopathy, herbal therapy, chiropractic, osteopathy, and traditional Chinese acupuncture. Another type is more unusual and offers a more dramatic and spectacular cure for specific serious diseases but without a lot of scientific research or supporting documentation for methods, such as megavitamins or shark cartilage. It is important to distinguish these two types when considering AT. The following are some of the typical questions people ask about AT: Why do patients seek AT? What forms may help certain illnesses? What forms are potentially harmful or useless? How can AT complement conventional medicine? How can AT healing be balanced with conventional therapy? These questions present a challenge to conventional counseling and therapy.

Western or conventional therapies have become a cultural institution of their own defined by their own cultural assumptions, both explicit and implicit. Conventional therapies have tended to rely on insight and objective consciousness, are progress-oriented, assume a mind–body dichotomy, value efficiency, require empirical proof, and tend to separate the individual from the context. These assumptions have a great deal of power, especially in ambiguous situations, and Western people have a strong emotional attachment to conventional assumptions—even when there is sometimes contrary evidence. In any case, the conventional assumptions themselves are seldom examined and frequently confused with fact. Conventional assumptions are typically implicit in the ways counseling is taught and practiced.

We can best examine AT assumptions by examining conventional assumptions. Some examples of conventional or Western assumptions provided by Tart (1975) are that the universe was created spontaneously or accidentally and has always been as it now is, that there is no purpose or reason for the universe, that the universe is "dead," and that physics is the study of the real world and hard sciences are better than soft sciences.

Assumptions about people are that the purpose of life is to maximize pleasure and minimize pain; the universe is harsh, uncaring, and unresponsive; our purpose is to conquer the universe; we are the supreme life form and probably the only intelligent life form; lower organisms exist for the benefit of humans; and only humans are conscious.

Assumptions about the mind–body dichotomy suggest that the body is a passive servo-mechanism of the brain, the physical body is the only one we have, death is the inevitable end of human life, physical death is the termination of consciousness, personality gives people their unique identity, and the loss of personality is pathology.

Assumptions about knowledge suggest that knowledge is a hypothesis and not direct or certain, knowledge can be transmitted in writing, written words are least ambiguous and most accurate, logical inconsistency proves invalidity, faith means believing in things that are not real, intuition is a lucky guess, symbols are physical objects with emotional meanings, and beliefs do not affect the real world.

Assumptions about emotions suggest that emotions are electrical/chemical shifts, interfere with logic, should be suppressed or eliminated, have no place in scientific work, and are self-serving and animal functions.

Assumptions about learning are that it involves electrochemical changes, intellectual learning is the highest form, people with a high IQ are better learners, memory is not as reliable as objective records, one's only memory is of one's own life experiences, the only memories we have access to are our own, and desiring things is the basic motivation of life.

Assumptions about perception are that we can only perceive the physical world through our nervous system and that perception is selective and biased.

Assumptions about social relationships are that suffering is caused by others, no normal person likes to suffer, progress comes from improving society, scientific progress is cumulative, and our civilization is steadily progressing and is the best in all history as we learn to control the universe.

By contrast, the alternative assumptions by some non-Western societies may include the following:

1. A newborn infant is the result of previous lives.
2. Self is both individual and cosmic at the same time.
3. Social relationships are more important than individualism.
4. Maturity requires continuous dependency.
5. Personality is molded by duty and guilt sanctions.
6. Behavior is molded by parent–child relations.
7. Experience is more useful than logic to interpret behavior.
8. Rigid authority relationships do not inhibit development.
9. Life is dialectical.
10. Truth is paradoxical.

Conventional Western therapies and AT are compatible and complementary, if we begin by looking at the basic assumptions and starting points of each system. Each system recognizes alternative methods to achieve similar goals, and in that way AT and conventional therapies can contribute to one another's success.

3. Specific Non-Western Therapies

The separation of Asian and Western cultures sometimes obscures more than it illuminates (Nakamura, 1964). The common features of one hemisphere are either partly or imperfectly understood in the other hemisphere or were conspicuous in a particular country at a particular time and then generalized to include the whole hemisphere. The assumptions underlying Asian psychological thinking relate to basic collective or corporate philosophical assumptions of the self in a context of human existence. In Asia, there is much less emphasis on individualism and more emphasis on a corporate identity that balances aspects of the self. Likewise, there is a more positive interpretation of dependence and interdependencies within the unit, the family, and society. The family plays a particularly significant role as a model for defining the balance of roles for institutional social relationships of society. Many Asian cultures define the personality in relational terms, focusing on the relationship connections between individuals rather than on the individuals themselves. The emphasis in these Asian systems is mainly on the structure of family, clan, class, and state through which individuals relate to one another. Asian thinking is by no means unimodal, however, and has many different approaches to cognition.

Benesch and Ponterotto (1989) suggested that Asian clients rely more on intuition than reason in their worldviews. The "Eastern consciousness disciplines" assume that (a) ordinary consciousness is not the optimal state, (b) higher states of "multiple consciousness" exist, (c) people can attain higher states of consciousness through training, and (d) verbal communication about the higher states of consciousness is necessarily limited.

Psychological explanation is not a Western invention. Ancient India had developed a variety of personality theories, originally based on the *gunas,* or attributes of the mind, dating back to Vedic literature of about 800–500 BC. Each succeeding religion and philosophical system in India modified views of personality in its own way, generally emphasizing practical aspects of organizing, classifying, and understanding persons in relation to the family, society, and abstract values.

The development of psychological concepts in India went through a period emphasizing magic, in which people tried to understand nature, and a period emphasizing human concerns, as in Buddhism, in which inner harmony and psychic consciousness became the key to freedom. Awareness of suffering is a constant theme of Indian psychology, whereby the wise person escapes enslavement to selfishness by realizing the true nature of the universe.

Buddhism emphasizes the four Noble Truths and the eightfold path. The four Noble Truths are that (a) all life is subject to suffering, (b) desire to live is the cause of repeated existences, (c) the annihilation of desire gives release from suffering, and (d) the way of escape is through the eightfold path. The eightfold path is right belief, right thought, right speech, right action, right livelihood, right effort, right mindfulness, and right concentration to escape from desire. These ideas spread throughout Asia to influence the understanding of personality in a variety of settings.

When Buddhism was imported to China around the first century BC, it was modified to emphasize the social responsibility of Buddha's ethical teaching. The Chinese have been fairly characterized as valuing common sense and utilitarian ways of thinking. Even their philosophical teachings were based on practical subjects and included everyday examples of morality, politics, and a lifestyle that would result in successful living.

The indigenous Chinese view of personality developed from the teaching of Confucius (551–479 BC), which emphasized aspects of "characterological theory." The basic aspects of this view emphasize the notions of face, filial piety, and proper conduct. The notion of face brings out an individual's felt moral worth, assessed according to her or his loyalty to her or his group rather than according to universal principles, with social deviance controlled more by public shaming than private guilt. Filial piety describes a compliant and submissive posture toward authority. Proper conduct (*li*) defines the duty of persons and the necessity of observing proper forms of conduct for each social situation. The task of Chinese philosophy is to describe the "way" (Tao) to perfection of the personality along practical lines, synthesizing Confucian this-worldliness and Taoist otherworldliness to achieve "sageliness" within and "kingliness" without (P. Pedersen, 1983a).

Hsu (1985) described the very concept of being a person (*jen*) in Chinese culture as involving a dynamic balance, which he called *psychosocial homeostasis*. For every living human being, *jen* (personhood) is not a fixed entity. Like the human body, it is in a state of dynamic equilibrium. It is a matrix or a framework within which every human individual seeks to maintain a satisfactory level of psychic and interpersonal equilibrium, in the same sense that every physical organism tends to maintain a uniform and beneficial psychological stability within and between its parts (Hsu, 1985, pp. 33–34).

Cheung (1986) described empirical studies of both normal and abnormal Chinese participants that demonstrate multiple causal attributions and coping strategies for problem solving, suggesting an interactional paradigm. Psychological variables, somatic factors, and situational contexts all contribute to the Chinese understanding of the psychological. A systems model is more adequate to examine the multiple factors and to prescribe treatment. This interactional approach is similar to the biopsychological model of medicine gaining popularity in Western medicine.

The Japanese, influenced by both India and China, adapted and expanded these models of balance and harmony through the uniquely Japanese perspective of Zen. Zen Buddhism believes that persons who are emancipated from the dualistic bondage of subjectivity and objectivity of mind and body are awakened to their own true nature, or the condition of *Satori* or enlightenment. In that state, the person is finely tuned to the reality both inside and outside. Reynolds (1980) in his Zen center emphasized "phenomenological operationalism," during which the uneasy mind is refocused and regulated.

Relationships in Japanese culture stress groups rather than persons. Whereas the basic social unit in the West is the individual, and groups of individuals create a society, the Japanese society is more accurately understood as an aggregation of family units. Considerable importance is attached to esteem of the hierarchical order, with each person well defined in her or his role. Special attention is given to the family, clan, and nation as instrumental in defining loyalty through mutual exchange of obligation.

Role behavior becomes the means of self-realization for the modern Japanese. The individual is dedicated to and inseparable from her or his role, probably dating back to basic Confucian values embodied in the samurai elite of the 19th century. Carefully prescribed role relationships, beginning with the family, have contributed significantly to the stability of Japanese society despite rapid social change, at the cost of deemphasizing a sense of personal self. Achievement is not considered an individual phenomenon but rather the result of cooperation, both collaterally and hierarchically, in the combined and collective efforts of individuals. DeVoss (1973) noted, "Internalized sanctions make it difficult to conceive of letting down one's family or one's social groups and occupational superiors. In turn, those in authority positions must take paternal care of those for whom they have responsibility" (p. 185). Horizontal relationships among equals are not emphasized in traditional Japanese culture. Social cohesion and social control are exercised through participation in organizations directed to community betterment. How the individual feels about participating is beside the point. One is expected to meet the social expectations of others as one subordinates self to social role (DeVoss, 1973).

The Japanese self-consciously strive for higher goals to realize their ego ideal and are further motivated in this direction by a family-related, shame-oriented drive to be successful. The lifestyle is defined by attitudes toward work, illness, and death, whereby the person is duty bound to repay obligations. The ideals of self-denial are prominent in Japanese culture. The traditional Japanese family provides models through the father's omnipotence in the household and a mother whose task is to maintain harmony in the family.

The individual reconciles tension by living in accord with prescribed roles within family and society. The source of conflict most likely to occur is between individual ambition and role responsibility. Mental health, therefore, depends on keeping these two opposing tendencies in balance, so that the individual can move freely from masochistic hard work in the workplace to narcissistic relaxation at home, without either tendency taking control. It is necessary for the individual to transcend these categories by balancing them without weakening either tendency.

4. The Role of Individualism in Counseling

Describing, understanding, and helping individuals has been a central theme in the concepts of psychology and counseling as an application of those concepts. However, the notion of the individual is different across cultures. A Westernized description of the self is that of a separate, independent, and autonomous individual, guided by traits, abilities, values, and motives that distinguish that individual from others. The contrasting notion of person in many non-Western cultures emphasizes relationships, connections, and interdependencies in which that person is defined in a context and in which the individual is not separated from the unit to which he or she belongs. Berry et al. (1992) described the more individualistic cultures as more *idiocentric,* emphasizing competition, self-confidence, and freedom, whereas collectivistic cultures are more *allocentric,* emphasizing communal responsibility, social usefulness, and acceptance of authority. Collectivist cultures emphasize equality more than equity. The collectivist rules of justice, however, only apply to "insiders," so that the more collectivist cultures treat outsiders the same as persons are treated in individualist cultures. It is possible to find individualism and collectivism in the same person at the same time, suggesting that individualism and collectivism may not be opposites but rather independent variables.

Christopher (1992) described the role of individualism in psychological well-being from a Western perspective. Individualism is described as a "disguised ideology" that has shaped the social sciences to uncritically adopt individualistic notions of the good life. Until the implicit individualism in the social sciences has been identified and made explicit, it will be difficult to transfer the theory and practice of counseling to cultures that are less accepting of individualism.

Lukes (1973) identified the implicit values of individualism to include the dignity of the person, the priority for autonomy or self-direction, the need for privacy, and the goal of self-development. The notion of individuals as inherently worthy and dignified was based on a religious understanding of humans and later extended to the secular applications in the "natural rights" of man, growing out of the Enlightenment. The importance of autonomy disregards social commitments and obligations in favor of critical rational thought, growing out of the European Middle Ages. The importance of privacy resulted from turning inward for spiritual growth and insight. Self-development and realization of one's potential as a value grew out of the Renaissance, making the individual the focal point.

Lukes (1973) went on to describe the different varieties of individualism.

1. Methodological individualism suggests that explanations of social behavior are not accurate or are incomplete unless they are grounded in facts and empirical data about individuals.
2. Political individualism defines the basis of authority in the purposes and uses of power by individuals.
3. Economic individualism is a justification of self-serving economic behaviors and their deregulation by outside authority.
4. Religious individualism refers to the direct connection between the individual and God without intermediaries.
5. Ethical individualism describes the individual as the criteria of moral evaluation and the basis of moral judgment.
6. Epistemological individualism presumes that knowledge is primarily a property of individuals.

Individualism is a viewpoint that has shaped modern Westernized lifestyles in profoundly important ways. The heart of individualism is a metaphysical position of "the person as a disengaged or abstract self living in a disenchanted world" (Christopher, 1992, p. 105). Individualism presumes that the road to freedom requires that persons should be instrumental, rational, and expressive of themselves. Psychological well-being depends on individualistic indicators of health and illness. The uncritical acceptance of individualism has led to cultural bias in counseling that is captured by either objectivism on the one hand or relativistic subjectivism on the other. Individualism has been closely linked to modernization, and individually held attitudes, values, motives, or dispositions have been considered a necessary precondition for modernization. Changes in the environment provide opportunities for modernization by individuals with the appropriate attitudes, values, and beliefs.

Heilbronner (1975) pointed out the negative consequences of Westernized values such as individualism. Civilization is threatened by (a) overpopulation, particularly in less industrialized countries; (b) the spread of nuclear weapons and methods of mass destruction to countries that have been exploited in the past; and (c) the demands of technological advancement on limited environmental resources. The Westernized lifestyle toward growth and development is spreading to Third World cultures that seek to overcome social problems through economic growth and materialistic consumption. This has resulted in a less favorable climate of social satisfaction. Heilbronner sought the alternative to industrial destruction in preindustrial societies. Although science, technology, and industrialization have promoted material comforts, they have been less successful in promoting psychological well-being. The same individualistic cultural patterns that may have been adaptive at one stage of social development may require modification toward a more ecological perspective of preindustrial societies of our past and perhaps postindustrial societies of our future as well.

5. The Power of Unintentional Racism

Racism has been identified as a natural consequence of Westernized individualism. Individualism becomes a vivid example of unintentional bias by many counselors. Counselors who presume that they are free of racism seriously underestimate the social impact on their own socialization. In most cases, this racism emerges as an *unintentional* action by well-meaning, right-thinking, good-hearted, caring professionals who are probably no more or less free from cultural bias than other members of the general public. *Racism* is defined as a pattern of systematic behaviors resulting in the denial of opportunities or privileges to one social group by another. These behaviors are observable, measurable, verifiable, and predictable. Racism can refer to aversive behavior of individuals or of institutionalized social groups. Overt racism is intentional, in which a particular group is judged inferior or undeserving. Covert racism is unintentional, in which misinformation or wrong assumptions lead to inaccurate assessments or inappropriate treatments. Covert unintentional racism is less likely to be changed because there is no awareness of dissonance between intention and action. The unintentional racist may behave in ways that are even contradictory to that person's underlying motives (Ridley, 1989).

According to Sedlacek and Brooks (1976), most racism is unknowing or unintentional: People are unaware of the racist effects of their behavior. The key to changing the unintentional racist lies in examining basic underlying assumptions. While these culturally learned basic underlying assumptions control our behavior, our perceptions or understanding of rational behavior, and our definition of "truth," they usually remain unexamined. There are no courses in "underlying assumptions of counseling," nor is this a frequent area of research except perhaps in research on perception. There is rather the "assumption" that we all have the same understanding.

We depend on scientific objectivity to protect us from unintentional racism. In at least some cases, however, the very research on which we have depended to identify data-based truth contains implicit, unexamined assumptions that have continued this unintentional racism. Segall et al. (1990), in a review of human behavior in global perspective, pointed out the continuation of unexamined assumptions with regard to research on intelligence: "Much of the writing and thinking about race and intelligence has been sloppy, irrational, politically motivated, and extremely costly in human terms" (p. 100). The controversy surrounding Jensen's (1969) research on intelligence and racial identity has demonstrated how both sides of the argument cite "scientific" evidence in support of their position. There are many other examples of research on intelligence in multiracial societies in which one group has been politically and economically dominant and in which the less powerful groups have been targets of discrimination justified on the basis of "racial differences" in intelligence. These attitudes toward culturally different groups can be traced to "scientific racism" (Guthrie, 1976; Williams, 1978) and Euro-American ethnocentricism in psychology (White, 1984). D. W. Sue (1981) described the "genetic deficiency" model, which promoted the idea that Whites were superior to Blacks and other non-White populations for biological reasons. These beliefs have been traced to the early scientific writings of Charles Darwin and Sir Frances Galton. The scientific arguments for racial discrimination persist particularly in the literature about culturally biased tests. Lifton's (1986) book *The Nazi Doctors* is overpowering in its documentation of how some of the most advanced and distinguished scientists of that time could be so profoundly misled by their unexamined assumptions about racial issues with disastrous consequences. Herrnstein and Murray's (1994) book *The Bell Curve* provides another example of how science can be used to promote a political agenda in the measures of IQ and racial membership. Even good science can become bent by bad assumptions.

6. Formal and Informal Alternatives

From a systems perspective, counseling can occur in an informal as well as a formal mode. The place where counseling occurs as well as the method by which counseling is provided is defined by a balance of formal and informal support systems. The combination of formal and informal methods and contexts creates a dynamic combination of indigenous support systems that define our personal culture.

Although most research on support contains similar assumptions, definitions of support vary greatly (Caplan, 1976; Cobb, 1976). The kinds of support frequently mentioned include emotional support (feelings of closeness, intimacy, esteem, and encouragement), tangible goods and assistance, intellectual advice or guidance, and supportive socialization (Pearson, 1990). The accurate identification of social support networks helps to prevent disorder by the early detection of problems and referral to appropriate helpers (Gottlieb & Hall, 1980) and by meeting basic human needs for affiliation and attachment. The literature on counseling is now providing more data on the importance of indigenous support systems to mediate the functions of counseling (Pearson, 1990).

Figure 3.1 shows the full range of methods and contexts through which support systems function, from the most formal (in which rules, structures, and definite expectations apply) to the more informal (in which spontaneity and the lack of defined structures apply). The figure reveals a paradigm for describing the range of formal and informal support systems. The incorporation of formal and informal support systems has been included in previously published literature. Figure 3.1 incorporates the full range of previously identified possibilities for analyzing how the formal and informal systems complement one another. These combinations include a range of alternatives appropriate in various culturally diverse settings.

FIGURE 3.1

A Three-Dimensional Model of Counseling Services Methods

	Formal Method	Nonformal Method	Informal Method
Formal context	1 Office-scheduled therapy	4 Mental health training	7 Mental health presentation
Nonformal context	2 Community mental health	5 Support groups friends	8 Family and service
Informal context	3 Professional advice	6 Self-help groups	9 Daily encounter

Each cell of Figure 3.1 depicts a different combination of formal and nonformal features of counseling methods in various counseling contexts. Each cell in the figure illustrates a different meaning.

1. A formal method and formal context are involved when the counselor-specialist works with a fee-paying client in a scheduled office interview. Counseling as a professional activity occurs mostly in this cell.

2. A formal method and nonformal context are involved when the counselor-specialist works by invitation or appointment with a client in the client's home, office, or community. Semiformal meetings with individuals, families, or groups of foreign students are often best scheduled for locations outside the counseling office. A location that is more familiar to the client can make it easier to establish rapport when discussing personal problems.

3. A formal method and informal context are involved when the counselor-specialist is consulted about a personal problem by a friend or relative at a party or on the street. In some cultures, it is important for the person requesting help to be accepted as a friend before it is appropriate for that person to disclose intimate problems. When I counseled international students at the University of Minnesota, I first would have to be "checked out" at nationality-group parties or approached about personal problems informally on street corners and only later—if I passed the test—in an office or formal setting.

4. A nonformal method and formal context are involved when a person not functioning in the "role" of counselor is asked for psychological help or to provide a professional service, training, or presentation. When I counseled for 6 years in universities in Asia, it became clear that the functions of a counselor were not well understood. The concept of a medical doctor was clear, but the counselor was more a special kind of "teacher." To accept help from a teacher was honorable and increased one's status in the community. Consequently, it was frequently useful to describe counseling as a special kind of teaching and learning interaction. An Asian student would be quite comfortable asking her or his teacher for advice and help on a personal problem.

5. A nonformal method and nonformal context are involved in the various support groups organized by persons to help one another through regular contact and an exchange of ideas, even though none of the participants are trained as a therapist. When I had Asian or other international students as clients who were unfamiliar with counseling, I frequently would ask them to bring a friend to the interview. The friend, although not trained as a counselor, would function almost as a cotherapist by providing constant support, clarifying the content of formal counseling interviews, and helping me to understand the client by acting as mediator and interpreter. This can be especially useful if there is a language problem between the client and counselor.

6. A nonformal method and informal context are involved when self-help groups and popular psychology are used as resources. A frequent indicator of culture shock is withdrawal from support groups and increased

isolation from groups of others. There are various self-help groups, such as Alcoholics Anonymous and other organizations for addicts, single persons, veterans, or those who share the common bond of a traumatic experience. Similarly, there is much literature on positive thinking or advice giving that is a frequent source of help. My Chinese clients frequently first consulted the Confucian proverbs for advice and sought counseling only when the proverbs seemed inadequate.

7. An informal method and formal context are involved when a listener receives considerable assistance in solving a psychological problem from a formal, scheduled presentation or activity even if that was not the explicit intention of the program. In non-Western cultures, much of what we call counseling in Western settings occurs through religious institutions. Family meetings and activities also provide valuable vehicles for the functions of counseling and leave a great vacuum by their absence. These institutions are not primarily psychological, nor is their primary purpose to promote mental health. The ritualistic context, however, is often formal and contributes significantly to healthy mental attitudes.

8. An informal method and nonformal context are involved when family and friends provide help to an individual. In many Asian cultures, it would be unacceptable to go outside the family or a very close circle of friends to disclose personal problems. In some situations, a foreign student under stress while in the United States may be helped by making contact with relatives or close friends who can serve as a resource and context for casual and indirect conversations that can promote healthy mental attitudes.

9. An informal method and informal context are involved in daily encounters in which individuals receive help spontaneously and unexpectedly from their contacts with other people, whether that help is intended or unintended. Spontaneous recovery from crises or stress takes many forms. Imagine, for example, that it is a nice day and you are walking down the street. Someone smiles. You smile back. You feel better. Each culture teaches its own repertoire of self-help mechanisms for healing.

A comprehensive picture of formal and informal support systems helps to classify the different sources of psychological help. Without an adequate framework to identify the resources, counselors are likely to rely too heavily on more formal, obvious support systems and ignore the less obvious, informal alternatives. If counselors seek to translate counseling and therapy to culturally different populations, they will need to complement the diverse informal influences in clients' support systems. The formal and informal framework highlights the complexity of clients' indigenous support systems and also indicates the importance of matching the right method and context so that culturally skilled counseling can occur.

7. Conclusion

We are at the starting point in developing multicultural awareness about how conventional and alternative therapies can work together. First, we need to examine our own assumptions and the implicit assumptions in the therapies we teach and learn. Only those who are able to escape being caught up in the web of their own assumptions and maintain a balanced perspective will be able to achieve long-term competence in counseling. The dangers of cultural encapsulation and the dogma of increasingly technique-oriented definitions of counseling have been frequently mentioned in the rhetoric of professional associations in the social services as criteria for accreditation.

In their national plan for behavioral science research, the Basic Behavioral Science Task Force of the National Advisory Mental Health Council (1996) identified several areas in which social and cultural factors were evident in research literature about mental health. First, anthropological and cross-cultural research has demonstrated that cultural beliefs influence the diagnosis and treatment of mental illness. Second, the diagnosis of mental illness differs across cultures. Third, research has revealed differences in how individuals express symptoms in different cultural contexts. Fourth, culturally biased variations in diagnosis vary according to the diagnostic categories relevant to the majority population. Fifth, most providers come from a majority culture whereas most clients are members of minority cultures.

There is a pervasive awareness of change in the social sciences generally and among counselors in particular that will require rethinking our culturally learned conventional assumptions. J. A. Smith, Harre, and Van Langenhove (1995) contrasted the new with the old paradigms. The new paradigms emphasize applied understanding more than abstract measurement, finding meaning more than causation, social significance more than statistical significance, explanation more than numerical reductionism, holistic rather than atomistic perspectives, particularities more than universals, context-based more than context-free perspectives, and subjectivity as much as objectivity. The old and new rules are seamlessly connected in the cultural context of counseling with a connection to both conventional and alternative perspectives.

We are also at the starting point in developing multicultural awareness as a criteria for counseling. Only those who are able to escape being caught up in the web of their own assumptions and maintain a balanced perspective will be able to communicate effectively with other cultures. The dangers of cultural encapsulation and the dogma of increasingly technique-oriented definitions of counseling have been frequently mentioned in the rhetoric of professional associations in the social services as criteria for accreditation. To escape from what Wrenn (1962, 1985) called *cultural encapsulation,* counselors need to challenge the cultural bias of their own untested criteria. To leave our assumptions untested or, worse yet, to be unaware of our culturally learned assumptions is not consistent with the standards of good and appropriate counseling.

EXERCISE: The Outside Expert

Sometimes it is difficult for outside experts to understand information provided by a host culture. Patterns of response that are obvious and consistent from the host culture's point of view may seem frustrating, inconsistent, uncooperative, and even hostile to the outside expert who does not know the host culture's rules.

Request volunteers from the group to leave the room briefly and return as an "outside expert team" invited into the host culture to identify the group's problem and explore solutions. In a large group, you may select a separate team for every 8 or 10 participants to work simultaneously.

While the volunteers are outside the room, instruct the *remaining* participants in the three "rules" of their "host culture."

1. They may respond only by a "yes" or "no" to any question. All questions by the outside experts must be questions that can be answered yes or no.
2. Men may respond only to men and women only to women. Female participants will ignore all questions by male experts, and male participants will ignore all questions by female experts.
3. If the expert is "smiling" when asking a question, the same-sex participant will say "yes," but if the expert is not smiling when asking a question, the same-sex participant will say "no."

The experts return and are instructed about the first rule, that all their questions must be answered "yes" or "no," to give them a clue about the host culture's rules and to reduce frustration. The experts are encouraged to work individually and to roam the room asking as many participants yes/no questions as possible, speaking loudly enough so that other participants can hear as data are gathered. After about 10 minutes, the experts report back to the group on the nature of the host culture's problem with suggestions for solutions.

Typically, the experts have generated an elegant interpretation of their data based on the yes/no responses. When the experts have shared their observations, thank them, lead a round of applause for their contribution, and *then reveal the other two cultural rules.* The discussion may emphasize the importance of understanding a culture's rules before collecting data. Participants learn to recognize that inconsistency may be by the outside expert (sometimes smiling, sometimes not) as well as by the host culture people and that what one person says may differ from what the other person hears. Discussion should emphasize the *process* of entering the host culture as an outside expert.

When debriefing participants, these frequently observed patterns might be helpful:

1. The experts frequently disregard nonverbals such as gender or smiling, which profoundly shape their data.
2. The experts frequently experience the host culture as inconsistent when actually it was the expert who was inconsistent, sometimes smiling and sometimes not smiling.
3. The experts frequently describe the host culture in negative terms ("I wouldn't want to spend summer vacation there!") when in fact the host culture was trying to be hospitable within the limits of its rules.
4. The data gathered by the experts tell more about the expert's priorities than they do about the host culture.

OUTSIDE EXPERT EXERCISE

Participant Objectives:
1. To identify communication cues in an unfamiliar culture.
2. To gather information systematically from an unfamiliar culture.
3. To report ambiguities and stress factors from the interaction.

Learning Objective:
1. Misunderstandings occur between the expert and the host culture whenever behavior is not interpreted in its cultural context.

CHAPTER 4

Developing a Cultural Identity

Major objective:

1. To describe the process of developing a cultural identity.

Secondary objectives:

1. To demonstrate culture shock as a change-promoting process in identity formation.
2. To describe alternative models of racial/ethnic identity development.
3. To define cultural identity development.

Identity is developed in a cultural context. Belonging to a cultural group means accepting the beliefs and symbols of that group as having meaning and importance in a profoundly personal sense. Identity includes personal elements such as one's name, social connections such as one's family, and cultural connections such as one's nationality and ethnicity. This combined description of identity has also been referred to as one's personality. As we become more aware of how ethnographic, demographic, status, and formal/informal affiliations have shaped our lives, we become more intentional in understanding our own identity through developing multicultural awareness. We become more aware of our cultural identity through contact with persons from other cultures who are different from ourselves, and we see ourselves in contrast.

Cultural identity is complicated. Sometimes within-group differences seem to exceed between-groups differences as we track the complex and dynamic salience of our own cultural self-identity across situations and times. This chapter presents an *orthogonal* model of cultural identity that allows each of us to belong to several cultures at the same time. Then we look at the literature on racial/ethnic identity development, and finally we look at the stages of culture shock as our identity is challenged by others who see things differently.

1. An Orthogonal Definition of Cultural Self-Identity

Oetting and Beauvais (1991) developed a theory of cultural identification that does not polarize cultures but instead acknowledges the simultaneous multiplicity of coexisting identities in each person. This orthogonal model recognizes that increased identification with one culture does not require decreased identification with other cultures. People can belong to many different cultures at the same time (P. Pedersen, 2000).

The five most frequently used alternative models of cultural identity are less complex than the orthogonal model but are also less adequate. The *dominant majority* model simply imposes a dominant culture on all minority groups, regardless of the consequences. The *transitional* model presumes a movement toward the dominant culture as an appropriate adjustment. The *alienation* model seeks to avoid stress from anomie by assisting persons in transition to make successful adjustments to some external norm. The *multidimensional* model presumes transition on several dimensions at the same time with different degrees of adjustment on each dimension. The *bicultural* model presumes that one can adapt to a new culture without losing contact with an earlier culture. The *orthogonal* model, however, suggests that adapting simultaneously to any one culture is independent from adapting to many other cultures, thus providing an unlimited combination of patterns that combine the preceding five alternative models as each being partially valid, depending on the situation. The orthogonal model presumes a higher level of complexity and a more comprehensive inclusion of cultural identities. The orthogonal model offers several advantages:

1. Cultural groups may exist in association with one another without isolating themselves or competing with one another.
2. Minority cultures need not be eliminated or absorbed to coexist with the dominant majority culture.
3. A permanent multicultural society may be possible that is multifaceted and multidimensional without becoming a melting pot imposed by the dominant culture or anarchy and chaos imposed by the different competing cultural minorities.
4. Conflicts of value and belief do not present insurmountable barriers but may be combined in a realistic pluralism. Although some primary values and beliefs of each cultural group cannot be compromised, other secondary values and beliefs can be adapted and modified to fit a changing society.
5. Cultural conflict may become a positive rather than a negative force from the perspective of shared common-ground expectations, even when the culturally learned behaviors of minorities are perceived to be different and seemingly hostile to the dominant culture.

6. Members of minority groups may be less inclined toward militancy when their survival is not threatened. Personal and social advancement requires an environment that is safe enough that people can take risks with one another. Without safety, no one will take the risk. Without risk, little or no learning occurs.
7. Interaction between minority and majority cultures may be less destructive for all parties. The orthogonal model describes a win-win outcome for conflict among culturally different peoples.
8. There are economic advantages of releasing resources previously consumed by cultural conflict. Imposed and enforced harmony is expensive and frequently ineffective in the long run. Voluntary harmony promotes the best interests of everyone if it can be achieved through willing cooperation.
9. There are already models of orthogonal relationships in healthy bicultural and multicultural individuals or social units. These models have appeared briefly but have then usually been overcome by the need for power by a dominant majority or the need to protect special interests by a hostile minority. Pluralism is neither easy to achieve nor simple to maintain. However, the alternatives are likely to be more expensive in the long term.

Although Erikson (1968) emphasized the importance of autonomy and initiative development during the childhood years in his classic model of identity, it is also true that his psychosocial concepts defined the individual self in the context of this community's values, norms, and social roles. Whereas Erikson's model favors the individualistic worldview and perhaps the more masculine roles, the notion of a "separated self" is now being replaced with a notion of "self-in-relationship," in which the sense of self reflects the relationships between people. Bond-Claire, Pilner, and Stoker (1998) introduced a new way of thinking about intrapersonal competence in which the self is the object of implicit mental models as it relates to successful functioning in adulthood. They looked at how individuals function on their own terms, free from any particular external social norm for success. This makes the cultural context central to self-identity.

The individualized self, rooted in individualism of the Western world, is being overtaken by a more familial self, typical of the global majority, as best described by Geertz (1975):

> The Western conception of the person as a bounded, unique, more or less integrated motivational and cognitive universe, a dynamic center of awareness, emotion, judgment and action organized into a distinctive whole and set contrastively both against other such wholes and against a social and natural background is, however incorrigible it may seem to us, a rather peculiar idea within the context of the world's cultures. (p. 48)

The more corporate notion of a relational self is integrated into the orthogonal perspective.

2. Theories of Self-Identity

Theories of self-identity frequently fail to take into account the significance of social identification in the definition of self. *Social identities* are self-definitions that are more inclusive than the individuated self-concept (Brewer, 1991). The orthogonal self-identity becomes a link between the individual self or selves and the social context in which that individual self or selves exist.

The sociocultural context guides the definition of self in several ways (Markus & Kitayama, 1991). One way is through independent self-construal, in which the self is perceived as a separate identity with internal characteristics that are stable across situations regardless of context. This perspective is typical of the more individualistic cultures. An alternative way more typical of collectivistic societies connects the notion of self to societal roles and relationships. This interdependent self-construal is relationship centered, requiring conformity and seeking harmony over personal goals. This interdependent self depends more on context than internal attributes.

Kagitcibasi (1996) characterized Western psychology as affirming the separated self as a healthy prototype basic to the prescriptive nature of applied psychology. When this expresses itself as selfishness, self-centeredness, and a lack of social commitment, psychology becomes more a part of the social problems for non-Western cultures than part of the solution. The individualistic Western cultural ethos favored by American psychology draws a clear and narrow boundary between the self and nonself, contrary to the construal of self in many non-Western cultures. However, because American psychology has a dominant position and is self-contained, the individualistic perspective is often assumed to be universal. The linking of the social with the individual perspective is essential to the development of multicultural awareness.

Culture is the context in which all behaviors are learned. Imagine yourself surrounded by thousands of people whom you have met, learned from, and come to appreciate in your lifetime. Each of these culture teachers has taught you something that you have incorporated into your identity. You do not have just one cultural identity; rather, thousands of different potentially salient identities are presented by ethnographic, demographic, status, and affiliation groups as they take turns whispering advice into your ear.

Imagine the thousands of culture teachers sitting in your seat with you, talking with you and talking among themselves about you as you interact with them or listen passively. These metaphorical voices are not a schizophrenic episode but the healthy and normal behavior of most thinking people. Spengler, Strohmer, Dixon, and Shivy (1995) defined thinking as multidimensional: "We recognize that multiple world views of reality lead to multiple sources of evidence and ways of explaining and predicting human behavior" (p. 508). Developing multicultural awareness of your identity means observing yourself, finding patterns in complex data, challenging faulty inference, and being guided by each person's cultural context.

While theories of cultural or ethnic identity development disagree regarding the highest or final stage of identity development, they generally agree that the lowest stage is where people are captured by racism and prejudice. The most frequently encountered examples of racism and prejudice are displayed by what White (1984) called a "Euro-American ethnocentricity." According to this perspective, the criteria for normal behavior, personal beauty, and competence are based on characteristics associated with a dominant culture in the European and later Euro-American traditions.

Liberation movements for women, minorities, the disabled, the elderly, and other special populations in the 1960s and 1970s began to accept the idea that judging all populations by a narrow standard was racist and dominated by prejudice. Special populations began to develop their own separate criteria for group identity. White (1984) developed a seven-dimension psychology of Blackness. Jones and Korchin (1982) described research about how psychology is understood in the Third World, with Khatib and Nobles (1977) describing African peoples, Tong (1971) describing the Chinese, and Martinez (1977) describing the *LaRaza* psychology of Hispanics and others. Also at about this time, McGoldrick, Pearce, and Giordano (1982) began developing criteria for "White" ethnic groups as culturally defined populations. A wide range of psychologies classified specific groups of "Third-World minorities," ethnocultural groups, and specific special populations according to different and separate characteristics.

Erikson's (1968) stages of identity development theory apply less accurately to minority groups than to the dominant European American culture. The early development of typologies for describing stages of identity development for Black Americans (Cross, 1971; Thomas, 1971), Asian Americans (D. W. Sue & Sue, 1972), and Hispanics (Szapocznik, Kurtines, & Fernandez 1980) stimulated research in a wide range of ethnic identity stage-based models.

The process of identity development is essentially linked to cultural factors. D. W. Sue (1977) described a two-dimensional model matching locus of control with locus of responsibility. His model is divided into four cells. The first cell matching internal control and internal responsibility describes dominant culture values and is achievement oriented. The second cell matching internal control and external responsibility is where people have the power to change if given the chance but where their typical response is to attack the system and challenge the value of counseling. The third cell matching external control and internal responsibility is similar to the role of oppressed minorities, where self-hatred and marginality are problems. The fourth cell matching external control and external responsibility is where the system is blamed for any and all failures and where people need to learn appropriate coping skills.

Acculturation strategies describe the ways in which an individual or group relates to the dominant society (Berry et al., 1992). By combining ideas from the literature on cultural change and intergroup relations, Berry et al. designed a model based on two issues. The first central issue is the extent to which the individual or group members want to conserve their own cultural background as opposed to giving up their cultural traditions. The second central issue is the extent to which the individual or group members want interactions with members of other groups in the larger society as opposed to turning away from other groups. Berry et al.'s (1992) conceptual framework posits four alternative styles of acculturation.

> When an acculturating individual does not wish to maintain culture and identity and seeks daily interaction with the dominant society, then the *assimilation* path or strategy is defined. In contrast, when there is a value placed on holding onto one's original culture and a wish to avoid interaction with others, then the *separation* alternative is defined. When there is an interest in both maintaining one's original culture and in daily interactions with others, *integration* is the option; here there is some degree of cultural integrity maintained, while moving to participate as an integral part of the larger social network. Integration is the strategy that attempts to make the best of both worlds. Finally, when there is little possibility or interest in cultural maintenance (often for reasons of enforced cultural loss), and little possibility or interest in relations with others (often for reasons of exclusion or discrimination), then *marginalization* is defined. (pp. 278–279)

Kitano (1989) provided a model that is also divided into four cells looking at the two dimensions of assimilation and ethnic identity. The first cell is described by a high level of assimilation but a low level of ethnic identity in which people lump themselves together as "Americans" without differentiation. The second cell is described by a high level of assimilation and a high level of ethnic identity in which people are bicultural or multicultural in their orientation. The third cell is described by a high level of ethnic identity and a low level of assimilation, for example, new immigrants or some very traditional or isolated and separatist cultural groups. The fourth cell is described by a low level of assimilation and a low level of ethnic identity, for example, dropouts or persons alienated from society at all levels.

3. Ethnic Identity Development Theories

Thomas (1971) provided a five-stage model of "Negromachy" to cut through the confusion of Black ethnic identity development as a process. His first stage was one of withdrawal. His second stage was one during which individuals testify to what they believed. His third stage involved processing information on or about the Black heritage. His fourth stage involved actively working through Black subgroups. His fifth and final stage was "transcendental," in which each person is a member of humanity in a membership that goes beyond groups. It is significant that Thomas's model moves in a divergent direction from a narrow to a broad focus.

Cross (1971), writing independently at about the same time on the topic of Black ethnic identity, came up with a four-stage model. His first stage was preencounter, where the world is described as "anti-Black." His second stage involved an encounter that validated the person's Blackness. His third stage involved immersion and a deliberate rejection of non-Black values. His fourth stage emphasized internalization to sharply define a secure sense of Black identity. Cross's early descriptions were "convergent," moving from a broad to a narrow focus in identity development. Cross (1991) later expanded his earlier design to move from a broad focus to a narrow convergent focus midway in the identity development process and then toward a broader divergent focus at the highest stages.

Jackson (1975) also presented a Black identity development model with four stages. The first stage emphasizes passive acceptance of things as they are. The second stage emphasizes active resistance to the way things are. The third stage involves "redirection" to find new ways and to make changes. The fourth stage is internalization of identity by taking the best elements of all previous stages. Marcia (1980) based his research on Erikson's (1968) stages of crisis in ego identity formation, incorporating stages of identity diffusion, foreclosed identity, and, finally, an achieved identity. Delworth (1989) built on Marcia's work to focus on gender-related aspects of identity development. Relationships form a central aspect of identity development for women. Ponterotto and Pedersen (1993) discussed still other examples of stage-graded models of identity development.

Most stage development models suggest that individuals experience three to five phases or stages of cultural identification. First, there is an identification with the dominant culture in a preencounter, conformity, or traditional stage. Second, there is an awakening to the impact of racism in a transitional encounter or dissonant stage. Third, there is an identification with one's own ethnic group. Fourth, there is an internalization and integration of both cultures. The literature on Nigrescence, or Black racial identity, has led the research literature about ethnic identity development formation.

Helms (1985), in the best-known stage model, characterized stage-based identity development models as putting the responsibility for adaptation on the minority individual rather than society, which tends to blame the victim. The research on ethnic identity development models has described an alternative framework. Standard identity development models do not account for the adaptation process in change and assume that identity will develop in a linear, continuous process. Helms's (1985) five assumptions about minority development models summarize the extensive literature on development of an identity by minority peoples. These five assumptions pervade the literature on developing a minority identity.

1. Minority groups develop modal personality patterns in response to White racism.
2. Some styles of identity resolution are healthier than others.
3. Cultural identity development involves shifts in attitudes involving cognitive, affective, and conative components.
4. Styles of identity resolution are distinguishable and can be assessed.
5. Intracultural and intercultural interactions are influenced by the manner of cultural identification of the participants. (Helms, 1985, p. 241)

Helms (1984, 1990) has been a leader in researching the various minority identity models. In her own cognitive development model, she traces the development of racial consciousness from historical and sociocultural information, through skill building and cognitive/affective self-awareness, and finally to cultural immersion. Helms (1990) summarized the literature on Nigrescence theories of identity development. Most theories defined the process of moving from less healthy White-defined stages of identity to more healthy self-defined racial transcendence, even though the labels of different stages were different for each theory. Helms also pointed out the similarity of content in how stages are described by Akbar (1979), Banks (1981), Cross (1971), Dizzard (1970), Gibbs (1974), Gay (1984), Jackson (1975), Milliones (1980), Thomas (1971), Toldson and Pasteur (1975), and Vontress (1971), even though each researcher worked independently, reacting to racism and prejudice in society. Helms (1990, p. 30) summarized the stages regarding Nigrescence identity development.

Helms's work in ethnic and racial identity development has resulted in many research studies. Helms (1984) and Parham and Helms (1981) demonstrated that counselors must be particularly aware of their own stage of multicultural development and respect their clients' stages as well. Parham and Helms found that Black students in the preencounter stage preferred White counselors, whereas those in the other three stages of their paradigm had varying degrees of preference for a Black counselor.

Helms (1990) described each stage as a worldview used to organize information about self and society, related to the person's maturation level. The first stage, Preencounter, is divided into an "active form" in which the person deliberately idealizes Whiteness or denigrates Blacks, or a "passive form" in which the Black is assimilated into White society. The second stage, Encounter, deals with Blacks who are confronted by racial affronts and indignities and are searching for their own Black identity. The third stage, Immersion, is where the Black person withdraws into a stereotyped Black perspective that is internally defined. The fourth stage, Emersion, is when the Black person develops a nonstereotyped Black perspective. The fifth stage, Internalization, is when the Black person moves toward a positive, internalized perspective of Black identity. The sixth category involves Commitment to that positive internalized perspective. Helms's adaptation of these models in her Racial Attitudes Identity Scale summarizes these perspectives into the four stages of Preencounter, Encounter, Immersion/Emersion, and Internalization.

E. Smith (1991) developed a model of ethnic identity development around conflicts experienced in a pluralistic society. These conflicts include the following:

1. Ethnic awareness versus ethnic unawareness.
2. Ethnic self-identification versus nonethnic self-identification.
3. Self-hatred versus self-acceptance.
4. Self-acceptance versus other-group acceptance.
5. Other-group rejection versus self-acceptance.
6. Other-group rejection versus self-rejection.
7. Ethnic identity integration versus ethnic identity fragmentation or diffusion.
8. Ethnocentrism versus allocentrism.

These conflicts are experienced as phases in identity development that must be resolved for development to occur. The salient conflicts go through four phases or stages.

> *Phase 1: Preoccupation with self or the preservation of ethnic self-identity.*
> During this phase, contact with other groups may be either positive or negative but they are usually negative. The person preserves ethnic identity with ego defense mechanisms or by identifying with the aggressor.
> *Phase 2: Preoccupation with the ethnic conflict and with the salient ethnic outer boundary group.* During this phase, the person is preoccupied with seeking refuge or safety in one's own community. Anger, guilt, or remorse is typical of this period.

Phase 3: Resolution of conflict. During this phase, there is an attempt to go beyond the experiences of previous stages so that the heightened awareness or tensions become less salient. The person searches for a solution to the conflicts of previous stages.

Phase 4: Integration. The person integrates previous experiences toward a comprehensive ethnic identity. If the person is unsuccessful in integrating the previous experiences in a positive resolution, the result will be confusion regarding ethnic identity.

E. Smith (1991) went beyond conceptualizations of ethnic identity as a response to ethnic or racial oppression and offered 18 propositions regarding ethnic identity development within the context of minority–majority status.

1. Developing ethnic identity means making one's ethnic membership salient.
2. Developing an ethnic reference group means depending on that group for one's social identity.
3. Sometimes individuals identify with a different ethnic reference group.
4. Each ethnic group has signs and symbols indicating allegiance and membership.
5. Persons construct a social order based on "we" and "they" relationships.
6. Ethnic identity is different for majority than for minority group members.
7. The status of one's ethnic group determines whether one's identity is positive or negative.
8. Positive self-esteem results from accepting one's ethnic membership group as a positive reference group.
9. For ethnic minorities, minority status is a source of stress.
10. Ethnic minorities differ in their psychological accommodation of the majority.
11. In pluralistic societies, members of minority and majority groups share one another's salient conflicts.
12. In pluralistic societies, members of minority and majority groups experience the same patterns of conflict.
13. Members of majority and minority groups know the psychological dynamics of their salient conflicts.
14. Persons experiencing salient conflicts go through four phases.
15. Individuals use defense mechanisms when their ethnic identifications are conflicted.
16. A complete ethnic identity requires resolution of salient conflicts.
17. Both race and ethnicity influence an individual's ethnic identity.
18. One's career development depends on maintaining salient reference group perspectives of ethnic identity.

Recent research on ethnic identity development has emphasized salience as a primary concept. Cross (1991) modified his earlier (Cross, 1971) views on Black ethnic identity development summarized by Helms earlier in this chapter.

Cross's (1991) first stage, Preencounter, is a resocializing experience describing how assimilated as well as deracinated, deculturalized, or miseducated Black adults are transformed. Persons at this stage are distinguished by their value orientation, historical perspective, and worldview in which race has limited personal or negative personal salience.

The second stage, Encounter, is where the person's old identity seeks to defend itself against change. Something significant happens to challenge the old identity as a kind of "culture shock." The issues of ethnic identity become personally salient and highly emotional.

The third stage, Immersion/Emersion, is a "transition period" during which the old perspective is demolished and a new frame of salient reference is put in place. The person is immersed in a new world of Black culture to which the person is dedicated and loyal. Emersion is the process of emerging from the emotionality and sometimes oversimplifications of the immersion period. This stage is very powerful and traumatic, sometimes resulting in regression, fixation, or dropping out of involvement with Black issues.

The fourth stage, Internalization, is the working out of problems from the transition period. A thoughtful and considered salience occurs ranging from nationalism to bicultural or multicultural perspectives. Racial identity concerns are now matched to other identity concerns such as religious, gender, career, class, and role in a reduction of dissonance and a reconstitution of personality.

The fifth stage, Internalization/Commitment, represents the long-term translation of Black identity into a comprehensive life plan or commitment. It may be necessary to recycle through the previous four stages from time to time or from issue to issue as the person or situation changes. Nigrescence does not result in a single ideological stance such as Black nationalism or Afrocentrism but is more broadly focused on the wide range of potentially salient identities resulting from the first four stages.

Cross described his earlier (1971) theory of Nigrescence as a pyramid moving convergently from the broad foundation of preencounter to the apex of internalization. Cross described his recent (1991) theory of Nigrescence as more of an "hourglass" shape converging in the transition period of Stage 3, Immersion/Emersion, and then moving to a broad focus in Stages 4 and 5 of Internalization and Internalization/Commitment.

B. C. Kim (1981) described an Asian American identity development model in which conflict is resolved in a five-stage progress from a negative self-concept and identify confusion to a positive self-concept and positive identification with Asian Americans. The first stage, Ethnic Awareness, occurs when the person becomes aware of ethnocultural origins, often through family members or relatives. The second stage, White Identification, is often linked to the time when children begin attending school. A sense of being different tends to alienate Asian children from their own ethnic background. The third stage, Awakening to Social Political Consciousness, is when the Asian American recognizes her or his minority group membership. The reassessment of White values and attitudes, although traumatic, leads to a more positive self-concept. The fourth stage, Redirection to Asian American Consciousness, is when the person develops a sense of pride and active participation in developing his or her role within an Asian American identity. The fifth stage, Incorporation, results in a secure balance of the various identities as potentially salient under different conditions.

Arce (1981) also presented a model of Chicano identity whose transitional phases of forced identification, internal quest, acceptance, and internalized ethnic identity closely resemble the stages in other theories of ethnic/racial identity development.

The minority identity development model combines elements of the previous models in a comprehensive framework. This model, presented by Atkinson, Morten, and Sue (1983, 1998), describes development in five stages (see Figure 4.1).

1. Conformity: preference for values of the dominant culture to those of their own culture group.
2. Dissonance: confusion and conflict toward dominant cultural system and their own group's cultural system.
3. Resistance and immersion: active rejection of dominant society and acceptance of their own cultural group's traditions and customs.
4. Introspection: questioning the value of both minority culture and dominant culture.
5. Synergetic articulation and awareness: developing a cultural identity that selects elements from both the dominant and minority cultural group values.

The theories of racial/ethnic identity development provide a structure for looking at identity development in other populations as well. Recent research on White identity development has applied the patterns and theories of minority identity development to the majority populations. Ponterotto and Pedersen (1993) reviewed the most prominent theories of White identity development. They described the work of Phinney (1990) linking ethnic/racial identity development to more broadly based theories of identity development. Ethnic/racial identity is seen as an important component of self-concept, especially for adolescents. The primary issues of stereotypes and prejudice toward their

FIGURE 4.1

Summary of Minority Identity Development Model

Stages of Minority Development Model	Attitude Toward Self	Attitude Toward Others of the Same Minority	Attitude Toward Others of a Different Minority	Attitude Toward Dominant Group
Stage 1: Conformity	Self-depreciating	Group depreciating	Discriminatory	Group appreciating
Stage 2: Dissonance	Conflict between self-depreciating and appreciating	Conflict between group depreciating and group appreciating	Conflict between dominant-held views of minority hierarchy and feelings of shared experience	Conflict between group appreciating and group depreciating
Stage 3: Resistance and immersion	Self-appreciating	Group appreciating	Conflict between feelings of empathy for other minority experiences and feelings of culture centrism	Group depreciating
Stage 4: Introspection	Concern with basis of self-appreciation	Concern with nature of unequivocal appreciation	Concern with ethnocentric basis for judging others	Concern with the basis of group depreciation
Stage 5: Synergetic articulation and awareness	Self-appreciating	Group appreciating	Group appreciating	Selective appreciation

Note. From *Counseling American Minorities: A Cross-Cultural Perspective* (5th ed.) by D. R. Atkinson, G. Morten, and D. W. Sue, 1997, Copyright 1997, The McGraw-Hill Companies. Adapted with permission of The McGraw-Hill Companies.

group and contrasting value systems require the person to make choices. Those who successfully resolve these two issues develop an *achieved* ethnic identity, whereas those who fail develop a *diffused* or *foreclosed* identity. Borrowing from Tajfel (1978), Berry and Kim (1988) described the alternative outcomes of ethnic identity conflicts as follows:

1. Alienation or marginalization from their own cultural group.
2. Assimilation into the dominant culture.
3. Withdrawal or separation from the dominant culture.
4. Integration or biculturalism in which both their own ethnic identity and their connection with other social groups are potentially salient.

Phinney's (1990) model of ethnic identity has three stages to track the process of exploring ethnic group issues that provide still another alternative framework. The initial stage involves ethnic identity diffusion or foreclosure, in which persons accept the values and attitudes of a dominant culture. Persons at this stage do not necessarily prefer the dominant group perspective, but the issue has little personal salience for them. The second stage of identity search and moratorium involves exploration of ethnic identity issues, often as the result of an encounter experience or personal crisis. The third stage of ethnic identity achievement is when racial/ethnic identity issues have become salient and the person becomes more accepting of her or his new ethnic identity in a healthy bicultural or multicultural identity.

Hardiman (1982) examined race and gender issues in the context of social identity theory in a five-stage White identity model. Social identity includes conscious or unconscious membership that contributes to a person's conception of herself or himself. Hardiman looked at gender, occupation, religion, and White racial identity as contributing to that self-perception.

The first stage of Hardiman's model, No Social Consciousness, is when the person does not recognize or accept the restrictions of any particular social role and presumes to act spontaneously or independently. In the second stage, Acceptance, the person is suddenly aware of her or his social role and is profoundly changed to conform with that role. The third stage, Resistance, results in critical analysis of restrictions imposed by the social role resulting in rebellion and some rejection of social pressure to conform from others who share the same social role. The fourth stage, Redefinition, involves adapting the rules of the person's social role to fit the circumstances and rediscovering the importance of that social role in this new personalized context. The fifth stage, Internalization, integrates insights from the previous four stages into this newly defined social role or identity.

Hardiman (1982) developed her White racial identity theory on the autobiographies of four White women and two White men. In the first stage, the individuals operated naively from their own needs, extending from birth to about age 4 or 5 years. The second stage was a transition period emphasizing acceptance and role learning that extended into adult years. The third stage involved resistance to the "myths" they had learned and an emotionally painful reaction toward their own "Whiteness." The fourth stage redefined their identity in a more positive direction, acknowledging both strengths and limitations. The fifth stage internalizes and establishes the new identity as their own.

Helms (1984) also developed a White identity model with six stages and two phases. During the first phase, Abandonment of Racism, the first three stages occur. The first stage of Contact involves initial limited contacts between Whites and Blacks or other racially defined groups, and they realize that Blacks and Whites are treated differently. The second stage, Disintegration, is when the White person acknowledges and understands the benefits of being White while feeling guilty for enjoying these benefits. The third stage, Reintegration, involves accepting a belief in White superiority when the guilt and self-blame of previous stages turns into anger and aggressiveness.

During the phase of Defining a Nonracist White Identity, the White person enters the fourth stage, Pseudoindependence, during which responsibility for racism is acknowledged and an alternative nonracist identity is sought out. The fifth stage, Immersion/Emersion, involves the hard work of developing a new identity and gathering accurate information. The sixth stage, Autonomy, describes an end-goal of openness and flexibility through self-actualization.

Ponterotto's (1988) four-stage model of racial consciousness was developed with White counselor trainees in mind. Ponterotto relied on Helms's (1984) earlier work applied to graduate students studying multicultural counseling. The first stage of Ponterotto's model is Preexposure, when the White students had little awareness or interest in multicultural issues and were quite comfortable with the status quo. The second stage, Exposure, involved confrontation with multicultural issues, often through taking a course on multiculturalism. The students become aware of racism and are motivated by guilt and anger to make changes. The third stage, Zealot-Defensive, is when the students become pro-minority and anti-White in their attempt to make things right. The fourth stage, Integration, is when the students process their anger and guilt feelings toward a more balanced perspective. Ponterotto and Pedersen (1993) identified a variety of tests for measuring White identity development. It is important to synthesize the various measures of racial/ethnic/cultural identity development and to recognize the important of cultural factors for identity development among all populations.

4. Culture Shock

Culture shock is a profoundly personal encounter with persons from a different culture (P. Pedersen, 1995b). The experience of culture shock will not be the same for any two persons or for the same person at two points in time. Pedersen collected more than 300 examples of culture shock across the various stages while teaching on the Institute for Shipboard Education from the University of Pittsburgh. The 350 upper level undergraduate students collected incidents to demonstrate psychological constructs from their classes. These incidents provide concrete and explicit examples of culture shock. Kalvero Oberg (1958) introduced the concept of culture shock to describe anxiety resulting from losing one's sense of when and how to "do the right thing." This adjustment process involves a nonspecific state of uncertainty, in which the persons do not know what others expect of them or what they can expect of others, with emotional, psychological, behavioral, cognitive, and physiological consequences.

The most frequently cited indicators of culture shock include the absence of familiar cues about how to behave, the reinterpretation of familiar values about what is good, an emotional disorientation ranging from anxiety to uncontrollable rage, a nostalgic idealization of how things used to be, a sense of helplessness in the new setting, and a feeling that the discomfort will never go away. Variations on the culture shock label with similar characteristics have included culture fatigue, language shock, role shock, and pervasive ambiguity. Any new situation such as a new job, divorce, graduation, being fired, being arrested, cancer, or radical change involves some adjustment of role and identity that might result in culture shock.

The culture shock experience has been classified into stages or categories (Adler, 1975) such as (a) initial contact, (b) disintegration of the old familiar cues, (c) reintegration of new cues, (d) new identity formation, and (e) biculturalism. Each stage is described in terms of its perceptions, emotional range, behaviors, and interpretations. These stages have been described as a "U-curve" or a "W-curve" when the person returns "home," going from higher to lower to higher stages of personal adjustment.

The U-shaped adjustment curve associated with culture shock describes a process similar to the stages in developing cultural identity to be discussed later in this chapter. The first stage of initial contact has been called the "tourist" or "honeymoon" stage because the visitor experiences this new experience as exciting and intriguing and is living in a kind of fantasy about the new experience. The person has not really "left home" yet in terms of his or her real identity.

The second stage begins when the full impact of differences hits the person in ways that can no longer be ignored. The person experiences loneliness and responds with depression or self-blame and withdrawal. Being "different" leads to many failures in the new setting and a feeling of helplessness.

The third stage begins with anger and fighting back "against" the others in this new setting. Self-blame turns into hostility, rejection, and attacks against the new setting to protect the person's self-esteem, and the person redirects the blame for failure.

The fourth stage begins when both similarities and differences are recognized and the person becomes more self-assured. The person can see both strengths and weaknesses in the new setting that demonstrate what should be done even though the person cannot yet figure out how to do it.

The fifth stage ideally leads toward a bicultural or multicultural identity that includes competence in both the old and new setting. The person can see what needs to be done and is developing the skill to respond appropriately.

The W-shaped adjustment curve describes both entry and reentry as duplicating the same process. This shape begins Stage 1 in the upper left, Stage 2 along the left side, Stage 3 at the bottom, Stage 4 along the right side, and Stage 5 at the upper right showing change from high to low to high adjustment over time.

Church (1982) discussed 11 empirical studies in support of the U-curve hypothesis. These data support the general hypothesis through the first three stages in an inverted "J-curve" but do not support a full recovery to the fully functioning levels the person experienced back home. Five other studies Church (1982) cited did not confirm the U-curve hypothesis. Whether the lack of proof relates to inadequate measures of change or the U-curve construct's lack of validity, the U-curve continues to flourish as a convenient description of the developmental process.

Furnham and Bochner (1986) discussed some problems with the U-curve hypothesis. First, there are many dependent variables to consider, such as depression, loneliness, homesickness, and other attitudes. Second, the definition of a U-shape is uneven because different persons start out at different levels of original adjustment adequacy and then change at different rates. Third, research on interpersonal aspects of culture shock seems more promising than the intrapsychic aspects. In any case, the smooth, linear process of adaptation suggested by a U-curve oversimplifies the erratic and elusive reality. Not enough is known about how the stages relate to each other in terms of their relative importance, the order of occurrence, the groups most vulnerable, and the progression of change (Furnham, 1988).

The early research on culture shock compared it to a "disease" which resulted in disability and which could be cured with the right treatment. Culture shock was described as a "stress reaction" resulting from disorientation regarding values, norms, and expectations resulting from change and adaptation, and a "deficit" of resources for an appropriate response. Gudykunst and Hammer (1988) emphasized uncertainty reduction as an essential deficit resulting in culture shock: "The reduction of uncertainty and anxiety is a function of stereotypes, favorable contact, shared networks, intergroup attitudes, cultural identity, cultural similarity, second language competence, and knowledge of the host culture" (p. 132). Stephen and Stephen (1992) linked culture shock to fear of negative psychological consequences such as loss of control or frustration, negative behavioral consequences through exploitation or derogation, negative evaluations or stereotyping by outgroup members, and negative evaluations or rejection by ingroup members for having contact with outgroups.

Other recent research on culture shock has emphasized the "growth" or "educational" model. The experience of acculturative stress is not entirely negative but may include a positive and creative force to stimulate, motivate, and enhance long-term change. People develop skills and abilities through culture shock that may not otherwise be available. Acculturative stress (Berry et al., 1992) is not necessarily a negative process. Kealey (1988) found that many persons who were successful abroad had experienced intense culture shock. Culture shock is a learning experience that leads to greater self-awareness and personal growth. This educational–developmental approach to culture shock is beginning to replace the disease–deficit descriptions of culture shock. On the one hand, there is the possibility of relatively harmonious change through culture shock and acculturation; on the other hand, culture shock can result in severe psychological conflict.

Furnham and Bochner (1986) highlighted the potentially positive consequences of culture shock, advocating a skill-learning response to the culture shock experience. These skills may include language learning, turn taking in conversation, learning rules of communication, knowing the protocol of politeness, identifying communication styles, and learning appropriate nonverbal behaviors. Learning appropriate skills will enhance multicultural competence and increase the likelihood of success in the host culture. These skills include (a) knowing the rules for interpersonal communication; (b) accommodating the effect of biological factors, demographic characteristics, and geopolitical conditions; and (c) understanding the characteristics of their own culture from the host culture viewpoint. Culture shock may be viewed as a specialized form of learning and educational growth, combining a social skills model with a culture-learning model to increase the potentially positive consequence of multicultural contact.

Thomas Coffman (see Coffman & Harris, 1984) described culture shock as having six identifying features: cue problems, value discrepancies, an emotional core, a set of typical symptoms, adjustment mechanisms, and a pattern of emergence over time. When the cues or messages we receive in another culture are confusing, it is usually because familiar cues we have learned to depend on are missing, important cues are there but not recognized as important, or the same cue has a different meaning in the new culture. Many of the problems in culture shock involve learning to deal with new cues. Familiar values define the meaning of good, desirable, beautiful, and valuable. Each culture values its own behaviors, attitudes, and ideas. Although the visitor does not need to discard familiar values, he or she must recognize alternative value systems in order to adapt to a new cultural system.

Culture shock has an emotional core and produces a heightened emotional awareness of the new and unfamiliar surroundings whether as a sudden "shock" or as a gradual "fatigue" that occurs over a period of time. The emotional effect of this experience may include anxiety, depression, or even hostility ranging from mild uneasiness to the "white furies" of unreasonable and uncontrolled rage.

The specific symptoms of culture shock focus either on dissatisfaction with the host country or on idealization of the home country. The host culture is criticized as being peculiar, irrational, inefficient, and unfriendly. The visitor is likely to fear being taken advantage of, being laughed at or talked about, and not being accepted, and he or she wants to spend more time around people from his or her home culture. The visitor might develop a glazed, vacant, or absentminded look nicknamed the "tropical stare," or withdraw for long periods by sleeping or being otherwise inactive. Minor annoyances in the host culture become exaggerated, and the few remaining links with the home culture, such as mail from home, become extraordinarily important.

Strategies for adjustment that worked in the home culture might not work for the visitor in a new host culture, so that the visitor needs to spend a greater amount of energy in making adjustments and learning new strategies. Direct confrontation and openness might facilitate adjustment in the home culture. Defensive strategies might range from hostile stereotyping and scapegoating of the host culture to "going native" and rejecting the visitor's own home culture.

Culture shock is likely to last over the visitor's entire stay in the unfamiliar culture, reappear in a variety of forms, and not be limited to an initial adjustment. As familiar cues are replaced by unfamiliar cues, the visitor experiences a genuine identity crisis, requiring either that the former identity be disowned or that multiple identities for each of the several cultures encountered be created and maintained. In either case, the visitor is required to reintegrate, confront, and challenge the basic underlying assumptions of his or her personality.

Coffman (see Coffman & Harris, 1984) made suggestions for visitors experiencing or anticipating culture shock.

1. The visitor needs to recognize that transition problems are usual and normal in the stress of adjusting to a strange new setting. The visitor can be helped to recognize, understand, and accept the effects of adjustments in the context of a host culture support system.
2. The maintenance of personal integrity and self-esteem becomes a primary goal. The visitor often experiences a loss of status in the new cul-

ture, where the language, customs, and procedures are strange or unfamiliar. The visitor will need reassurance and support to maintain a healthy self-image.

3. Time must be allowed for the adjustment to take place without pressure or urgency. Persons adjust at their own rate and recognize that their reconciliation with the host culture, although painful, will enhance their future effectiveness.

4. Recognizing the patterns of adjustment will help the visitor make progress in developing new skills and insights. Depression and a sense of failure will be recognized as a stage of the adjustment process and not as a permanent feature of the new experience.

5. Labeling the symptoms of culture shock will help the visitor interpret emotional responses to stress in the adjustment process.

6. Being well-adjusted at home does not ensure an easy adjustment in a foreign culture. In some cases, visitors uncomfortable "back home" may find it easy to adjust to a foreign culture. In extreme cases of maladjustment, visitors are more likely to carry their "back home" problems with them into the new culture. With existing measures, it is difficult to predict a hard or easy adjustment for most individuals.

7. Although culture shock cannot be prevented, preparation for transition can ease the stress of adjustment. Preparation might include language study, learning about the host culture, simulating situations to be encountered, and spending time with nationals from the host culture. In all instances, the development of a support system is essential to helping the visitor reconstruct an appropriate identity or role in the new culture.

In reviewing the literature about culture shock, a recurring theme is the opportunity for learning, the process or stages of adjustment, the identifying features, and suggestions for minimizing its negative effects in a subjective reevaluation of individual identity. The key to understanding and controlling the effect of culture shock lies within the visitor as well as in the manipulation of the environment.

Ruben and Kealey (1970) found that in at least some cases sojourners from the Canadian International Development Agency who had undergone intensive culture shock during transition abroad were ultimately more productive than those who had experienced little or no culture shock. Perhaps those who are most aware of their own subjective perceptions experience more shock. For whatever reason, culture shock teaches lessons that perhaps cannot be learned in any other way, and in that respect culture shock contributes to developing a multicultural identity. Considerable research has been done on international or intercultural adjustment, but thus far there are few if any widely accepted guidelines or measures.

5. Conclusion

Theories of identity development from Erikson (1968), Horney (1967), and others have long established the importance of the sociocultural context in identify formation. Until recently, the measures of identity have been defined by the dominant culture, with other minority populations having to either adapt to those dominant culture characteristics or suffer the consequences. The research on racial/ethnic/cultural stages of identity development has made a significant contribution to research on identity development generally. Although there are many differences across the various research models studying racial/ethnic/cultural identity development, the general patterns apply across the various models.

First, there is a clear differentiation between lower and higher levels of development regarding the person's identity. This development is usually related to intentional/unintentional, conscious/unconscious, or articulate/inarticulate aspects. In some cases, the lower levels of development correlate with measures of illness or personal inadequacy whereas higher levels of development correlate with healthy competent functioning.

Second, it is clear that culture relates to the process of personal identity development in profoundly meaningful ways. Culture, broadly defined, describes the significant experiences that lead the person to defined roles. It should be clear to the reader that measures of identity development that disregard cultural aspects are likely to be inaccurate and inadequate.

Third, identity development indicates a process similar to culture shock, in which individuals are confronted by themselves and by others who are different from themselves. This culture shock process is where much of the learning takes place, resulting in identity development.

Minority populations and particularly Black minority authors from at least the last 200 years in the United States began the process of reflecting on culture and identity issues in social, political, and economic situations. In most cases, these persons were not psychologists, although the implications of their ideas were certainly psychological. As we examine racial/ethnic/cultural identity development as a process, it is important to recognize these ideas as having a history that goes far beyond the last several decades.

EXERCISE: Drawing Your Culture

Sometimes our verbal facility in describing our culture betrays us by abstracting the less rational and more emotional aspects of our cultural influences. By drawing the symbols that describe what our culture means, it is possible to escape from the preconceived format we usually use to describe our identity.

Divide the group into units of about three to five persons sitting in a circle. If possible, arrange for the group to sit around a table. Provide each individual with a sheet of paper that may be ordinary typing paper or newsprint, depending on the space available. Provide each individual also with a pen or pencil. If possible, provide participants with pens and pencils of different colors or felt tip markers if the paper is large enough.

Ask each individual to spend about 5 to 10 minutes drawing his or her culture. Participants may draw pictures of events in their lives that have influenced them in their culture. They may also draw any combination of designs, doodles, or lines that have meaning to them in terms of their culture. They may not, however, draw or write any words on their paper.

At the end of the predetermined time limit, ask the participants to stop drawing. Then ask them each in turn to present their drawing, with explanations of what the symbols or drawings mean, to the other members of their small unit. Each member of the unit should be instructed to spend about the same amount of time, about 5 minutes, describing and explaining the drawing to their unit members so that each person has the same opportunity, and all units will complete their explanations at about the same time.

When all members of all units have completed their explanations to the other members of their unit, you may ask each unit to report back to the larger group on any particularly useful insights they discovered during the exercise. This exercise is useful for articulating some of the nonverbal, symbolic, or less rational and more emotional aspects of our culture that are often difficult to describe in words.

DRAWING YOUR CULTURE EXERCISE

Participant Objectives:
1. To draw the figures or symbols important to their cultural identity.
2. To explain or express the figures or symbols they have drawn to other members of a small group.
3. To listen and understand the figures or symbols other members of a small group have identified as important to their cultural identity.

Learning Objective:
1. Our cultural identity contains nonverbal, nonrational, and symbolic elements that are difficult to express using language.

CHAPTER 5

The Patterns of Cultural Systems

Major objective:

1. To become aware of cultural patterns and relationships between individuals and groups.

Secondary objectives:

1. To separate objective facts from subjective inferences.
2. To describe culture as objective values to be discovered.
3. To describe culture as a construction of explanations based on experiences.
4. To describe a personal cultural orientation through the cultural grid.

Culture is complex but not chaotic. We understand culture through understanding patterns of cultural systems. These patterns are defined by personalized assumptions, attitudes, and opinions of individuals. Culture is the internalized perspectives shared by persons at a particular time and place. Cultural systems are the networks of relationships between individuals and groups who share the same perspectives.

I have discussed the importance of awareness to identify underlying assumptions and how those assumptions control behaviors through culturally learned expectations and values. I have demonstrated how two persons who are guided by different culturally learned assumptions might disagree without one necessarily being right and the other necessarily being wrong. When two individuals or groups do not share the same culturally learned assumptions, the likelihood for misunderstanding and conflict is high.

There is a new field of "cultural psychology" that combines anthropology and ethnopsychology that is especially strong among cognitive scientists focused on cultural patterns.

The basic idea is that our representations of reality (including social and psychological reality) become part of the realities they represent; and many casual processes are constraining precisely because of our representations of them and involvement with them. A central goal of cultural psychology is to examine the way people make personal use of their customary practices, traditional institutions, symbolic and material resources, and inherited conceptions of things to construct a world that makes sense and to constitute a life-space in which they can feel at home. (Stigler, Shweder, & Herdt, 1990, p. vii)

This chapter explores the implications of these cultural patterns for counseling.

1. Discovering Dispositional Values

Cultural systems are the structures we use to organize our experiences and to explain the experiences of others. These systems are divided into objective and subjective culture (Triandis, 1980). Objective culture includes verifiable information such as names, ethnicity, gender, age, education, kinship relationships, economic background, and occupation, to name a few of the more obvious. These indicators of culture are objective because they can be verified by independent observers. Subjective culture is more difficult to verify and includes feelings, beliefs, conceptions, judgments, hopes, intentions, expectations, values, and meanings. Subjective culture is inferred rather than observed directly. Both objective and subjective culture are important but must be distinguished to prevent the confusion of mistaking inferences for factual information.

Values are more often products of a person's subjective culture, and attempts to treat values as objective verifiable facts have not been very successful. Values define the boundaries of cultural systems and are therefore very important for communicating across cultures. A cultural value does not require external proof or outside verification to be accepted as true. Groups depend on similar values to communicate with one another and explain their identity, as was demonstrated earlier. Values become a yardstick for groups to include or exclude individuals from their group. Groups with different value systems experience conflict or disagreement because they experience the same events differently. Each group begins from different assumptions and therefore makes different inferences. Examples of conflict between Arabs and Jews in the Middle East, of nationalities in Eastern Europe, or of ethnic groups in the United States demonstrate clearly the conflict resulting from groups who presume different beliefs or values or who express the same values in different ways.

The value differences may result from different national affiliations, different ethnic identities, or different social roles. At the level of nations, the people are separated by their country's role in world affairs, languages, and political loyalties. At the ethnic level, the people are separated by competing with one another for the same pool of limited national resources, with some ethnic groups having more power than others. People who are separated by their social roles as administrators, housewives, hard hats, or other special interest groups use exclusion to build their membership's visibility and to enhance their own solidarity.

The problem with differentiating cultural systems solely by their values is that cultures are more complicated and dynamic than traditional value perspectives seem to suggest. The description of cultures by their values suggests that culture is a trait or "disposition" to do one thing and not do another. Values presume a constancy over times, places, and persons that denies the very dynamic nature of culture. People who value "kindness" may sometimes act unkindly. People who value "fairness" may sometimes act unfairly. This variability applies to people who presume to share the same cultural values and priorities. These people act differently from one another even though they maintain the same cultural disposition according to their values. The more clearly defined and absolute these cultural categories are, the more likely they are to bend the data to fit their own rigid framework of standard topologies, mixing fact with inference.

The best-known value typology was designed by Kluckhohn and Strodtbeck (1961). Kohls (1979) provided a useful overview of the Kluckhohn and Strodtbeck model (see Figure 5.1).

The first orientation is toward human nature. Some people have an optimistic and positive view of others, whereas other people have a more negative view. Most people take a middle position, waiting to judge others until they have more data about their positive or negative intentions. Premature judgment of other people is perhaps the single most frequent source of error in producing multicultural misunderstandings.

The second orientation is toward the person's relationship to nature. This orientation resembles the internal and external locus-of-control concepts in psychology. Westernized "low-context" cultures tend to put a more positive meaning on internal locus of control, whereas other "high-context" cultures are more accepting of external locus of control.

The third orientation is toward time, with some cultures valuing the past and other cultures valuing the future. Understanding a culture's historical background is essential to developing multicultural awareness about that culture. Westernized cultures have a reputation for putting more emphasis on the future than on the past.

The fourth orientation is toward activity. Westernized cultures have a reputation for valuing activity and proactive behavior. A frequently quoted English language expression is, "If you don't know what to do, at least *do* something." An equivalent common Chinese expression is, "If you don't know what to do, at least *don't do* anything." A task-oriented person is likely to be uncomfortable in a culture that values relationship building more than task accomplishment.

FIGURE 5.1

Kohls' Interpretation of the Kluckhohn–Strodtbeck Model

Orientation		Range	
Human Nature	Most people can't be trusted.	There are both evil people and good people, and you have to check people out to find out which they are.	Most people are basically pretty good at heart.
Relationship to Nature	Life is largely determined by external forces, such as God, fate, or genetics. A person can't surpass the conditions life has set.	Humans should, in every way, live in complete harmony with nature.	Humans' challenge is to conquer and control nature. Everything from air conditioning to the "green revolution" has resulted from having met this challenge.
Sense of Time	Humans should learn from history and attempt to emulate the glorious ages of the past.	The present moment is everything. Let's make the most of it. Don't worry about tomorrow; enjoy today.	Planning and goal setting make it possible to accomplish miracles. A little sacrifice today will bring a better tomorrow.
Activity	It's enough to just "be." It's not necessary to accomplish great things in life to feel your life has been worthwhile.	Humans' main purpose for being placed on this earth is for their own inner development.	If people work hard and apply themselves fully, their efforts will be rewarded.
Social Relationships	Some people are born to lead others. There are leaders and there are followers.	Whenever I have a serious problem, I like to get the advice of my family or close friends on how best to solve it.	All people should have equal rights and complete control over their own destiny.

Note. From *Survival Kit for Overseas Living For Americans Planning to Live and Work Abroad* (3rd ed., p.135) by L. R. Kohls, 1996, Yarmouth, ME: Intercultural Press. Copyright 1996 by Intercultural Press, Inc. Reprinted with permission.

Finally, under the Kluckhohn and Strodtbeck (1961) model, attitudes toward social relations likewise are assumed to be different from one group to another. The power structure in hierarchical cultures is authoritarian—from the role of the father in a family to the ruler in the state. In other cultures, equality is emphasized and each individual group member is allotted equal power. In a third alternative, the group as a unit is expected to manage power and control its own members.

Carter (1991) provided a review of counseling research on the Kluckhohn and Strodtbeck (1961) model of value orientations. Carter pointed out that understanding a culture's values is essential for understanding the uniqueness of that culture as well as for defining similarities for appropriate interaction across cultures. Kluckhohn and Strodtbeck's model has a long history of use across disciplines in the social sciences, resulting in measures of cultural difference, frameworks for comparing cultures, development of culturally sensitive treatments, measures of counselor effectiveness, identification of cultural preferences, and organization of cultural information. The presumption is that mismatches of cultural values will inhibit the delivery of psychological services and complicate the communication process.

Carter (1991) recognized the limitations of Kluckhohn and Strodtbeck's (1961) approach for studying within-group and between-groups patterns of cultural similarity and difference. However, he is persuasive in documenting how studying historical and cultural values will help counselors understand racial and ethnic inequalities across culturally different people. Values are useful for learning about one's self as a starting point for learning about culturally different alternatives. Values provide a framework for organizing historical knowledge about cultures as long as the value labels are not confused with the more complicated cultural realities and inferred values are not treated as objective fact.

Cultural values have stimulated a great deal of research relevant to counseling. Stewart (1972) developed a list of value perspectives for "American" and "Contrast American" organized around Kluckhohn and Strodtbeck's (1961) categories to demonstrate cultural differences. This Contrast American simulation has been useful in establishing cultural differences. Ibrahim (1991) developed a measure of worldview as a mediating variable in counseling and development interventions. Her work on this worldview measure is based on Kluckhohn and Strodtbeck's framework of human nature, social relationships, nature, time orientation, and activity orientation. Carter and Helms (1987) developed a measure of White racial identity attitudes and cultural values; Szapocznik, Kurtines, and Fernandez (1980) developed a measure of Cuban values; and Trimble (1976) measured aspects of Native American Indian cultures, all from Kluckhohn and Strodtbeck's framework. D. W. Sue and Sue (1990) described

Kluckhohn and Strodtbeck's framework as "one of the most useful frameworks for understanding differences among individuals and groups" (p. 138). The value orientation framework of Kluckhohn and Strodtbeck has made a significant contribution toward the discovery of cultural values in different cultures.

2. The Construction of Cultural Patterns

Constructivism challenges the realist and objectivist versions of science. Neimeyer (1993) described the boundaries of constructivist assessment. This viewpoint is based on the premise that people do not have direct access to a singular, stable, and fully knowable external reality. All of our thinking is culturally embedded, interpersonally forged, and necessarily limited. According to the constructivist perspective, emphasis is placed on personal meaning, the influence of relationships on creating meaning and the subjective nature of knowledge, and judgment of methods more according to their viable utility than their independent validity. This approach assumes that people are actively oriented toward a meaningful understanding of life, that they are denied direct access to any external reality, and that they are continuously developing or changing. McNamee and Gergen (1992) provided a theoretical basis for social construction in counseling and therapy, pointing out the implications for client–counselor relationships and for the practice of counseling.

A study of the constructionist perspective begins with an examination of the self. The European and American psychological literature describes self as self-contained, self-reliant, independent, standing-out-in-a-group, egocentric, a centralized equilibrium structure, selfish, a distinctive whole set contrastively against other such wholes, and rationalistic (Hermans, Kempen, & Van Loon, 1992). In a global context, this Euro-American perspective is fairly exotic and ethnocentric. A dialogical view of the self, by contrast, goes beyond the limits of rationalism and individualism to the "stories" and dialogues people have told about themselves to understand where they fit in the world. The self is constructed by defining its social connections and plurality of relationships. "The embodied nature of the self contrasts with conceptions of the self found in mainstream psychology, which are based on the assumption of a disembodied or rationalistic mind" (Hermans et al., 1992, p. 23).

Hermans et al. (1992) described how a person "constructs" her or his own theory of self in a sociocultural context. In their definition, the self is "dialogical," transcending the boundaries of both individualism and rationalism. They trace the history of the constructionist perspective back to the Italian philosopher Giambattista Vico, the German philosopher Vaihinger, and the American psychologist George Kelly (Mahoney, 1988). Vico credited human nature with a creative force of "ingenium" by which people change the physical world and create history by constructing relationships. Vaihinger identified the importance of "fiction" as a scientific instrument for going beyond the "hypothesis" of reality as we experience it toward constructing a higher development of thought. Kelly's notion of personal constructs contends that understanding depends on the alternative interpretations available to us. Kelly's constructs are the criteria by which some things are seen to be alike and others to be different in a way that challenges objective reality (Hermans et al., 1992).

If we describe the world as objective, we assume that people's different perceptions of the world are to a greater or lesser extent inaccurate. It assumes that our differing beliefs and perceptions about the world are not relevant. We describe the world independent of its context, and our experiences are judged by absolute measures of logical rationalism. Our experiences, however, describe a subjective world of imagination and reality that is defined by metaphors (Lakoff & Johnson, 1980). Reality is not the discovery of absolute truth but an understanding of the complex and dynamic relationships between events. Life is a narrative of interacting stories in which there are many roles (Bruner, 1986; Sarbin, 1986) that locate the self in a cultural context. The dialogical description of self describes the construction of culture in a personal context, not as an abstraction but as a product of our experienced relationships (Howard, 1991).

Steenbarger (1991) applied the contextualist theme of a divergent reality to counseling and development as an alternative to linear stage-based convergent hierarchies. Steenbarger identified three problems of the linear development "growth" models:

1. In their emphasis on linearity, stage-based models cannot account for the complexity of human development. Change is rarely unidirectional but more often multidirectional.
2. In their emphasis on invariant sequences of structural unfolding, stage-based models cannot account for important situational influences in the developmental process. Growth occurs through interactions with the environment rather than through the independent unfolding of intrapersonal aspects.
3. In an attempt to reduce development to uniform sequences, stage-based theories assume the consistency of troublesome value premises. The objective norms implied by a fixed uniformity are in conflict with a multicultural and culturally diverse reality around us. The alternative is to view development in a context of person–situation relationships.

According to social role theory, the self is a social construction from roles that have been internalized through interactions with others as described by the works of Goffman, Mead, Sarbin, and Allen (discussed in Steenbarger, 1991). The person is not unfolding from a unitary core so much as constantly *becoming* while shifting the salience of alternative selves or roles. As the sociocultural context changes, so the salient self also changes to accommodate and adapt. In this context, counseling is the process by which a person constructs and deconstructs reality.

The life span approach to development is also contextual in emphasizing the multidirectionality of life plans and psychosocial adaptation. The emphasis is not on traits or behaviors but on the "goodness of fit" between person and environment. Throughout one's life span, the person develops by responding to crises in a dialectical and continuously changing trajectory as described by Steenbarger (1991) and the research he cited.

3. Synthetic Cultures

Hofstede (1980, 1986, 1991) provided an example of synthetic-constructed patterns of similarities and differences among participants from more than 55 different nations around the world. The resulting data were factor analyzed into four dimensions. The first dimension was distributed from High to Low Power Distance measures. The second dimension was distributed from Weak to Strong Uncertainty Avoidance measures. The third dimension was distributed from Individualist to Collectivist perspectives. The fourth dimension was distributed from Masculine to Feminine perspectives. These constructs were used to describe patterns of similarity and differences in the distribution of responses across countries. A synthetic culture laboratory was developed in which groups of individuals take on stereotyped identities according to one or another of these cultural dimensions to demonstrate the importance of subtle cultural differences between groups (Hofstede & Pedersen, in press; P. Pedersen & Ivey, 1993).

The four dimensions describe how patterns of thinking, feeling, and acting were constructed differently by different populations throughout the life span. Hofstede (1991) described these patterns as "mental programs" that provide "software" for the mind to function. Each person reacts to the social environment in different ways by constructing a perception of reality that is functional. Hofstede equated this mental software with culture as "the collective programming of the mind which distinguishes the members of one group or category of people from another" (p. 5). Culture is distinguished from the universally shared characteristics of human nature on the one hand and from the uniquely individualized characteristics of personality on the other. Culture is programmed both in response to the universal characteristics of human nature and the specialized perspectives of personality.

Cultural differences are manifested in four ways, according to Hofstede (1991). First, symbols of words, gestures, pictures, or objects express cultural meaning to the individual. Second, heroes provide role models for the individual's behavior. Third, rituals demonstrate collective activities that are socially essential for persons within that culture. Fourth, values express a broad range of tendencies and preferences that have a functional purpose within each culture.

The four cultural dimensions in Hofstede's (1991) model describe patterns of preference. Although the dimensions were derived from patterns of how people constructed their culture, once they are abstracted the cultural patterns themselves may function as typologies, describing ideal and alternative perspectives or types. Real cases, however, almost never correspond to a single ideal type. The cases themselves are complex and much more multidimensional than any one type would suggest. The artificiality of these four synthetic types does present an opportunity, however. P. Pedersen and Ivey (1993) developed four synthetic cultures for generating four contrasting styles of applying microcounseling skills in a culture-centered approach to counseling. Each of the four synthetic cultures represents one of Hofstede's "types," with alpha representing high power distance, beta representing strong uncertainty avoidance, gamma representing strong individualism, and delta representing strong masculinity. Because none of these synthetic cultures occur in the real world, they become a safe setting to practice multicultural counseling skills and increase the counselor's repertoire of cultural styles.

The practical implications of each cultural tendency are indicated by Hofstede (1986, pp. 312–314) as they might apply to the educational setting (see Figures 5.2–5.5).

In reviewing Figures 5.2–5.5, it is apparent how the culture for each group was constructed as a functional response to the situation and relationships between persons in responding to Hofstede's (1986) questionnaire. Although no individual or group can fairly be labeled by one or another extreme on the four dimensions, individuals will construct their own identity about self and cultural relationships, incorporating and combining responses similar to these lists of preferences.

4. A Personal–Cultural Orientation

Rather than labeling persons according to their culture, it might be more functionally useful to understand the ways that different cultural influences lead individuals to behave in a particular way through constructing a *personal–cultural orientation* toward the situation or event. Accuracy in assessment and interpretation requires that we understand each person's behavior in the sociocultural context in which that behavior occurred. Behaviors are frequently interpreted and changed without regard to their sociocultural context, resulting in misattribution and inaccurate data. Perhaps the most important reason for understanding a person's cultural context is to facilitate accuracy in

FIGURE 5.2

Differences in Teacher–Student and Student–Student Interaction Related to the Individualism Versus Collectivism Dimension

Collectivist Societies	*Individualist Societies*
• Positive association in society with whatever is rooted in tradition • The young should learn; adults cannot accept student role • Students expect to learn how to do • Individual students will only speak up in class when called on personally by the teacher • Individuals will only speak up in small groups • Large classes split socially into smaller, cohesive subgroups based on particularist criteria (e.g., ethnic affiliation) • Formal harmony in learning situations should be maintained at all times (T-groups are taboo) • Neither the teacher nor any student should ever be made to lose face • Education is a way of gaining prestige in one's social environment and of joining a higher status group ("a ticket to a ride") • Diploma certificates are important and displayed on walls • Acquiring certificates, even through illegal means (cheating, corruption), is more important than acquiring competence • Teachers are expected to give preferential treatment to students (e.g., based on ethnic affiliation or recommendation by an influential person)	• Positive association in society with whatever is "new" • One is never too old to learn; "permanent education" • Students expect to learn how to learn • Individual students will speak up in class in response to a general invitation by the teacher • Individuals will speak up in large groups • Subgroups in class vary from one situation to the next based on universalist criteria (e.g., the task "at hand") • Confrontation in learning situations can be salutary; conflicts can be brought into the open • Face-consciousness is weak • Education is a way of improving one's economic worth and self-respect based on ability and competence • Diploma certificates have little symbolic value • Acquiring competence is more important than acquiring certificates • Teachers are expected to be strictly impartial

Note. In contrasting the collectivist societies with the individualist societies, we are examining the differences between the United States and Third World countries. Individualism has an important function in the theory and practice of counseling. It is useful to identify the specific ways in which a collectivistic and contrasting perspective may construct quite a different reality in which to live. (Figures 5.2–5.5 from "Cultural Differences in Teaching and Learning," by G. Hofstede, 1986, *International Journal of Intercultural Relations, 10,* pp. 301–320. Copyright 1986 by Pergamon Press. Reprinted with permission.)

FIGURE 5.3

Differences in Teacher–Student and Student–Student Interaction Related to the Power Distance Dimension

Small Power Distance Societies	*Large Power Distance Societies*
• Stress on impersonal "truth" that can in principle be obtained from any competent person	• Stress on personal "wisdom" that is transferred in the relationship with a particular teacher (guru)
• A teacher should respect the independence of his or her students	• A teacher merits the respect of his or her students
• Student-centered education (premium on initiative)	• Teacher-centered education (premium on order)
• Teacher expects students to initiate communication	• Students expect teacher to initiate communication
• Teacher expects students to find their own paths	• Students expect teacher to outline paths to follow
• Students may speak up spontaneously in class	• Students speak up in class only when invited by the teacher
• Students allowed to contradict or criticize teacher	• Teacher is never contradicted or publicly criticized
• Effectiveness of learning related to amount of two-way communication in class	• Effectiveness of learning is related to excellence of the teacher
• Outside class, teachers are treated as equals	• Respect for teachers is also shown outside class
• In teacher–student conflicts, parents are expected to side with the student	• In teacher–student conflicts, parents are expected to side with the teacher
• Younger teachers are more liked than older teachers	• Older teachers are more respected than younger teachers

Note. In contrasting small power distance societies with large power distance societies, it is useful to consider the importance of power relationships in counseling across cultures. The importance of power relationships across cultures has already been identified. It is important to recognize that an equal distribution of power is preferred in some but not all cultures and that other cultures are quite comfortable with an unequal distribution of power.

the assessment and interpretation of a person's behavior. The *cultural grid* is an attempt to demonstrate how a personal–cultural orientation is constructed.

A. Hines and Pedersen (1980) developed the cultural grid to help identify and describe the cultural aspects of a situation, to help form hypotheses about cultural differences, and to explain how to train people for culturally appropriate interactions. The cultural grid is an open-ended model that matches social system variables with patterns of behavior, expectation, and value in a personal–cultural orientation to each event (A. Pedersen & Pedersen, 1985).

FIGURE 5.4

Differences in Teacher–Student and Student–Student Interaction Related to the Uncertainty Avoidance Dimension

Weak Uncertainty Avoidance Societies	*Strong Uncertainty Avoidance Societies*
• Students feel comfortable in unstructured learning situations; vague objectives, broad assignments, no timetables	• Students feel comfortable in structured learning situations; precise objectives, detailed assignments, strict timetables
• Teachers are allowed to say "I don't know"	• Teachers are expected to have all the answers
• A good teacher uses plain language	• A good teacher uses academic language
• Students are rewarded for innovative approaches to problem solving	• Students are rewarded for accuracy in problem solving
• Teachers are expected to suppress emotions (and so are students)	• Teachers are allowed to behave emotionally (and so are students)
• Teachers interpret intellectual disagreement as a stimulating exercise	• Teachers interpret intellectual disagreement as personal disloyalty
• Teachers seek parents' ideas	• Teachers consider themselves experts who cannot learn anything from lay parents, and parents agree

Note. In contrasting weak uncertainty avoidance societies with alternatives, it is important to recognize that some cultures appreciate and function well in a highly structured setting whereas others require more spontaneity. The counselor will need to function differently in these two contrasting cultural settings, applying more or less structure appropriately.

The cultural grid provides a means of describing and understanding a person's behavior in the context of learned expectations and values. This more complicated approach to culture takes a broad and comprehensive perspective of culture beyond the traditional limits of fixed categories or dimensions. The cultural grid makes it easier to separate cultural from personal variables by identifying patterns of similarities and differences in the attributions or expectations attached to an action or behavior.

The cultural grid is an attempt to demonstrate a relational personal–cultural orientation to the cultural context by separating behaviors from expectations. A. Hines and Pedersen (1980) developed the cultural grid to help identify and describe the complexity of a cultural context in a way that connects the personal and the cultural perspectives. The cultural grid matches the social system (cultural teachers) variables with the individual or personal variables of what people do and why they do it in a personal–cultural orientation to each cultural context. The cultural grid provides a strategy to describe, understand,

FIGURE 5.5

Differences in Teacher–Student and Student–Student Interaction Related to the Masculinity Versus Femininity Dimension

Feminine Societies	*Masculine Societies*
• Teachers avoid openly praising students	• Teachers openly praise good students
• Teachers use average student as the norm	• Teachers use best students as the norm
• System rewards students' social adaptation	• System rewards students' academic performance
• A student's failure in school is a relatively minor accident	• A student's failure in school is a severe blow to his or her self-image and may in extreme cases lead to suicide
• Students admire friendliness in teachers	• Students admire brilliance in teachers
• Students practice mutual solidarity	
• Students try to behave modestly	• Students compete with each other in class
• Corporal punishment severely rejected	• Students try to make themselves visible
• Students choose academic subjects in view of intrinsic interest	• Corporal punishment occasionally considered salutary
• Male students may choose traditionally feminine academic subjects	• Students choose academic subjects in view of career opportunities
	• Male students avoid traditionally feminine academic subjects

Note: In contrasting the societies displaying characteristics more traditionally associated with a feminine role from those societies traditionally associated with a masculine role, it is important to suspend value judgments. This dimension is perhaps the most controversial of the four dimensions and to the extent that one seems more natural the opposite extreme may seem less appropriate.

and act upon each person's behavior as constructed by the cultural context in which that behavior was learned and displayed (P. Pedersen & Ivey, 1993).

As shown in Figure 5.6, the "inside-the-person" or intrapersonal cultural grid provides a conceptual framework for demonstrating how cultural and personal factors interact in a combined relationship. The cultural grid links each behavior or action to an expectation or reason behind that action, and each expectation to a value learned from the cultural teachers.

Each cultural context is complicated and dynamic, influenced by many cultural teachers from the individual's cultural context, who take turns at being salient according to each time and place. An awareness of one's cultural iden-

FIGURE 5.6
The Intrapersonal Cultural Grid

Social System Variables	Behavior	Expectation	Values

Ethnographic
  Nationality
  Ethnicity
  Religion
  Language			

Demographic
  Age
  Gender
  Affectional orientation
  Physical abilities			

Status
  Social
  Economic
  Political
  Educational			

Affiliation
  Formal
    (like family or career)
  Informal
    (like a shared idea
    or belief)			

tity requires being able to identify how each action is the expression of specific expectations, how each expectation developed from specific values, and how each value was learned from one or more cultural teachers in the cultural context. The cultural teachers might come from family relationships such as relatives, fellow countrypersons, ancestors, or those with shared beliefs. Power relationships based on social friendships, sponsors and mentors, subordinates, supervisors, or superiors may provide cultural teachers. Other memberships with co-workers, organizations, gender or age groups, and workplace colleagues may contribute cultural teachers. A wide range of nonfamily relationships, friendships, classmates, neighbors, or ordinary people may also have contributed teachers.

The intrapersonal cultural grid is intended to show the complex relationships among what a person did (behavior), why the person did it (expectation), and where the person learned to do it. Judging other people's behavior out of context, or without regard to why the person did it and where the person learned it, is likely to be misleading at best and totally wrong at worst. It is not easy to discover why people do what they do. Many if not most of us often do not know ourselves why we do what we do, not to mention where we learned to do it. This is no quick and easy answer to understanding behaviors in their cultural context. However, unless the behavior is understood in context, that behavior is very likely to be misunderstood.

The interpersonal cultural grid (see Figure 5.7), on the other hand, is an attempt to describe the relationship between people or groups by separating what they do (behaviors) from why they do it (expectations). The interpersonal cultural grid includes four quadrants. Each quadrant explains one large or small part of any relationship between two individuals or groups. There will be some data in all four cells for any relationship, but the salience may change from one cell to another over time as the relationship changes.

In the first quadrant (see Figure 5.7), two individuals have similar (perceived positive) behavior and similar (perceived positive) reasons or expectations for doing that behavior. The relationship is congruent and harmonious. There is a high level of accuracy in both individuals' interpretation of one another's behavior and the positive shared expectations or reasons behind that behavior. Both persons are smiling (behavior), for example, and both persons expect friendship. There is little conflict in this quadrant and few surprises.

In the second quadrant, two individuals act differently or perceive the other's action in negative terms, but they still share the same positive expectations or reason for doing what they did. There is a high level of agreement in that both persons expect trust, friendliness, and safety, for example, but there is a low level of accuracy because each person perceives the other's behavior or action as negative, wrong or inappropriate, and probably hostile. This quad-

FIGURE 5.7
The Interpersonal Cultural Grid

Behavior

		Same	Different
	Same or Positive	I (Harmony)	II (Cross-cultural conflict)
Expectation	Different or Negative	III (Personal conflict)	IV (War)

rant is characteristic of cultural conflict in which each person is applying a self-reference criterion to interpret the other person's behavior. The conditions described in the second quadrant are very unstable, and unless the shared positive expectations are quickly found and made explicit, the salience is likely to change toward the third quadrant, favoring the more powerful of the two. It is important for at least one of the two people to discover and identify the presence of shared positive expectations for trust, respect, safety, and fairness in their different cultural contexts, despite the apparent differences in their behaviors as they express those reasons.

In the third quadrant, the two persons have the same behaviors but now they have different or negative expectations or reasons. The similar behaviors give the appearance of harmony and agreement through displaying the desired behavior or action, but the hidden different or negative expectations and reasons for acting will ultimately destroy the relationship. Although both persons are now in disagreement, this might not be obvious or apparent. One person may continue to expect trust and friendliness, whereas the other person is now negatively distrustful and unfriendly, even though they are both presenting the same smiling and glad-handing congruent behaviors. If these two people discover that at an earlier time they shared positive expectations or reasons for working together, they might be able to salvage the relationship and return to the second quadrant, reversing the escalating conflict between them. If the difference in expectations or reasons is ignored or undiscovered, the conflict will ultimately move to the fourth quadrant.

The fourth quadrant is where two people have different or negative expectations and they stop pretending to be congruent. The two persons are now "at war" with one another and may not even want to increase harmony in their relationship any longer. They may just want to hurt one another. Both persons are in disagreement, and that disagreement is now obvious and apparent. This relationship is likely to result in hostile disengagement. It is very difficult to retrieve conflict from the fourth quadrant because one or both parties have stopped trying to find shared positive expectations. Unfortunately, most conflicts between people and groups remain undiscovered until they reach the fourth quadrant. An appropriate prevention strategy would be to identify the conflict in behaviors—as indicated in the second quadrant—early in the process, when those differences in behaviors might be a positive resource, as long as there are shared positive reasons or expectations for behaving, thereby allowing the parties to build on their common ground without losing integrity.

Therefore, as described in the cultural grid, two people or groups may both share the same positive expectations or reasons for what they do but continue to act differently. They may both want trust, but one may be loud and the other quiet. They may share respect, but one may be open and the other closed. They may both believe in fairness, but one may be direct and the other indirect. They may value efficiency, but one may be formal and the other informal. They may both seek effectiveness, but one may be close and the other distant. They may want safety, but one may be task oriented and the other relationship oriented. Only when each behavior is assessed and understood in its own cultural context does that behavior become meaningful. Only when positive shared expectations can be identified will two individuals or groups be able to find and build on common ground without sacrificing integrity.

5. Conclusion

This chapter has described several alternative ways that cultural patterns have been used to interpret behavior along with the advantages and disadvantages of each. In each explanation, it seems clear that culture is not an external force but an internalized perspective of reality as we know it. If culture is indeed within the person, then developing a multicultural identity becomes an essential part of personal development. We need to go beyond the obvious labels used to describe individual and collective cultural identities. We need to recognize the constructive principles of cultural patterns as we adapt our identity to each new context. We need to understand the process of developing an identity as a complex but not chaotic series of stages or categories. Finally, we need to see our multicultural identity as a synthesis of the many cultures in our lives. This synthesis is both complex and dynamic, shaping both our expectations and our behaviors. We construct our own cultural identity.

As we continue to develop our multicultural awareness, knowledge, and skill, a clear and accurate perception of our own multicultural identity becomes an essential element. Our ability to shape and influence our environment, bring about desired changes, and find harmony with others depends on knowing ourselves and our cultures.

EXERCISE: Nested Emotions

Sometimes it is difficult to interpret what someone from another culture is feeling. Our emotional response to a situation is usually mixed, emphasizing conflicting feelings. Interview a particularly articulate participant from a contrasting culture on an emotionally loaded simulated role play situation for about 3 minutes. As an alternative, have the resource person talk about a situation in which he or she had strong positive or negative feelings. After the interview, distribute a rating sheet listing 10 or more emotions, such as love, happiness, fear, anger, contempt, mirth, surprise, determination, or disgust. Beside each emotion, provide a semantic differential ranging from 1 (*least*) to 10 (*most*), asking participants to describe the degree of emotional feeling *they thought* the interviewee was feeling *while in the role* of the person being interviewed. Ask the interviewee also to complete the semantic differential indicating how he or she was *actually* feeling while in the role of the person being interviewed.

When everyone has completed their semantic differentials, ask the interviewee to read the number indicating a degree of feeling he or she checked for each of the 10 items and to explain the reasons for that choice while the participants check the accuracy of their *perceptions* about what the interviewee was feeling. The discussion that follows might emphasize clues to identify nested emotions for the interviewee's culture and highlight emotions that are particularly difficult for an outsider to detect.

THE NESTED EMOTIONS EXERCISE

Participant Objectives:
1. To estimate the degree of each emotion displayed by the resource person.
2. To determine the degree of each emotion reported by the resource person.
3. To identify cues to emotional expression in different cultures.

Learning Objective:
1. Emotions are always complicated and perception will differ from reality.

CHAPTER 6

Unanswered Research Questions on Multicultural Counseling

Major objective:

1. To review questions about multicultural counseling to which we do not know the answer.

Secondary objectives:

1. To identify topics for funded research on multicultural counseling.
2. To suggest dissertation topics on multicultural counseling.
3. To define the limits of our knowledge about multicultural counseling.
4. To stimulate the identification of other unanswered questions about multicultural counseling.

The domestic context of multicultural relations has been characterized by political influence and socioeconomic impact in the search for "equality." The basis of dissatisfaction, ironically, was written into the idealist promises of the U.S. Declaration of Independence that "all men are created equal." As a nation, we have experienced a social revolution that has idealized a state of equality among races, sexes, generations, and peoples. We have been taught that only those who make use of their opportunities and develop special skills can be assured of their fair share. The concept of equality is thereby diluted to a power struggle, granting us the equal right to become unequal, as perceived by the minorities, through competing with one another (Dreikurs, 1972). Bryne

Parts of this chapter are reprinted from P. Pedersen, R.T. Carter, & J.G. Ponterotto (1996), "The cultural context of psychology: Questions for accurate research and appropriate practice," *Cultural Diversity and Mental Health, 2,* 205–216. Reprinted with permission of John Wiley & Sons.

(1977) pointed out how the perception of equality has politicized the delivery of counseling services in the North American social context. Aubrey (1977) likewise pointed out the trend in counseling to emphasize normal developmental concerns of individuals to the exclusion of a special group's concerns in the name of equality. In many ways, the White, dominant-culture researcher finds himself or herself in a dilemma by wanting to contribute but not being sure how to do so (P. Pedersen, 1993).

With the civil rights movement of the 1950s, the militancy of minorities for change gained momentum. With the growth of the community mental health movement of the 1960s, mental health care became the right of all citizens and not just the wealthy or middle-class dominant majority (Atkinson et al., 1983; LeVine & Padilla, 1980). The issues of feminism and popular dissent nurtured by the anti-Vietnam War movement fostered a climate of discontent during which protest was accepted and in some cases even demanded. The stigma of discrimination became synonymous with any attempt to treat groups differently. D. W. Sue (1981) suggested, however, that minority groups may not be asking for equal treatment as much as for equal access to power. Differential treatment is not necessarily discriminatory or preferential.

Multiculturally skilled counseling is necessarily and inevitably different across cultures in providing an appropriate counseling service for each group and individual. With increased publications on minority group counseling in the late 1970s and 1980s, these differences have led to a great deal of confusion in the use of terms like *race, ethnicity, culture,* and *minority* (Atkinson et al., 1983). The term *race* technically refers to biological differences, whereas *ethnicity* rightly refers to group classifications. People of the same ethnic group within the same race might still be culturally different. Other items such as *culturally deprived* or *culturally disadvantaged, culturally different,* and *culturally distinct* were created to explain why a minority group is out of step with the majority population. Minorities, then, are groups of people singled out for unequal and different treatment and who regard themselves as objects of discrimination (Atkinson et al., 1993). Research on multicultural counseling issues have attempted to clarify these issues.

An accurate psychological assessment, a meaningful psychological interpretation, and an appropriate psychological intervention require that behaviors be understood in their cultural context in which those behaviors were learned. As counselors and psychologists become more aware of the complex and dynamic cultural contexts in which behaviors are learned, we become aware of the many "unanswered questions" about the cultural context of counseling and psychology. In August 1995, Robert Carter from Columbia Teachers College, Joe Ponterotto from Fordham University, Jim Nageotte from Sage Press, and Paul Pedersen from Syracuse University organized a 2-day conference focusing on unanswered questions about multicultural counseling and psychology. The forum was intended to raise questions and discuss answers about research gaps, appropriate theory, and competent practice.

1. The Need to Identify Unanswered Questions

Most conferences focus on lengthy presentations by a small group to a relatively passive audience of listeners. There is usually little or no time for questions and discussions of issues after the presentations. Recognizing the considerable expertise in the audience that is typically underutilized, the conference organizers designed a conference focused on discussion without formal presentations. The plan was to move directly to the discussion of previously identified stimulus questions so that the audience could more actively participate.

In the process of identifying priority questions for discussion, the conference organizers hoped to do the following:

1. Identify topics for dissertations on culture and mental health issues.
2. Identify networks of resources for collaborative research and publication on the cultural context of counseling and psychology.
3. Mobilize the synergy of the group working together in generating answers to difficult questions.
4. Produce a document recording ideas from the discussion for dissemination to other interested colleagues in the field.
5. Experiment with an innovative conference design that focuses on discussion rather than presentations.

The facilitators were invited to identify questions on the basis of their extensive publications and visibility as leaders in the field of multicultural counseling. There are, of course, many other professionals who are also well known in the field but who were unavailable to participate.

The conference was organized as a "think tank" with 27 conversation groups focusing on a different set of pressing questions about the latest research, current and emerging theory, and insights from across the country on the theory and practice of multicultural counseling. There were no formal presentations. Each session was led by a facilitator who had identified from three to five difficult and "unanswered research questions" about the cultural context of psychology and counseling, which were then discussed by the whole group. The emphasis was on small group discussion with full audience participation throughout.

This chapter attempts to highlight selected issues raised in the discussion groups at the conference. The discussion organizes the questions and answers into three groups: those emphasizing awareness of cultural assumptions, those emphasizing knowledge about particular cultures, and those emphasizing the skills needed to provide accurate and appropriate direct service to clients in their cultural contexts.

2. Questions About Cultural Awareness

Most of the questions about cultural awareness related to underlying assumptions about culture, defining culture-related terms and identifying "starting points" for accurately interpreting counseling data in its cultural context.

2.1. Farah Ibrahim from the University of Connecticut–Storrs asked what variables are defined as *culture* and why those variables are so controversial.

- Are we watering down the definition of *culture* until it becomes meaningless?
- Is culture more "personal" and less abstract than other constructs?
- Is there an implicit assumption that in the United States there is only one culture?
- Do we need an operational definition and more terms to define it?
- Is culture also a process in which people from different groups have different narratives?
- Is culture a conversation about sharing power?
- Is gender also anchored in a cultural context?
- How does culture mediate gender?

2.2. Don C. Locke from the University of North Carolina at Asheville asked why we need so many "umbrella" terms to define racial and ethnic groups and "who speaks for multiculturalism?"

- Can only "insider" group members speak for the group in a narrow rather than a broad focus?
- Can we organize the confusion of terminology about multiculturalism and the wide range of emotions attached to these terms?
- Do the political aspects of culture further increase the controversy in culture-related language?
- Can we agree on what culture is?
- Is clearly defined terminology essential to a meaningful discussion?

2.3. Frederick Leong from Ohio State University challenged the following underlying assumptions of a linear, positivistic, and empirical approach to epistemology.

- How do we integrate culture-general (etic) with culture-specific (emic) models and theories in cross-cultural counseling?
- Can a multicultural perspective help counseling become more multidimensional?
- Is part of the problem in counseling the tendency to look at one variable independently from others while ignoring the complex cultural context?
- Does each individual function at all three levels—universal, individual, and group—simultaneously?
- Do complex adaptive systems theories suggest a means of identifying complex and dynamic cultural patterns through chaos theory and complexity theory in which many interactive variables are combined?

2.4. Janet Helms from the University of Maryland focused on the definition of terms and the importance of "race."

- Has the dominant White culture invented terms like *ethnicity* because they are uncomfortable with "race" issues?
- Do factors of guilt and shame complicate "racial" issues, especially for the dominant culture?
- Can people who have such different cultural values and access to power even communicate about race issues?
- Is race a pseudobiological term that has sociopolitical meaning?
- Can we start by developing scales to assess race or racism and by being more active in organizations?

2.5. Robert Carter from Teachers College, Columbia University, focused on how race issues influence therapy.

- Do we all operate within a culture using language to communicate meaning across geographical boundaries?
- Is race different from the other cultural categories as a more permanent characteristic that was used to construct society?
- Does race evoke emotion and therefore tends to be "untouchable"?
- Is race a real part of both the client's and the counselor's perspective?
- Does race influence human development and personality through perception?
- Does race function like gender in making a difference?
- Can we get anywhere if we do not agree that we all have a "race"?
- Is most counseling research about race the "White" race?

2.6. Grace Powless Sage from the Indian Health Service, Blackfeet Community Hospital, Browning, Montana, asked what basic competencies are necessary when working with American Indians.

- How does one integrate traditional and contemporary healing practices in respect to the historical tension between traditional and contemporary healing practices?
- How are *power* and *control* defined in the American Indian worldview?
- Do the words *normal, healthy, healing,* and *wellness* have the same meaning in the American Indian context as elsewhere?
- How does indigenous self-determination play a role in the identity and understanding of American Indians in their communities?
- How does one address the urban versus rural reservation and generational differences among American Indian communities?
- Is the American Indian identity more than a race?
- Has the romanticization of American Indian identity contributed to the confusion?
- Given the history and training of traditional clinical psychology programs, is there a need to consider a "high-context" worldview and a history of colonial ("Whitening processes") exploitation, appropriation, and extermination as part of the context?

2.7. Timothy Thomason from Northern Arizona University asked what we need to know to provide culturally appropriate assessment and intervention services to American Indians.

- Do we need more participatory action model approaches on treatment programs?
- Do we need better criteria of effectiveness in alcohol treatment programs?
- Do we need to learn more from indigenous, traditional approaches to Indian healing?
- Do we need to redefine *mental health* in the American Indian context?
- Do we need better indigenous assessment measures?
- Do we need a more appropriate theory regarding culturally appropriate counseling and psychological services for American Indians?
- Do we need psychotherapeutic methodologies that incorporate storytelling, talking circles, and sweat-lodge/vision quest perspectives?
- Do we need a more spiritual emphasis regarding healing processes?

2.8. Paul Pedersen from the University of Alabama at Birmingham asked questions about the generic application of multiculturalism to all counseling and psychological interventions.

- Can we find "common ground" between dominant culture and minority member colleagues and clients?

- How can we identify the changing salience of broadly defined cultural variables in an interview?
- Can we compensate for cultural bias in the theory and practice of counseling without throwing out theories, tests, and conventional psychological procedures?
- Is there an alternative to relativism and absolutism in describing guidelines for ethical behavior in multicultural settings?
- Is cultural encapsulation getting better or getting worse in fields of applied counseling and psychology?
- How can we demonstrate the positive value of making all theories of counseling more "culture-centered"?
- How can we get textbooks, tests, and professional guidelines to make their underlying assumptions explicit rather than implicit?
- If behavior is learned and displayed in a cultural context, then how can that behavior be assessed accurately, interpreted meaningfully, and changed appropriately without regard for that cultural context?

3. Questions About Cultural Knowledge

Some of the discussions emphasized the need for specific facts and information about the cultural context as a necessary step in giving appropriate care. The emphasis on meaningful knowledge presumed accurate assumptions about the cultural context in the first place.

3.1. Harold Cheatham from Pennsylvania State University asked about the danger of doing "too much" for the client and moving "too far" outside the traditional counseling model.

- As the counselor works to make sense of the client's issues within the context of multiculturalism, when does the counselor begin to do too much for the client?
- How does the counselor determine when this boundary has been reached or crossed?
- Are there guidelines for the practice of the counselor extending himself or herself beyond the counseling walls, or is this a decision the counselor must make?
- After years of struggle, how do you envision the end product of equality among culture, gender, and lifestyle?
- What would it look, sound, and feel like to live in that environment?
- How would members of the society at large interact with one another (socially, in business, in education, in government) as neighbors?
- To what images do we strive?

- How do/can we train counselors to assess the extent to which their own backgrounds affect their working relationships?
- Is it fairly well established that various ethnic groups have different orientations to factors and values, such as family, community, time, and age?
- Counselors need to be aware of these differences across groups, but do they also need to be aware of within-group differences (e.g., within-group distribution and variability of time orientation)?
- How do we prepare counselors to assess and work within the individual client's within-group differences?

3.2. Oliva Espin from San Diego State University asked about women's roles when a group migrates to an unfamiliar society.

- Are behaviors necessarily modified, requiring migrants to become more rigid and "traditionalizing" the roles and behaviors, especially of women and girls, to protect their culture?
- Do many conflicts of migrant groups relate to male–female relationships?
- Does the provider want to be respectful of the migrant's culture but not condone violence or the denial of opportunities for women in the host society?
- Is cultural sensitivity a way of condoning injustices?
- Should culture be preserved at the expense of women who "carry culture on their backs"?
- Is the acculturation–adaptation process different for women and men?
- Can an immigrant/refugee woman preserve cultural identity while acculturating or adapting to U.S. society?
- Is narrative research, which allows women to tell their stories, useful?
- Why do so many of us come from immigrant families where, once the immigrants have "blended," the stories of pain are forgotten?
- Do migrants become scapegoats of social problems in the stereotype?
- Do providers need more sensitive training to provide for migrants in an equitable way?

3.3. Nadya Fouad from the University of Wisconsin–Milwaukee asked questions about how gender differences or sexual preference differences influenced career choices, making dominant culture heterosexual males the criterion group for everyone else.

- Do we need new norms that are sensitive to different cultural contexts?
- Do we need to reevaluate traditional career development theories regarding their cultural sensitivity?

- Do realistic choices that look at satisfaction as well as satisfactoriness in a balanced perspective need to be defined for minority group persons?
- How does vocational choice affect identity issues in multicultural contexts?
- Do traditional vocational concepts such as vocational maturity and stage/ladder focus on career development need to be redefined according to the cultural context and gender?
- Do the criteria of success need to be reexamined for majority and minority cultural contexts?
- Does the role of family need to be reintegrated into each cultural context as a complex and dynamic variable?
- Do power differences and issues of helplessness become especially important in career counseling across cultures?

3.4. Anderson Franklin from City University of New York asked questions about psychological invisibility and social marginalization, especially among African American men.

- Does *invisibility* mean being in a place where you are not acknowledged, are not recognized, have no sense of gratification, and are unsure if it is legitimate or valid to be present in that place?
- Do churches and cultural groups serve an important function in validating identity?
- Do issues of culture and race become more salient because of social marginalization, and does dissonance occur when "the best theory going" just does not fit?
- Does social marginalization have to do with the social indicators as represented by statistical measures of social inequities?
- By recognizing and valuing the importance of identity, can the counselor reduce the effect of marginalization and help the client struggle against invisibility and become more empowered?
- Is the Black male particularly vulnerable to marginalization without creating a Black male stereotype?
- Does the system determine visibility but perpetuate invisibility to protect itself?

3.5. Jane Fried from Northeastern University asked how we can energize a dialogue between counseling and the other social sciences.

- What is cultural "common sense" and how does it affect the cross-cultural counseling process?
- How do the emerging transdisciplines of cultural psychology and self-reflexive anthropology affect cross-cultural counseling?

- Are there useful ideas that emerge when one thinks of a counselor as a cultural/interpersonal ethnographer?
- Is counseling, as we have traditionally practiced it in the United States, functional a helping mode for people from sociocentric or theocentric cultures?
- How do community psychology and ecological counseling relate to emerging models of cross-cultural counseling?

3.6. Barbara Okun from Northeastern University asked questions about conflicting loyalties across cultures: class, gender, and professional socialization.

- Does our psychology training sometimes strengthen an inflexible perspective and prevent change by minimalizing the significance of gender, race, sexual orientation, class, and ethnicity on human development and behavior?
- Does the fear of change most often come from inside the group rather than outside the group?
- Are senior members of the group more threatened by change than junior members?
- Is this fear of change because senior members can lose power, or because junior members have more to risk (with regard to tenure and promotion)?
- Do "old boy" networks tend to enforce insider rules and protect against outsider intervention?
- Do culturally sensitive seniors have an imperative to mentor juniors for constructive change?
- Are simplistic solutions to complex problems used to create a false sense of unity within the group?
- Are the real problems and risks associated with taking on the system minimalized?
- Do factors of age and gender mediate questions of loyalty with others within the group, protecting the status quo?
- Is gender more salient than race?
- Is a critical mass within the group needed to generate energy for constructive paradigm shifts in a proactive rather than reactive effort?
- Are there training and clinical interventions for addressing issues of backlash and polarization on issues of acculturation?

4. Questions About Cultural Skill

A third category of discussion groups focused on skill-based direct service interventions or applications of culturally accurate awareness and culturally grounded knowledge. The questions and ideas brought out in discussion were action oriented.

4.1. Lillian Comas-Diaz from Transcultural Mental Health Institute, Washington, DC, asked questions about how cross-cultural practice might influence general psychological practice.

- Are the issues of managed care complicated by cultural issues, such as choice of caregiver, uninformed providers, advocacy of client's identity, and involvement of paraprofessionals?
- Can clinicians provide quality care if they cannot communicate accurately and meaningfully with their clients?
- Do providers of counseling and psychological services need to become more politically involved and historically aware beyond protecting the status quo?
- Is more training of counselors and therapists in culturally different perspectives from a practical as well as a theoretical perspective essential?
- Are changes in accreditation processes important to sanction cultural issues?
- Are both culture-specific and cultural-general approaches necessary?
- Does the *Diagnostic and Statistical Manual of Mental Disorders'* (4th ed.; American Psychiatric Association, 1994) attention to cultural issues define clinical skills in a cultural context rather than put culture in a clinical context?

4.2. Patricia Arredondo from Empowerment Workshops, Boston, focused on questions of organizational and business management practices.

- What language would best relate to the organizational setting and which multicultural models could be applied to business environments?
- Is it important to broaden the multicultural discussion from solely clinical to the more inclusive organizational context?
- Does diversity in organizations require that we emphasize relationship factors as they relate to empowerment and ultimately to the "bottom line"?
- Do organizations resist putting personal issues ahead of bottom-line factors and the dominant culture in organizations, and are they especially resistant to change by persons of color?
- Do top-down model changes start at the top and work their way down?
- Is change uncomfortable because it disrupts the hierarchy at the personal and organizational levels, or are there other reasons that might explain the phenomenon of resistance?

- Can coalitions be formed to facilitate constructive change and help systems adapt?
- Is the "culture of organizations" about fluidity and adaptation to chaos?
- Why are diversity issues still not considered a high priority in organizations and instead met with "quick-fix" strategies?
- What would be the incentives for organizational leaders to participate in diversity training even when they are themselves minority group members?

4.3. Richard Brislin from the East West Center, Honolulu, Hawaii, focused on questions of multicultural training.

- Which classroom activities simulating intercultural experiences tend to work best for training?
- Are groups that are more culturally diverse easier to teach than homogeneous and particularly dominant culture groups?
- Can we learn our cultural patterns from persons of other cultures who see us differently than we see ourselves?
- Is working together to accomplish a task or going "somewhere where you're different" an effective training approach?
- Do minority persons, who experience the consequences of "being different" more than dominant culture persons, resent the "obligation" to teach or train their dominant culture peers and feel this can become another example of their "being used"?
- Does good training need to provide a safe environment where people can take risks?
- Is it frustrating for the instructor to meet the widely divergent training needs of students?
- Is good training based on clearly defined goals, investment of emotional energy, and favorable conditions for cultural contact, based on careful homework and scientific methods that focus on both content and process?

4.4. Ann Kathleen Burlew from the University of Cincinnati focused on questions of getting published in the multicultural area.

- Are mainstream journals more valuable for promotion tenure review even though they will be less receptive to culture-based articles?
- Are traditional research methods more highly regarded even though they may be less appropriate?
- Are the authors most qualified to write about culture often overwhelmed by their own practical involvement?
- Are the most recognized assessment measures typically not validated with minority populations?

- Is more emphasis on mentoring needed to recruit new authors for special issues of mainstream journals?
- Does more emphasis need to be placed on "Whiteness" as well as "Blackness" factors?
- Does there need to be a higher level of commitment to multiculturalism by mainstream journals and the dominant culture?
- Does the polarization of quantitative versus qualitative methodology and research versus practice applications need to be reconciled?
- Do practice-based criterion groups need to be developed to advise researchers writing for publication?
- Will the quality of multicultural publications be enhanced when there is an effective network linking people doing culturally responsive research with people publishing culturally responsive research?

4.5. J. Manuel Casas from the University of California, Santa Barbara, raised questions on the implementation of a Multi-Agency Integrated System of Care designed to provide services that are comprehensive, truly integrated, child centered, family focused, autonomy building, community based, rationally managed, and culturally competent.

- To accomplish this goal, do we need to identify the most effective methodologies for assessment, define effectiveness in working with culturally distinct groups, identify appropriate skills, develop more culturally appropriate instruments, and generate racial/ethnic criteria for each target population?
- What are the steps that need to be taken to identify and/or develop culturally sensitive and appropriate measures to assess the effectiveness of an integrated system of care with racial/ethnic minority populations?
- What are the steps that need to be taken to measure the cultural competency of the service providers?
- How can we more effectively train diverse service providers to design and implement effective and community based integrative systems of care that are earmarked for racial/ethnic minority populations?
- What are defining characteristics that determine the most effective interventions for children and families from diverse sociocultural backgrounds?
- When working with culturally different groups, should successful outcomes be measured by statistical or clinical significance?
- When designing a community-based system of care, what are the best sources of information for assessing needs and in turn developing effective interventions?

- Do political priorities often overshadow humanitarian priorities when implementing integrated systems of care in racial/ethnic minority communities?

4.6. Michael D'Andrea from the University of Hawaii asked questions about competencies for working with culturally diverse client populations.

- Why are those competencies not more prominent in accreditation rules, and why are multicultural competencies not more strongly advocated by the American Counseling Association and other professional counselor organizations?
- Why is the American Counseling Association considering including multicultural competencies in its guidelines for certification and accreditation?
- Do we need to identify indigenous helping frameworks as alternatives to traditional counseling approaches?
- Do we need to distinguish between personal and cultural dimensions of identity as we develop competencies?
- Do competencies need to be not just evaluated but also activated toward culture-sensitive change?
- Are minorities "expected" to have more cultural competence than dominant culture counselors according to the stereotype?
- How important is "comfort" as an outcome measure of competence?
- How do we address colleagues unwilling to become competent?
- Does conformity to the status quo inhibit new competencies with the focus often on the provider rather than the consumer?

4.7. James Jackson from the University of Michigan asked questions about multicultural research paradigms.

- Do we need to examine "natural" linkages among cross-ethnic and cross-national approaches to research?
- Do we need to untangle biological, structural, and social factors to distinguish the "universal" processes from those that are culturally bounded?
- What are the differences and similarities among descriptive comparative, comparative outcome, and comparative process research?
- Are ethnic differences merely the result of exposure to a different context?
- Do we need to step outside the U.S. domestic scene to understand how ethnic groups in other countries define themselves?
- Does each country define dominant and subordinate groups differently?
- Does counseling claim to consider social variables but tend to disregard many contextual factors and focus on the "dominant" groups in the United States and elsewhere?

- Is the basis of subjugation economic more than moral?
- Has neuroticism and pathology in the dominant group been functional, and does being a bigot result in higher levels of stress?
- Do we need to disentangle adaptive behaviors from those that are culturally determined?
- Can the sending–receiving model of research complement other approaches?
- Are complexity and context the crucial bases for cross-cultural research?

4.8. Sunkyo Kwon from Humboldt University, Berlin, Germany, raised questions about bridging information gaps through the Internet.

- Why does the research of many non-U.S. based scholars, however valuable, never reach a larger audience?
- Why do colleagues currently working on culture-related problems work in unnecessary isolation around the world?
- Why are there uncountable numbers of datasets around the world that have never been fully analyzed or examined comparatively?
- Where and how does the accumulated body of scientific knowledge about cross-cultural counseling and psychology become established?
- Do problems of reconciling diversity, merging information, synthesis, dissemination, and the research–practice gap inhibit coordination of valuable information?
- Is there a lag in disseminating or publishing information that leads to isolation?
- Do computers introduce e-mail, usenet, file transfer protocols, World Wide Web, and other facilities to reduce the lag time of information dissemination?
- Do colleagues from more industrialized countries benefit most from computer technology, and can it lead to domination by an elite upper class?
- Do we need new skills to manage information overload?

4.9. Joseph Ponterotto from Fordham University asked questions based on trends for the future.

- How can we bring colleagues from the subfields of psychology—often working in isolation—together to address more holistically multicultural issues?
- Would an interdisciplinary knowledge base assist both research and practice?
- What are the future trends in counseling, clinical, social work, family

psychology, and other subfields of psychology, and how can counselors and psychologists from these different disciplines work together?

- Do we need to know ourselves first and to listen carefully, focusing more on self-awareness as a professional competency?
- Do we need to know the historical, political, and spiritual context before intervening?
- Why has the field of counseling taken leadership in promoting multiculturalism and interdisciplinary connections among the subfields of psychology?
- Does change need to accommodate emotional as well as intellectual data about culture, requiring that we create a "safe place" to exchange ideas?
- Do Whites need to become more actively involved, perhaps as part of multicultural teams for research, teaching, and training?

5. Conclusion

The conference on unanswered research questions attempted to (a) bring together colleagues interested in the cultural context of psychology to exchange ideas, (b) identify some of the research gaps regarding the cultural context of psychology, (c) generate connections between networks of colleagues for future collaboration, (d) try on the model of a conference without presentations but that is almost entirely discussion-focused, (e) stimulate dissertation research and publications on new ideas about multiculturalism, and (f) provide opportunities for support and sharing among colleagues working on multicultural issues.

Although the conference was not evaluated in any formal sense, the feedback from participants has been uniformly positive, and anecdotal data suggest that the conference had valuable meaning to most if not all participants. A continuing theme of the conference emphasized the importance of activism and the dangers of passivity regarding the cultural context of counseling. We need to model more active and less passive alternatives in our research about cultural contexts. The traditionally passive model of one presenter reading a paper to hundreds of highly trained passively listening colleagues is not an efficient way to disseminate understanding. It is not just the content of the services we provide but also the process by which we provide that content that is in need of change.

The historical spread of counseling has been documented in a wide range of cultures. Although mental health problems are similar across cultures, the labels have changed from one culture to another over time. What has changed has been the complex classification of the environments in which counseling is being applied and the categories of problems, illness, difficulty, or crisis. A specialized counseling industry has developed to meet this need. The number of consumers as well as the number of providers is rising in proportion to the increasing modernization–urbanization process and the weakening of the traditional family, villages, and institutional support systems. Although the labels of counseling might be new, the functions of how help is provided are probably not new.

EXERCISE: Critical Incidents

The effectiveness of a training program usually is determined by its relevance to solving specific practical problems of a participant. Problem situations can themselves become valuable training tools. A critical incident occurs in a brief (5–6 minute) period of time, requires a decision to be made, and has serious consequences if a wrong decision is made but does not clearly show which decision is the right one ahead of time. For this training situation, the incident should involve persons from culturally different backgrounds. Collect examples of problem situations or decisions that have no easy answers, project serious consequences, and occur with some frequency.

You might divide participants into problem-solving groups to discuss the *cultural element* and perceived *conflict* within each situation, along with an *intervention* plan for dealing with the situation.

You also might ask individuals to respond to a situation (a) as they would *like* to respond, (b) as they think they *should* or are *expected* to respond, and (c) as they actually *would* respond in real life. By distinguishing among these three levels of response choices, you might open up a discussion on response alternatives participants face in real life.

CRITICAL INCIDENTS EXERCISE

Participant Objectives:
1. To identify culturally appropriate responses to a situation.
2. To identify personally preferred responses to a situation.
3. To examine the influence of cultural norms in responding to a situation.

Learning Objective:
1. Situations are defined by both personal and cultural considerations.

CHAPTER 7

The Ethical Dilemma of Multicultural Counselors

Major objective:

1. To critique ethical guidelines from a multicultural perspective.

Secondary objectives:

1. To examine measures of cultural equity in counseling.
2. To review historical trends emphasizing multiculturalism in society.
3. To examine the dangers of cultural encapsulation.
4. To examine ethical models applied to multicultural counseling.
5. To examine the American Counseling Association's ethical guidelines.

All behaviors are learned and displayed in one particular cultural context while they are typically perceived by others from the perspective of a different cultural context. We evaluate the behaviors of others from the perspective of our own cultural context and, consequently, are vulnerable to misattribution in judging the behaviors of others (P. Pedersen, 1997b, 1997c, 1997d). We are faced, then, with a cultural dilemma in which behaviors that might be ethical in one cultural context may be judged unethical in a different cultural context. It is therefore important to evaluate the behavior of others in the cultural context in which that behavior was learned and displayed (Cortese, 1989).

Changing demographics and increased awareness of special interest groups defined by gender, age, socioeconomic status, and lifestyle suggest an increased potential for cultural misunderstandings in the future. This increased diversity

Parts of this chapter are reprinted from P. Pedersen, (1997a), "The cultural context of the American Counseling Association Code of Ethics," *Journal of Counseling and Development,* 76, 23–29. Reprinted with permission.

presents problems and opportunities for evaluating ethical behavior. Hopkins (1997) pointed out the implications of increasing diversity in American society for defining standards of ethical behavior:

> In other words, will we see a change in Corporate America's ethical and moral standards as different cultural, ethnic, racial and interest groups, whose ethical and moral beliefs may be in conflict with mainstream America's, become a dominant force in the workplace? As individuals and groups from diverse cultures and backgrounds enter the workplace, they will not automatically shed their ethical and moral values at the door. The issue becomes whether, and to what extent, their ethical and moral values will alter existing ethics paradigms in organizations. (p. 16)

A report by the Basic Behavioral Science Task Force (1996) of the National Advisory Mental Health Council (NAMHC) documents the extent of cultural encapsulation of mental health services. First, anthropological and cross-cultural research has demonstrated that cultural beliefs influence the diagnosis and treatment of mental illness. Second, the diagnosis of mental illness differs across cultures. Third, research has revealed differences in how individuals express symptoms in different cultural contexts. Fourth, culturally based variations in diagnosis vary according to the diagnostic categories relevant to the majority population. Fifth, most providers come from a majority culture whereas most clients are members of minority cultures. If the standard practices of mental health services are themselves encapsulated, as suggested by the NAMHC report, then the criteria for ethical judgments need to be relocated outside the patterns of accepted conventional practice.

1. The Purpose of Ethical Codes

Ethical guidelines are a necessary but not sufficient condition for promoting ethical behavior. Codes of ethics are intended to promote ethical behavior by guiding counselors in good practice, protecting clients, safeguarding the counselor's autonomy, and enhancing the profession (Mappes, Robb, & Engels, 1985). Herlihy and Corey (1996) described the most basic functions of an ethics code as educating members about sound ethical conduct, providing a mechanism for professional accountability, and providing a catalyst for improving practice. Recognizing that no ethics code can address every situation, they described ethical codes as combining rules and utilitarian principles in ways that require interpretation. Ethical guidelines need to be interpreted not only in each situation but also in each cultural context. Clients or counselors from different cultural backgrounds might follow the same ethical guideline in the same situation by displaying different behaviors. Clients or counselors from an individualistic culture will interpret ethical guidelines about freedom and responsibility through different behaviors than will clients or counselors from a collectivistic culture. For this reason, to the extent that ethical guidelines are reduced to a list of rules, they tend to impose one set of behaviors—presumably the behaviors of a dominant culture—on all groups without regard to the client's or counselor's diversified cultural background.

The American Counseling Association (ACA) ethical guidelines tend to define ethics in terms of rules, checklists, principles, and guidelines for members to follow. To the extent that these objective guidelines reflect the culturally learned perspective of a dominant culture, the universal application of those rules, checklists, and principles create a dilemma for conscientious minorities.

Several strategies have been suggested for providing explicit guidelines but still allowing room for interpretation of those guidelines in each cultural context, without unfairly imposing rules of the dominant culture on minorities. Herlihy and Corey (1996) distinguished between *mandatory ethics*, which means to function according to minimum legal standards, and *aspirational ethics*, which means to function at a higher standard in accordance with the spirit behind the literal meaning of the code. In this way, fundamental values are identified while recognizing that different cultures may express those values through their own different culturally learned behaviors. Jordan and Meara (1990) distinguished between principle ethics, which focus on rational, objective, universal, and impartial principles mandating actions and choices, and virtue ethics, which focus on the counselor's motives, intentions, character, and ethical consciousness that recognizes the need to interpret principles differently in each cultural context.

The danger of any ethical code is that it might enforce the moral standards of the group in power. A fair and just code of ethics needs to do more than reflect the cultural values of those who wrote the code. As explained by Corey, Corey, and Callanan (1998), ethics describe moral principles or guidelines adopted by an individual or group to provide rules for right conduct. Morality involves the evaluation of any action according to some broader cultural context or religious standard. Thus, conduct that is evaluated as moral in one society may not provide exact and uniform answers to the moral dilemmas of counselors and clients in a culturally diversified society.

Kitchner (1984) described four of the basic moral principles that provide a foundation for the ethical code of counselors. These four principles of autonomy, beneficence, nonmalficence, and fairness are presumed to be universally valued regardless of the counselor's or client's cultural context. It is difficult to relate these moral principles to the subheading of the ACA code of ethics, although the moral principles pervade each of the subheadings and will be evident in the examples of systematic bias addressed later in this chapter. *Autonomy* refers to clients' freedom for self-determination. *Beneficence* refers to actions that promote the growth and development of the client. *Nonmalficence* means refraining from hurting clients. *Justice* or *fairness* refers to equal treatment of all people. Although these four principles may be valued across cultures, they are sometimes applied in culturally encapsulated ways. The 1995 ACA code of ethics continues to impose guidelines appropriate to the cultural context of the majority group on the quite different cultural contexts of multiple minority groups (LaFromboise, Foster, & James, 1996; P. Pedersen, 1994, 1995a).

2. Implicit Cultural Biases in the Ethics Code

The differences between the cultural context in which ethical codes were developed and the multiplicity of cultural contexts in which they are applied create a serious discrepancy (Ivey, 1987; Kendler, 1993; LaFromboise et al., 1996; Opotow, 1990). This discrepancy is evident in patterns of systematic cultural bias in the ACA code of ethics.

The Preamble to the *Code of Ethics and Standards of Practice* (ACA, 1995) states that "Association members recognize diversity in our society and embrace a cross-cultural approach in support of the worth, dignity, potential and uniqueness of each individual" (p. 1). This statement seems to imply that the code of ethics is based on a preference for individualism over collectivism, although that preference is not made explicit. Individualism applies to societies in which everyone is expected to look after themselves, whereas collectivism applies to societies in which people are integrated into cohesive groups that protect the members of the groups in exchange for their loyalty (Hofstede, 1991; U. Kim, Triandis, Kagitcibasi, Choi, & Yoon, 1994). A comprehensive code of ethics needs to respect the values of both individualistic and collectivistic cultural contexts. If that is not possible, the code of ethics at least needs to make its dependence on individualistic values explicit for the benefit of those who do not share the assumptions about the importance of the individual over the group.

Section A.1.c. on the counselor's effectiveness requires that "Counselors and clients regularly review counseling plans to ensure their continued viability and effectiveness, respecting the client's freedom of choice" (ACA, 1995, p. 2). The assumption that viable and effective measures are characterized by increasing the client's freedom of choice applies much more accurately to an individualistic context than to a collectivistic context. The client may belong to a family, organization, or unit and depend on that group for support. In such a case, an ethical counselor might want to explore the negative and positive consequences of encouraging freedom of choice to avoid what the individualistic counselor perceives as encumberment by responsibilities to the family or social unit. Female international students who return home after study in the United States, where they were counseled to fit in with the university culture, often describe a painful readjustment to their role back in their home country as wife, mother, or daughter in a context in which their freedom of choice is more limited or defined differently (P. Pedersen, 1991a). Both the long-term and short-term consequences of following the ethical guidelines in multicultural contexts need to be considered.

In Section A.6 on dual relationships, the assumption is that dual relationships with clients who share familial, social, financial, business, or close personal relationships with the counselor are to be avoided whenever possible, based on the assumption that the dual relationship might impair professional judgment and increase the risk of harm to clients. Herlihy and Corey (1997) asserted that not all dual relationships in counseling can be avoided, especially in smaller, more collectivist or rural communities. Herlihy and Corey further contended that not all dual relationships are harmful to clients. Most agree, however, that dual relationships provide the potential for a conflict of interest and exploitation. Haas and Malouf (1995) distinguished between friendships and counseling relationships. Friendships presume support, sharing, and mutual disclosure, whereas in counseling relationships trust, intimacy, and disclosure typically are not mutual in the American dominant cultural context. In other cultural contexts in which people are unaccustomed to depending on strangers or outsiders for advice and help and in which objective detachment would not be understood as facilitative, a dual relationship of reciprocal trust and "connectedness" may be required. Dual relationships are more likely to be hurtful in some cultural contexts than in others where it could be helpful or even necessary. Dual relationships by themselves are neither absolutely wrong nor absolutely right in all cultural contexts.

In Section B on confidentiality, there is an assumption about the importance of privacy, which again is not shared in all cultural contexts. In an individualistic culture, personal space and personal time are valued as property to be privately owned, and any infringement of those boundaries is considered a form of theft (Nelkin, 1984). "Time is money," as the saying goes. In other more collectivistic cultural contexts, the notion of personal privacy is less valued and may even be perceived as selfish or self-centered in ways that are destructive to the welfare of the community (U. Kim et al., 1994).

In Section E on evaluation, assessment, and interpretation, the "primary purpose of educational and psychological assessment is to provide measures that are objective and interpretable in either comparative or absolute terms" (ACA, 1995, p. 11). The implicit positivist, empirical, and linear assumptions seem to favor quantitative rather than more subjective qualitative methodologies as the criteria of accuracy. As the validity of nonlinear cultural perspectives gains credibility and the validity of subjective evidence becomes more accepted with the increased visibility of non-Western cultural contexts (Suzuki, Meller, & Ponterotto, 1996), it may become more appropriate to broaden the range of appraisal techniques that can be used ethically to include both objective and subjective measures, both quantitative and qualitative methodologies.

In describing the limitations of quantitative data to describe the Vietnam War, Goodman (cited in Yankelovitch, 1972) illustrated the importance of qualitative measures:

> The first step is to measure whatever can be easily measured. This is okay as far as it goes. The second step is to disregard that which can't be measured or give it an arbitrary quantitative value. This is artificial and misleading. The third step is to presume that what can't be measured easily really isn't very important. This is blindness. The fourth step is to say that what can't be easily measured really doesn't exist. (p. 286)

Dana (1993) recommended that a more broadly defined comprehensive model of assessment include (a) the client's level of acculturation, (b) questions that are phrased to fit the client's culture, (c) use of the client's native language, and (d) the use of culturally appropriate assessments. In some cases, the client's perspective will be nonlinear and subjective but important nonetheless.

3. The Cultural Encapsulation of the Ethics Code

Cultural encapsulation occurs when (a) reality is defined by a unidimensional cultural perspective, (b) cultural variations are ignored or minimalized, (c) disconfirming cultural evidence is ignored, (d) a technique-oriented strategy is applied across cultures, and (e) there is no evaluation of rival cultural viewpoints as valid (Wrenn, 1962, 1985). Cultural encapsulation has led toward dependence on a unidimensional authority in a multidimensional cultural context. The encapsulated counselor is trapped in one way of thinking that resists adaptation and rejects alternatives. A contrasting broader perspective leads counselors toward a more comprehensive understanding of alternatives and a more contextual application of theory (Wrenn, 1962, 1985). A second set of examples suggests that the ACA code of ethics is vulnerable to cultural encapsulation.

Item A.2.a., on respecting diversity, attacks discrimination and admonishes counselors not to "condone or engage in discrimination based on age, color, culture, disability, ethnic group, gender, race, religion, sexual orientation, marital status or socioeconomic status" (ACA, 1995, p. 2). A multidimensional perspective would recognize the necessity to discriminate between and among the many potentially salient cultural identities. Oetting and Beauvais (1991) described an "orthogonal" identity model based on many different but simultaneous cultural affiliations. Belonging to one group does not necessarily exclude belonging to many other groups at the same time. Each individual is a complex adaptive system for which salient identity is both complicated and dynamic in each context. A unidimensional perspective, in which differences are disregarded, is "color blind" to the potential and ever-changing balance of importance among the client's and the counselor's multiple simultaneous cultural identities. Applying a single encapsulated measure uniformly regardless of contextual differences oversimplifies and encapsulates counseling.

Section A.8. recommends against role diffusion by the counselor. "If it becomes apparent that counselors may be called upon to perform potentially conflicting roles, they clarify, adjust or withdraw from roles appropriately" (ACA, 1995, p. 3). To the extent that a collectivistic culture depends on overlapping relationships of role in the fabric of society, role diffusion is unavoidable. Most cultural contexts inevitably involve conflicting roles for participants, including the counselor. Rather than impose a simplistic encapsulated perspective, the counselor needs guidance on how to reframe these multiple roles in a way that is complementary and faithful to the intention of the guideline. In some cases, the counselor will not be able to give up the role of teacher, neighbor, friend, or boss in relation to his or her client.

Although Section E.5.b. requires that a client's "socioeconomic and cultural experience is considered when diagnosing mental disorders" (ACA, 1995, p. 12), the interpretation of that consideration is left entirely up to the individual counselor. Many of the other guidelines as well are open to interpretation according to the standards of accepted practice. The failure to define philosophical guidelines leaves providers open to imposing their own culturally encapsulated self-reference criteria.

The problem of cultural encapsulation can be addressed in the Preamble to the ACA code of ethics, as recommended by Kitchner (1986), to identify the cultural context of the ACA code of ethics. It is inevitable that assumptions are made in understanding and evaluating the ethical behaviors of self and others. Conscientious counselors and clients can interpret the ACA code of ethics in its cultural context to seek common ground in ethical principles. If the counselor or client disagrees with the underlying assumption, then the ethical guidelines that are based on those assumptions may be culturally encapsulated. Some general examples of philosophical assumptions are (a) the principle of altruism focused on real-world problems, (b) the principle of responsibility for counselors to both teach and learn in a reciprocal contact with other cultures, (c) the principle of justice that does not tolerate either intentional or unintentional exploitation, and (d) the principle of caring through trust and a personal investment in helping culturally different clients regardless of consequences. When ethical decisions are implicit, the counselors will base their thinking on those ethical philosophical principles most familiar to them and mistakenly presume that they are maintaining a high level of ethical standards. When those standards of accepted practice are themselves culturally encapsulated, they do not provide an adequate basis for an independent ethical judgment but rather tend to reinforce the ethical validity of the standard quo practices. A Southeast Asian refugee family might have their children taken away from them by the state for child-rearing practices the family might regard as traditional and honorable.

In Section G on research, there is no requirement to identify or differentiate the cultural context or background of research participants. This neglect can lead to the merging of data from participants across different cultural contexts and backgrounds. By not requiring researchers to identify the cultural context(s) in which data are gathered, the code of ethics contributes toward the creation of stereotypes and an imposed unidimensional interpretation of multidimensional data. These aggregate data can then be applied to individual cases, and disconfirming variance from the aggregate data can be dismissed as pathology.

Cultural encapsulation endangers the profession, the provider, and the consumer of counseling services. The irony is that those who are most encapsulated are least likely to recognize their own biases, and their judgment is more likely to be an artifact of their perspective than of the person or persons being assessed (Berry et al., 1992).

4. Favoring the Dominant Culture

The literature on cross-cultural psychology makes a distinction between culture-specific (emic) and culture-general (etic) aspects of behavior based respectively on the difference between specific phonemic patterns unique to each language and generalized phonetic patterns shared by all languages. According to Berry et al. (1992):

> Many researchers argue that behavior in its full complexity can only be understood within the context of the culture in which it occurs. In the emic approach an attempt is made to look at phenomena and their interrelationships (structure) through the eyes of people native to a particular culture. One tries to avoid the imposition of prior notions and ideas from one's own culture on the people studied. (p. 233)

When the counselors' perspectives are rooted in and shaped by their own cultural background, they are imposing their specific cultural viewpoint on others whose viewpoint is different. Only when these "imposed etics" have been modified to accommodate the other specific target cultures can "derived etics" be accomplished.

Code A.5.b. on personal needs and values requires that "Counselors are aware of their own values, attitudes, beliefs and behaviors and how these apply in a diverse society and avoid imposing their values on clients" (ACA, 1995, p. 3). There are several problems with this standard. First, the level of cultural self-awareness among counselors has been demonstrated to be low (Basic Behavioral Science Task Force, 1996). Second, counselors who lack cultural self-awareness are not likely to realize their deficit (Ridley, 1995). Third, accepted counseling practice is so rooted in values of the dominant culture that it would be difficult to separate those values from the practice of counseling. If the client believes in reincarnation, for example, then whose personality is being considered? The person(s) who were, or the person(s) who are yet to come? The problem is an unwillingness to admit to the practice of imposing majority culture beliefs on minority clients and, not acknowledging the discrepancy, there is little recognized need to move toward a derived etic that reflects the minority client's context.

J. Miller (1994) argued that there is no one universal morality of caring but rather alternative types of moralities that reflect the meaning systems of different cultural contexts. In her research comparing Americans and Hindus, Americans supported an individually oriented interpersonal moral code that stresses freedom of choice, individual responsibility, and a dualistic view of motivation, whereas Hindus supported a duty-based interpersonal moral code that stresses broad and socially enforceable interpersonal obligations and contextual sensitivity. In their research review, Gielen and Markoulis (1994) found that

> Whereas Western secular ideals emphasize the dignity and personhood of individuals, religious Tibetans emphasize the Buddha-nature inherent in everyone, Hindus uphold ideas of universal nonviolence (Ahimsa) and Confucianists focus on humanistic ideals of human-heartedness (jen). These cultural ideals are based upon different metaphysical assumptions but they all emphasize a concern for human dignity, solidarity and justice. Moral and cultural relativists have failed to perceive the underlying archetype that unites the moral imaginations of men and women living in different places and at different times. (p. 87)

There do seem to be core values across cultures, but those values are expressed differently by each culture.

Code A.10.c. discourages bartering for services. "Counselors ordinarily refrain from accepting goods or services from clients in return for counseling services because such arrangements create inherent potential for conflicts, exploitation and distortion of the professional relationship" (ACA, 1995, p. 4). This presumes a money economy to be more "fair" in every cultural context even though money, like goods, may mean something quite different for the very poor and the very rich. The emphasis should be more on fair and equitable exchange rather than the particular, in this case money, medium of exchange. As counselors move from affluent, urbanized settings into less affluent, rural, or Third World contexts, the presumption of a money economy is less warranted. The presumption is that an exchange of money is less likely to be exploitative than an exchange of goods or services. While the code acknowledges the possibility of exceptional cases in which goods and services can be exchanged for counseling, the preferred standard, not requiring special justification, is the exchange of money.

Code C.2. on professional competence emphasizes that "Counselors practice only within the boundaries of their competence, based on their education, training, supervised experience, state and national professional credentials and appropriate professional experience. Counselors will demonstrate a commitment to gain knowledge, personal awareness, sensitivity, and skills pertinent to working with a diverse client population" (ACA, 1995, p. 7). By these criteria and to the extent that the ACA has not yet endorsed any specific measures of multicultural competency, some authors consider that the ACA may itself be out of compliance (D. W. Sue et al., 1992). The danger is that the commitment to multiculturalism may be limited to supporting rhetoric with little serious effort to struggle with the multicultural issues. Until and unless specific and practical measures for ensuring multicultural competency are enacted, this discrepancy between the real conditions and the idealized rhetoric may be perceived by minority clients as hypocritical and an evasion of responsibility.

5. Examples of Specific Cultural Bias

If all behaviors are learned and displayed in a cultural context, then all tests, theories, and ethical guidelines are culturally biased to some extent when they are applied outside the cultural context of their origin. The appropriate response is not to discard tests, theories, and guidelines or to disregard culture bias but to develop strategies for culture-centered interpretation. Examples of specific cultural bias in the ACA 1995 code of ethics have been discussed and examples of systematic cultural bias are now identified and can be managed through culture-centered thinking. Ethical thinking is preferred to "rule-following" in competent counseling behavior.

All psychological measures and guidelines are biased to reflect the cultural context in which they were conceptualized, validated, and developed. This chapter seeks to identify a "third choice" to relativism (anarchy) or absolutism (tyranny) in the application of ethical guidelines to multicultural populations. The appropriate ethical response by counselors is not to discard all tests, theories, and guidelines for counseling services as flawed or to disregard cultural bias but rather to develop culture-centered interpretations of those guidelines that are neither relativistic nor absolutistic. As professionals, we are required to do the best job we can, recognizing that we are probably culturally biased, and then to eliminate or reduce that cultural bias as it becomes apparent to ourselves.

Relativism fails because it makes discussion of counseling guidelines impossible with each individual or group developing its own truth. Absolutism fails because it imposes the truth of a more powerful majority on less powerful minorities. The third option of cultural pluralism suggests that we recognize the elements of cultural bias in each guideline and make the cultural context central to our interpretation of that guideline with the goal of strengthening rather than weakening the relevance of that guideline.

It is not possible for an ethical guideline to fit all populations, settings, and situations. The following examples of cultural bias in the ACA (1995) code of ethics are not intended to diminish the importance of that ethical code but rather to describe a culture-centered interpretation of those guidelines that is neither absolutistic—"one size fits all"—or relativistic—"everyone for himself/herself."

In Code A.1.b., the guidelines imply that dependency is not a good or desirable feature and should be avoided or eliminated. Dependency would naturally be viewed as wrong in an individualistic society. There are many cultures, however, in which dependency is desirable and even essential to the healthy functioning of an individual in the collectivistic social context.

Example: According to Confucian belief, filial piety to the parent is extended by traditional Confucians to all figures of authority, including the counselor. Establishing a meaningful relationship with the counselor involves dependency on the counselor's advice, opinion, and direct guidance. Understanding the functional importance of the client's dependency will help the counselor work within the client's cultural context without seeming to "reject" the client on the one hand and without endangering the client's welfare on the other hand.

In Code A.1.c., the guidelines imply that freedom of choice is always desirable and nondestructive. In many traditional cultures, freedom of choice is seen as destructive of the social fabric because it disregards the responsibility and duty of the individual to the welfare of the society. Encouraging or imposing freedom of choice could have many unexpected negative consequences in a traditional society in which duty and responsibility are highly valued.

Example: You are working with a refugee family in which the unemployed husband takes out his hostility by verbally and physically abusing his wife. If his wife leaves the home, she will become an outcast of the refugee community of families, who believe one person's suffering is less destructive than breaking up the family. The alternatives of staying in an abusive situation and of leaving that situation are both destructive, requiring the counselor to understand the consequences of each choice before recommending a solution in each specific case.

In Code A.2.a., the guidelines recommend overlooking differences as a means of being "fair" and equitable in the application of the ethical guidelines. Absolute neutrality is probably not possible, much less desirable, as the counselor reflects his or her own cultural context. The tendency is to impose our own "self-reference criterion" on clients and assume that they want and need what the counselor would want and need in the same situation. The culturally different client may well value differences and not want those differences to be overlooked.

Example: The minority client is justifiably proud of her culture and the ways in which her values and beliefs are different from the conventional standards of the dominant culture. The counselor who imposes a self-reference criterion will disregard the cultural differences that distinguish the client's unique cultural identity and impose the counselor's own interpretation of cultural "norms," thinking he or she is being fair and equitable.

In Code A.3.c., the guidelines suggest that the counselor act *in loco parentis* or in a parental role when the parents are not available. The role of the family in many traditional cultures is vigorously protected against outsiders who are seen as separating a child from the family and sabotaging the credibility of the family by taking over the parental role.

Example: A bilingual and bicultural student lives two lives, one at home and the other at school, with the values of each often being in direct conflict with the other. The child's parents seek to discredit and unlearn the child's schooling as being foreign and White. By acting *in loco parentis*, the counselor protects the influence of the school but becomes the enemy of the child's family and places the child in a painful dilemma of having to choose between the school and the family.

In Code A.5.b., the guidelines suggest that counselors have or should have self-awareness, although considerable research to the contrary has demonstrated the lack of cultural self-awareness both among counselors and in counselor education programs. Self-awareness becomes more an aspirational goal as we seek to work with clients from different cultural contexts. The reality requires us to work with counselors and counselor educators who lack cultural self-awareness.

Example: A White male counselor working with a Black male client has a difficult time dealing with the client's diffuse anger and resistance, which seems directed toward the counselor. The client mentions the problems of "White privilege" that creates an insurmountable barrier between Whites and Blacks. The White counselor perceives the client's anger as inappropriate because the counselor has done nothing personally to deserve the client's anger. The White counselor lacks self-awareness of how the benefits of White privilege might appropriately be applied to him by the Black client.

In Code A.6.a., the guidelines presume that dual relationships are to be avoided. Dual relationships have characterized situations in which the counselor loses objectivity in working with the client or even intentionally/unintentionally exploits the client for the benefit of the counselor. Although dual relationships are frequently undesirable, working with a client from a more collectivistic context, rural area, or enclosed community might require counselors to relate with their clients through many different relationships in which multiple relationships are normal and even required.

Example: A client ran out of money to pay her counselor even though, in the counselor's opinion, further counseling would be needed. The counselor offered to continue the counseling sessions without payment until some future time when the client could conveniently pay for the counseling service. After continuing counseling for several months, the client filed a complaint with the counselor's professional counselor association that the counselor, by offering free counseling, was "incurring dependency" by the client on the counselor. The professional association determined that the counselor had violated the dual-relationship ethical guideline by offering to provide counseling at no charge, and the counselor was punished.

In Code A.8., the guidelines direct counselors to avoid or withdraw from conflict when working with multiple clients. There is increased recognition that advocacy and advice giving is an appropriate counseling response under specified circumstances, even though it might involve the counselor in "taking sides" in an argument. It is probably unrealistic to expect counselors to be completely neutral and entirely objective in the counseling process. In some cultures in which the counselor role is described as a teacher, counseling typically involves teaching, advice giving, and advocacy. Counselors who refuse to give advice are perceived as patronizing, uninformed, or otherwise ineffective.

Example: A counselor working with delinquent youths in an inner-city low-income population became aware that his client from a newly arrived immigrant family was being abused by the client's parents. The parents felt that physical punishment was appropriate and part of their role as caring parents and that failure to physically punish the child would indicate an unloving or uncaring family. Without getting into whether physical punishment was right or wrong, the counselor by taking sides was able to help the parents understand the serious legal consequences of physical abuse in this culture and help the family find other ways of responsible parenting.

In Code A.10.c., the guidelines presume that a money economy is preferred or superior to a barter economy in paying for counseling services. When barter is allowed, it requires a clear written contractual formal agreement. Although the intent of the guideline is to prevent client exploitation by counselors, it presumes that counseling always occurs in a formal setting with formal counseling methods. In many smaller or rural communities especially, counseling frequently occurs in nonformal or informal settings using nonformal or informal methods. With the increase in peer counseling and paraprofessionals, this tendency toward informal counseling is increasing.

Example: In a rural community, the preacher was providing important counseling services to his parishioners and anyone else who would come to him for help. In some instances, the counseling occurred through his sermons or even daily contact with the people in his community. The counseling seldom occurred in scheduled sessions, and there was never a written contract between the preacher and the client. Although the people had little money, they were able to share food and products from their small farms with the preacher in recognition of his important role in the community.

In Code B., the guidelines presume that privacy is universally respected and appreciated except to prevent clear and imminent danger to the client or others. Information, in an individualistic culture, is treated as property and accordingly protected by rights of privacy, whereas a more collectivistic culture would be more likely to share information as they would property within the family or collective social unit. Confidentiality is viewed quite differently in the collectivistic than in the individualistic context. In the collectivistic culture, the success of counseling depends more on social support through the family or social unit than the independent authority of any individual.

Example: A doctoral student in counseling came to my office to tell me he was dropping out of school because counseling was destroying his Laotian community by breaking up families. He organized his own counseling center in which groups of family and friends would discuss the problems of a particular family, with the family and significant others present, and determine the appropriate solution that valued the interests of the community over the welfare of any individual member. In Laotian culture, breaking confidentiality was a way of avoiding embarrassment by direct confrontation. Face-to-face communication was often less trusted than rumors and indirect hearsay information in which "leaks" in privacy served an important function.

In Code C.2., counselors are required to practice only within the boundaries of their competence, and failure to do so is a violation of the ethical guidelines. The Basic Behavioral Science Task Force (1996) of the NAMHC identified areas in which mental health services were culturally biased, cultural beliefs influenced diagnosis and treatment, diagnosis differed across cultural contexts, individuals expressed symptoms differently across cultures, diagnosis was typically guided by the cultural assumptions of the dominant culture, and most providers came from majority cultures while clients came from minority groups.

Example: An accrediting group visited a counselor education program to evaluate the competence of the faculty and teaching of counseling in the program. The members of the accreditation team were White middle-class men, as were the faculty in that counselor education program. The faculty members saw no need for a special course in multicultural counseling because cultural concerns were already being taught throughout the regular curriculum. The accreditation team decided that was a reasonable and appropriate conclusion.

In Code E.1., objective appraisal techniques are presumed to be preferred to more subjective assessments. With the increased attention to qualitative research and assessments and the rise of social postmodernism, the universal superiority of objective measures is being seriously questioned. It seems more apparent that qualitative and quantitative methods complement one another with each perspective clarifying different but related aspects of the assessment process.

Example: The counselor working in a retirement center whose residents scored extremely low on all objective tests of mental ability discovered that the residents responded quite differently to conversational interviews. Many if not most of the residents had previous backgrounds of leadership roles and high levels of competence in many areas of their community. The counselor soon realized that without gathering qualitative information from the interviews, the objective test data would lead to wrong and inappropriate conclusions.

In Code E.3. about informed consent, the guidelines assume that the counseling information, if presented in language the client can understand, meets the test of informed consent without any validation of that conclusion through feedback from the client. Informed consent requires two-way communication, not just "telling" the client but receiving feedback to validate that the message sent was the same as the message received.

Example: A non-English-speaking client comes to counseling and listens to the counselor explain the counseling process. The client knows enough English to follow the description but not enough to fully understand the meaning. When the counselor asks if the client understands, the client answers in the affirmative rather than be embarrassed by his lack of English language fluency.

In Code F.2., the guidelines assume that students learn from faculty but fail to recognize how faculty can also learn from students about the counseling process. A hierarchy of authority is described in the counselor education process whereby the students are placed in a consistently subordinate role, even though most good teachers will readily admit learning a great deal from their students in a reciprocal educational exchange.

Example: A minority group member of a counselor education program is being supervised by a White male who evaluates the student's counseling tapes negatively. The student works in a community agency with other minorities of the same ethnic background and claims that he is interpreting counseling skills appropriately to that minority client setting.

In Code H., the guidelines assume that the ethical guidelines are always adequate to determine right behavior for counselors in all situations. Given the reality of cultural bias in the counseling profession, it is quite possible that a counselor will need to decide whether to act in an ethical way while being "responsibly disobedient" to the ethical codes.

Example: The counselor knows that her particular client is right and that the system is wrong in this instance through imposing racist, sexist, and ageist rules on that particular client. The counselor is faced with a choice to protect the system against the client, knowing the system is wrong, or advocating for the client against the system.

The systematic biases in these ethical guidelines, and in many tests or theories of counseling, are the following:

1. Underlying assumptions are implicit rather than made explicit.
2. Counselors are guided by their own self-reference criterion.
3. Guidelines are to protect the provider rather than the consumer.
4. The dominant culture values are favored.

No single set of guidelines or rules will fit or apply to all multicultural situations in the same way. Every test, theory, and guideline will reflect the cultural assumptions of its origin. In attempting to interpret tests, theories, and guidelines to a multicultural population, one must ask the following four questions:

1. Is any basic human value being violated? (universalism)
2. Are the "best practice" behaviors of the particular client group being recognized? (relativism)
3. Is the intention of the provider honorable? (intentionalism)
4. What are the consequences? (consequentialism)

By approaching each decision through these four classical ethical systems, the counselor can learn to "think ethically" and reach the right conclusion. There are no firm and fixed guidelines for multicultural counseling, but there is a process of negotiation that will allow the counselor to find common ground without giving up integrity or forcing the client to give up integrity.

6. Some Positive Recommendations

Being rooted in behavioral science, moral principles, and ethical guidelines for counseling cannot be precisely validated or even inferred from empirical data, but case examples of behaviors can help identify the empirical consequences of good or bad ethics. Kendler (1993) spoke to psychology-related fields on this issue:

> Natural science psychology, to be successful, must abandon two seductive myths: (a) Psychology is able to identify ethical principles that should guide humankind, and (b) the logical gap between *is* and *ought* can be bridged by empirical evidence. In spite of these limitations, psychology can assist society in settling ethical disputes by revealing the empirical consequences of different policy choices, thus allowing society to make informed decisions as to which competing social policies to adopt. (p. 1052)

I have argued that the ACA ethical guidelines represent a culturally biased perspective that minimalizes the importance of worldviews of ethnocultural minorities. I have identified examples of cultural encapsulation in the ACA ethical guidelines. I have discussed the dangers of encouraging counselors to depend on their own self-reference criteria in evaluating their own ethical behavior. Finally, I have documented ways in which the ethical guidelines favor cultural values of the individualistic dominant culture. In this discussion, it is easier to identify ethical issues and problems than to identify meaningful alternative solutions. That difficulty in itself, however, does not negate the presence of serious problems.

The tendency of contemporary professional ethical guidelines for counselors is to deemphasize the responsibility of individual counselors for moral thinking, moral dialogue, and moral development (Rest & Narvaez, 1994). The function of ethical guidelines must go beyond describing safe options and help counselors deal with the moral dilemma of contrasting cultures: "Morality in the professions is not so much concerned with issues of rudimentary socialization. Rather, the issues involve deciding between conflicting values, each value representing something good in itself" (p. ix). The initial attempts to develop ethical guidelines for mental health services in the 1940s began by surveying providers' reaction to critical incident examples involving ethical choices (P. Pedersen, 1995a). The first set of ethical guidelines were derived in the multiple contexts of these incidents. To increase the ability of counselors for moral thinking, moral dialogue, and moral development, it might be useful to generate those incidents involving difficult ethical choices in a variety of contemporary cultural contexts to demonstrate by example how the same universally accepted values might be implemented in different and contrasting behaviors.

Multiculturalism has changed and is continuing to change the way in which counseling is understood, taught, and implemented. It is essential to modify the ACA code of ethics to provide meaningful guidelines for counselors in multicultural contexts. It is essential that counselors be able to differentiate between those positive and universally applied values on which their ethical judgments of goodness are based. The great diversity of contrary or sometimes contradictory behaviors by which those fundamental values are expressed varies in different cultural contexts (Shweder et al., 1990). This differentiation between positive, shared, common-ground values demonstrating similarities and culturally learned idiosyncratic behaviors demonstrating our individuality is fundamental to an adequate multicultural ethical code.

In 1971 the Committee on International Relations in Psychology for the American Psychological Association (APA) requested June Tapp to head a subcommittee of the APA on ethical considerations of cross-cultural research along with Lawrence Wrightsman, Harry Triandis, Herbert Kelman, and George Coelho. The recommendations of that committee are based on 2 years of consultation with cross-cultural psychologists from several countries and reactions to presentations at U.S. national and international professional meetings. The "advisory principles" of that group have been adapted by the International Association for Cross-Cultural Psychology (1978) and represent the best systematic attempt to deal with cross-cultural ethics by a psychological organization for psychological research thus far.

Tapp, Kelman, Triandis, Wrightman, & Coelho (1974) pointed out that a researcher's ethical obligation goes beyond avoiding harm to the participant to include demonstrations of how the research will enrich and benefit the host culture. In general, the benefit to the researcher is much clearer than the benefit to a host culture providing data. Tapp et al.'s recommendation for collaboration with the host culture is also seldom observed. It is often difficult to translate the implications of psychological research into useful outcomes for traditional people. Taft (1977) pointed out that most of us are so "psychologecentric" that we regard ourselves as having the right to mine our data from the places where we need it, provided we pay royalties to the natives (often, incidentally, in accordance with our own arbitrary concept of what is fair compensation) and provided we do not destroy the ecology irreparably. "In the latter respect, we are often not really much more conscientious than is the typical multi-national mining company" (Taft, 1977, pp. 11–12).

In her introduction to the special issue on ethics of *The Counseling Psychologist*, Kitchner (1986) pointed out that psychologists as a profession are better at identifying the ethical issues that face them than they are at thinking through how they ought to resolve them. This has resulted in a great revival of interest in applied ethics, increased government or administrative protection of human subjects, and increased numbers of court cases involving psychologists. In part, this interest in ethics has gone beyond ethical violations toward a positive appreciation for a client's own belief system. *Preventing harm* to the consumer and acting in such a way as to actually benefit the consumer applies the ethical principle of *beneficence* as a legitimate ethical obligation (Cayleff, 1986). These developments have contributed to a new interest in multicultural ethics.

7. The Consequences of Moral Exclusion

By better understanding the process of moral exclusion, we can better build a system of ethical guidelines for the future of counseling. This phenomenon is most evident in two nations at war, but subtle forms of moral exclusion are evident elsewhere as well.

Usually moral exclusion results from severe conflict or from feelings of unconnectedness as relationships are perceived. Opotow (1990) listed the rationalizations and justifications that support moral exclusion which help to identify otherwise hidden examples of moral exclusion (see Figure 7.1). Other examples of moral exclusion might include psychological distancing, displacing responsibility, group loyalty, and normalizing or glorifying violence. The list of examples is provided to demonstrate that moral exclusion can be so "ordinary" an occurrence that it fails to attract attention.

Moral exclusion is the obvious consequence of cultural encapsulation. The exclusion can occur in degrees from overt and malicious evil to passive unconcern. It is possible to be exclusionary by what one does not do as well as by what one does. Moral exclusion is pervasive and not isolated. It depends on those psychological and social supports that condone otherwise unacceptable attitudes, intentionally or unintentionally. "As severity of conflict and threat escalates, harm and sanctioned aggression become more likely. As harm doing escalates, societal structures change, the scope of justice shrinks, and the boundaries of harm doing expand" (Opotow, 1990, p. 13). What is need is a level of moral development that prevents moral exclusion.

Shweder et al. (1990) reviewed the cultural applicability of three theories of moral development. First, Kohlberg's cognitive developmental theory contends that a moral obligation has its origins in conventional or consensus-based obligations and that obligations are rooted in convention at the lower stages and natural law at the higher stages of development. Development depends on the cognitive ability to construct a detached and impartial viewpoint to evaluate right from wrong. Second, Turiel's social interactional theory separates morality from convention, whereas moral obligation results from social experiences related to justice, rights, harm, and the welfare of others. Third, there is a social communication theory that combines Kohlberg and Turiel in which moral obligation is based on a universal of learned cultural context that does not depend on either consensus or convention and in which there are no universals across cultures. In synthesizing the alternatives, Miller differentiated

FIGURE 7.1

Processes of Moral Exclusion

Process	Manifestation of Moral Exclusion
Exclusion-specific processes	
Biased evaluation of groups	Making unflattering comparisons between one's own group and another group; believing in the superiority of one's own group
Derogation	Disparaging and denigrating others by regarding them as lower life forms or inferior beings (e.g., barbarians, vermin)
Dehumanization	Repudiating others' humanity, dignity, ability to feel, and entitlement to compassion
Fear of contamination	Perceiving contact with others as posing a threat to one's own well-being
Expanding the target	Redefining "legitimate victims" as a larger category
Accelerating the pace of harm doing	Engaging in increasingly destructive and abhorrent acts to reduce remorse and inhibitions against inflicting harm
Open approval of destructive behavior	Accepting a moral code that condones harm doing
Reducing moral standards	Perceiving one's harmful behavior as proper; replacing moral standards that restrain harm with less stringent standards that condone or praise harm doing
Blaming the victim	Displacing the blame for reprehensible actions on those who are harmed
Self-righteous comparisons	Lauding or justifying harmful acts by contrasting them with morally condemnable atrocities committed by the adversary
Desecration	Harming others to demonstrate contempt for them, particularly symbolic or gratuitous harm
Ordinary processes	
Groupthink	Striving for group unanimity by maintaining isolation from dissenting opinion that would challenge the assumptions, distortions, or decisions of the group
Transcendent ideologies	Experiencing oneself or one's group as exalted, extraordinary, and possessed of a higher wisdom, which permits even harmful behavior as necessary to bring a better world into being

(continued)

FIGURE 7.1 *(continued)*
Processes of Moral Exclusion

Process	Manifestation of Moral Exclusion
Deindividuation	Feeling anonymous in a group setting, thus weakening one's capacity to behave in accordance with personal standards
Moral engulfment	Replacing one's own ethical standards with those of the group
Psychological distance	Ceasing to feel the presence of others; patronizing others and perceiving them with disdain (e.g., they are childlike, irrational, simple)
Technical orientation	Focusing on efficient means while ignoring outcomes; routinizing harm doing by transforming it into mechanical steps
Double standards	Having different sets of moral rules and obligations for different categories of people
Unflattering comparisons	Using unflattering contrasts to bolster one's superiority over others
Euphemisms	Masking, sanitizing, and conferring respectability on reprehensible behavior by using palliative terms that misrepresent cruelty and harm
Displacing responsibility	Behaving in ways one would normally repudiate because a higher authority explicitly or implicitly assumes responsibility for the consequences
Diffusing responsibility	Fragmenting the implementation of harmful tasks through collective action
Concealing the effects of harmful behavior	Disregarding, ignoring, disbelieving, distorting, or minimizing injurious outcomes to others
Glorifying violence	Viewing violence as a sublime activity and a legitimate form of human expression
Normalizing violence	Accepting violent behavior as ordinary because of repeated exposure to it and societal acceptance of it
Temporal containment of harm doing	Perceiving one's injurious behavior as an isolated event—"just this time"

Note. From "Moral Exclusion and Injustice: An Introduction," by S. Opotow, 1990, *Journal of Social Issues, 46,* pp. 10–11. Copyright 1990 by Blackwell Publishers. Reprinted with permission.

between mandatory and discretionary features of moral obligation. Rationally based moral codes may be based on natural law, justice, and harm as mandatory features and yet not founded on individualism, voluntarism, natural rights, secularism, or the idea of a social contract that are discretionary features.

Bad ethical behavior is not always deliberate. Goodyear and Sinnett (1984, p. 89) identified specific examples of how counselors might unintentionally violate a client's cultural values:

1. Misunderstanding who the client is.
2. Lacking knowledge or skills necessary for working with special populations.
3. Inserting prejudicial (although perhaps well-intentioned) attitudes and values into the assessment and treatment of special populations.
4. Failing to provide clients with information about the consequences of undergoing certain assessment or treatment procedures.
5. Failing to assume an activist stance when necessary to protect client populations in the face of abuses of authority wielded by others.

LaFromboise and Foster (1989) described in detail other examples of implicit institutionalized bias resulting in minority populations being underserved by counselors, the lack of multicultural courses in the counselor education curricula, the low visibility of multiculturalism in counseling textbooks, the ways counseling programs "get around" certification requirements of multiculturalism, the underrepresentation of minorities in counselor education programs, violations of cultural values in research about counseling, and the inadequacy of ethical guidelines for multicultural counseling.

Specific procedures and measures typically used by counselors have also been challenged as culturally biased. Lonner and Ibrahim (1989) suggested that accurate and ethical assessment in multicultural counseling requires (a) understanding the client's worldview, beliefs, values, and culturally unique assumptions; (b) understanding the client's culture specific norm group; and (c) using a combination of approaches including clinical judgment as well as standardized or nonstandardized assessment measures that might be appropriate. Standardized assessment measures raise problems of distinguishing between constructs and criteria, establishing equivalence, the effect of verbal or nonverbal stimuli, the role of response sets, the tendency to infer deficits from test score differences, and other examples of embedded Westernized bias. Even the psychological measures of ethical behavior itself seem to be biased. In reviewing cross-cultural research on Kohlberg's theory of moral development, Snarey (1985) discovered that cultural differences had not been taken into account and that the emphasis was better suited for an individualistic society than collectivist societies. Cortese (1989), on the other hand, examined gender and ethnic difference in making moral judgments and supported Kohlberg's methodological model as based on universals of moral judgment. Moral judgments across ethnic and cultural groups corresponded to Kohlberg's prediction and to his stages, even though a more interpersonal orientation to morality was evident. Segall et al. (1990) concluded that the Kohlbergian model of moral development reflects values of urban, middle-class groups. Gilligan's (1982, 1987) research additionally discovered a bias toward the male viewpoint in Kohlberg's theory as well. Ivey (1987) advocated for a more relational view of ethics in the form of a "dialectical inquiry" between the counselor providers and the consumer communities. Moral problems are viewed differently across cultures and must be dealt with differently.

8. Conclusion

We need to move toward a pluralistic perspective in form as well as function to accommodate the range of differences in culturally learned assumptions by which each individual interprets events. The more obvious cultural differences of nationality and ethnicity provide an opportunity to develop inclusionary perspectives that will increase our accuracy in dealing with the sometimes less obvious differences of age, gender, lifestyle, socioeconomic status, and affiliation. Until the ethical obligations of all counselors are seen and described in terms of increasing accuracy and relevance for multicultural counseling rather than for special selected interest groups, we are unlikely to see more than a token acknowledgment of cultural variables on the part of counseling professionals facing this ethical dilemma.

EXERCISE: "What You Said, Felt, and Meant in a Tape Recorder"

We tend to confuse messages about what others actually said, what they felt while they were saying it, and what they meant or intended by a statement. Cultural differences tend to confuse the accurate communication of messages even further. By separating these three functions, we may be better able to analyze the messages we receive and be more articulate about the messages we send.

Organize participants into two-person dyads, with one person designed as the "speaker" and the second person as the "listener." The speaker will speak for 1 minute about his or her culture, saying as much as possible within that 1-minute time period. The listener will then repeat back everything the speaker said, felt, and meant about his or her culture. The listener will have 1 minute to complete that task. Then the listener and speaker will discuss for 1 minute how complete and comprehensive the listener had been in repeating back what the speaker had said, felt, and meant. The speaker and listener may then exchange roles and begin the 3-minute process all over again in their different roles.

WHAT YOU SAID, FELT, AND MEANT
IN A TAPE RECORDER EXERCISE

Participant Objectives:
1. To attend accurately to the factual information being conveyed.
2. To articulate clearly the facts and inferences being conveyed.
3. To interpret the meaning and feelings being conveyed.

Learning Objective:
1. What someone says may be different from what he or she means or from what you think that he or she means.

CHAPTER 8

Constructive Conflict Management
in a Cultural Context

Primary objective:

    1. To demonstrate the advantages of making cultural issues central in constructive conflict management.

Secondary objectives:

    1. To describe a culture-centered approach to conflict management.
    2. To contrast Westernized with non-Westernized approaches to conflict management.
    3. To present alternative conflict management models from the Asia-Pacific region.
    4. To describe an interpersonal cultural grid for constructive conflict management.
    5. To examine the consequences of a culture-centered conflict management model for the future.

Recent literature on conflict management has given attention to sociocultural contextual factors in addition to structural, normative/prescriptive, individual-differences, and information-processing approaches (Kramer & Messick, 1995). At the same time, most empirical research on conflict has focused on the situational rather than the cultural context (Ting-Toomey, 1985). Lund, Morris, and LeBaron-Duryea (1994) described the significant and

Note. Parts of this chapter are reprinted from P. Pedersen (1999b) "Intercultural understanding: Finding common ground without losing integrity," in D. Christie, D. Wagner, and D. Winter (Eds.), *Peace, Conflict and Violence: Peace Psychology for the 21st Century,* Englewood Cliffs, NJ: Prentice Hall. Reprinted with permission from Prentice Hall.

increasing research to recognize the importance of culture in research on conflict and conflict management. Their research suggests that culture-centered models that incorporate culturally sensitive assessments of each conflict in its cultural context may be more appropriate than any universal intervention model.

1. A Culture-Centered Perspective

There are many opportunities for conflict as culturally defined special interest groups compete for limited resources. The increase in culturally defined conflict has profoundly changed the way conflict is successfully managed. Kruger (1992) observed:

> Dramatically changing demographics in the United States increase the likelihood that community disputes, often involving a public policy issue, will have race, ethnicity and national origin as a factor. Those called upon to assist in the resolution of such intergroup disputes include trained mediators, educators, community leaders, law enforcement executives, and elected or appointed officials. No longer can anyone who intervenes in an intergroup conflict assume that she or he has the tools necessary to understand and assist in properly resolving the dispute. (p. 1)

Conflict is a natural aspect of any relationship. The conflict may be positive (functional) or negative (dysfunctional). Negative conflict threatens to erode the consensus needed for growth and development. Positive conflict, when it is managed appropriately, is usually about less central or fundamental issues and takes place within the context of a general consensus. Positive conflict can actually strengthen group relationships, especially if different members of the conflicting groups share common ground values across cultures. According to Rabbie (1994):

> The importance of culture and cultural symbols in facilitating or hindering cross-cultural communications dictates a need to incorporate cultural attitudes and perceptions into models and theories of conflict analysis and conflict resolution. Models that were produced by Western specialists have continued to lack the proper tools to deal with non-Western nations, and thus they have remained largely irrelevant to those people. (p. 37)

The ways that conflicts are perceived and managed reflect culturally shared patterns of attitudes and beliefs. These patterns may involve punishing wrongdoers, repairing strained or broken relationships, depending on courts or the legal system, or relying on informal social pressure through teasing, gossip, exclusion, and supernatural forces. These typical ways of perceiving and responding to conflict are so natural to ingroup members of a culture that their assumptions typically go unquestioned and innovative alternatives are neglected. Fry and Bjorkqvist (1997) noted:

> To date many anthropological investigations of conflict resolutions have looked within particular cultures and have emphasized the culturally specific nature of conflict resolution processes . . . . On the other hand, many nonanthropological conflict-resolution sources have tended to focus on the modern complex societies of the West, and they sometimes convey an implicit assumption that conflict-resolution models and techniques are very generally applicable. (p. 9)

The impact of culture on conflict has important implications. First, groups in conflict might be limiting their alternatives to those within their specific culture. Second, given an appreciation of cultural complexity, they are discouraged from quick-and-easy answers or from forcing one cultural perspective on others. Third, by understanding a range of culturally different approaches to conflict management, groups increase their practical and theoretical options for managing conflict.

> We conclude that the source of conflict lies in the minds of people. External social conflict is a reflection of intrapsychic conflict. External control does not solve the roots of the problem: If we wish a conflict really to disappear, then a change in attitude is needed. Only when people learn to understand and respect each other can peaceful coexistence begin. (Bjorkqvist & Fry, 1997, p. 252)

Cultural systems are not abstract models of reality but are primarily guidelines for action through patterned activity that creates reality (Geertz, 1973). The cultural systems of two conflicting groups present fundamentally different interpretations of what is happening. Each group uses its own cultural standards to evaluate the actions of the other rather than the standards by which the others guide themselves. According to Dubinskas (1992):

> The task of the analyst is twofold. First, a cultural interpretation must present both of the contrasting native cultural systems to the reader so that they are both comprehensible and compelling as worldviews in themselves. Then the analyst must illuminate the contrasting native interpretations of each group by the other and show how these patterns contribute to the generation of conflict. (p. 189)

By understanding each conflict according to culturally constructed differences, we discover a unified platform for understanding the persistence and intensity of the conflict.

A culture-centered model of conflict management interprets the conflict in a cultural context that makes the conflict meaningful in terms of causes, processes, and effects. The cultural context provides data that the antagonists themselves might take for granted that can now be understood in a joint meaning-construction process. Dubinskas (1992) noted:

In a failing, conflictual process, two groups are blocked in their efforts to achieve agreement by a fundamental inability (or unwillingness) to interpret each other's position or perspective. In moving toward resolution, however, conflicting groups are actively seeking meaning in the other's actions as well as proactively trying to make their own actions understandable to that other. (p. 205)

By jointly constructing cultural meaning, the cultural differences are not erased, the cultural integrity of all parties is preserved, and a new basis for intercultural cooperation and coordination is constructed as a metaphoric bridge to an island of common ground for both sides of the dispute.

2. Western and Non-Western Alternative Models

Non-Western cultures have typically been associated with collectivistic perspectives, whereas Western cultures have typically been associated with individualistic value systems (U. Kim et al., 1994). Individualism describes societies in which the connections between individuals are loose and in which each individual is expected to look after him- or herself, whereas collectivism describes cultures in which people are part of strong cohesive ingroups that protect them in exchange for unquestioned lifetime loyalty (Hofstede, 1991).

The conflict between individuals in finite time, typical of a Westernized conflict, is quite different both in theory and in practice from collectivized conflict in an infinite time context. In many non-Western cultural conflicts, the ways to manage differences are found in quoted proverbs or stories and historical examples that instruct all parties about managing power differentials, handling disputes, locating mediators or go-betweens, and achieving mutually satisfactory settlements (Augsburger, 1992).

Watson-Gegeo and White (1990) preferred the term *disentangling* over conflict resolution or dispute management for describing conflict in Pacific Island cultures. Disentangling is more process than outcome oriented, and the image of a tangled net or line blocking purposeful activity has a practical emphasis as well as implying the ideal state in which the lines of people's lives are "straight." R. H. Katz (1993) likewise talked about "the straight path" as a healing tradition of Fiji with spiritual dimensions of health for the individual and for society. In a comparison between collectivistic and individualistic cultures, the nature of self becomes important. According to Augsburger (1992):

The self in most collectivistic cultures is maintained and defined through active negotiation of facework. By contrast, in Western societies the self is grounded intrapsychically in self-love, self-definition, and self-direction. In the solidarity of a collectivistic setting, the self is not free. It is bound by mutual role obligations and duties as it is structured and nurtured in an ongoing process of give-and-take in facework negotiations. In the West, there must be high consistency between public face and private self-image. In the East, the self is not an individual but a relational construct. (p. 86)

Another distinction between Western and non-Western models identifies the more complex, technologically advanced, and multi-institutional cultures as "low context," with some notable exceptions. Hall (1976) contrasted the American (low-context) with the Japanese (high-context) perspective regarding justice, for example. The Japanese trial puts the accused, the court, the public, and the injured parties together to work toward settling the dispute, in contrast with the protagonist–antagonist conflict model in an American court. The function of the trial in Japan is to locate the crime in context so that the criminal and society can see the consequence. In high-context systems, persons in authority are responsible for subordinates, whereas in low-context systems, responsibility is diffused, making it difficult to fix blame. Hall (1976) observed:

> Low context cultures generally refer to groups characterized by individualism, overt communication and heterogeneity. The United States, Canada and Central and Northern Europe are described as areas where low context cultural practices are most in evidence. High context cultures feature collective identity-focus, covert communication and homogeneity. This approach prevails in Asian countries including Japan, China and Korea as well as Latin American countries. (p. 39)

Gudykunst and Ting-Toomey (1988) associated low and high context with individualism and collectivism. Whereas members of low-context cultures view indirect conflict management as weak, cowardly, or evasive, members of high-context cultures view direct conflict management as impolite and clumsy. Whereas persons from low-context cultures separate the conflict issue from the person, those from high-context cultures see the issue and person as interrelated. Whereas low-context persons seek to manage conflict toward an objective and fair solution, high-context persons focus on the affective, relational, personal, and subjective aspects that preclude open conflict. Whereas low-context cultures have a linear and logical worldview that is problem oriented and sensitive to individuals, high-context cultures see the conflict, event, and all actors in a unified context. And whereas low-context cultures value independence focused on autonomy, freedom, and personal rights, high-context cultures value inclusion, approval, and association.

With data from a 1994 conference on "Conflict Resolution in the Asia Pacific Region," Jandt and Pedersen (1996) developed a series of 17 hypotheses about how high- and low-context cultures experience conflict differently.

1. In low-context cultures, *individual participants* must first accept and acknowledge that there is a conflict before resolution/mediation can begin.
2. In high-context cultures, *traditional groups* must first accept and acknowledge that there is a conflict before resolution/mediation can begin.

3. In low-context cultures, conflict and the resolution/mediation process must often be kept private.
4. In high-context cultures, conflict is not private and must be made public before the resolution/mediation process can begin.
5. In low-context cultures, societal conflict management is most effective in preparing an individual's skill for teaching individuals how to negotiate/mediate or resolve conflict reactively.
6. In high-context cultures, social conflict management emphasizes preventive measures by monitoring or mediating stress in a more proactive manner.
7. In low-context cultures, resolution and mediation are individually defined by the individuals involved in conflict.
8. In high-context cultures, conflict and its resolution and mediation are defined by the group or culture.
9. The role of internationals and the media from low-context cultures is not to intervene in conflicts in high-context cultures but to call public attention to the situation so that resolution/mediation can take place on its own.
10. In low-context cultures, settlements are usually devoid of ritual and spirituality.
11. In high-context cultures, settlements are most often accompanied by ritual and spirituality.
12. New arrivals from high-context cultures will not be served best by conflict resolution/mediation strategies developed in low-context cultures.
13. In groups combining high- and low-context cultures, the most powerful group's style of dispute resolution/mediation will predominate.
14. Low-context organizations in high-context cultures will avoid "traditional" alternative dispute resolution strategies and prefer court settlements.
15. Relying on courts to resolve/mediate conflict is regarded as a failure in high-context cultures.
16. Low-context cultures prefer dispute resolution/mediation to be face to face.
17. High-context cultures prefer to do dispute resolution/mediation through intermediaries.

Rubin, Pruitt, and Kim (1994) described conflict in Western cultures in terms of general strategies that vary in terms of outcomes and feasibility.

The strategies include contending (high concern for one's own outcomes and low concern for other's outcomes), problem solving (high concern for both one's own and the other's outcomes), yielding (low concern for one's own outcomes and high concern for other's outcomes) and avoiding (low concern for both one's own and other's outcomes). (p. 11)

Integrative solutions were judged the most desirable, longer lasting, and most likely to contribute to the relationship of parties and welfare of the broader community than compromises or arbitration. It would seem that the science of conflict management is moving toward Asian models.

3. Conflict in an Asian-Pacific Context

Barnes (1991), writing about conflict management in the Asia-Pacific region, described the four goals of traditional conflict as making rights effective, diverting the dispute from the court system, preserving social solidarity against change, and resisting the centralized legal bureaucracy. The Asia-Pacific perspective of these functions is unique in several ways, as described by a Chinese mediator.

> We who engage in mediation work should use our mouths, legs and eyes more often. This means we should constantly explain the importance of living in harmony and dispense legal education. We should also pay frequent visits to people's houses and when we hear or see any symptoms of disputes we should attempt to settle them before they become too serious. (Barnes, 1991, p. 26)

Conflict management in the Asian context has been described as face maintenance, face saving, face restoration, or face loss (Duryea, 1992). The concept of "face" is Chinese in origin as a literal translation of the Chinese term *lian*, representing the confidence of society in the integrity of moral character. Without moral character, the individuals cannot function in their community, so *lian* is both a social sanction for enforcing moral standards and an internalized sanction (Hu, 1945, p. 45). One loses face when an individual or group or someone representing the group fails to meet the requirements of their socially defined role or position. Face can become more important than life itself as the evaluation of the self by the community is essential to identity. What one thinks of oneself is less important than what one thinks *others* think. Ting-Tomey and Cole (1990) defined the concept of face in conflict management as important in all communications but especially in ambiguous conflict situations as defined by each cultural context and face-management strategy.

The traditional Chinese approach to conflict resolution is based on saving face for all parties by the choices made regarding personal goals and interpersonal harmony following the Confucian tradition (Hwang, 1998). First, giving up personal goals for the sake of interpersonal harmony requires *endurance*. Second, giving up interpersonal harmony for the sake of personal goals requires *confrontation*. Third, maintaining interpersonal harmony and personal goals at the same time requires *public obedience and private disobedience*. Fourth, maintaining interpersonal harmony more than personal goals requires *compromise.* Fifth, disregard for both interpersonal harmony and personal goals results in *quarreling* and the destruction of the relationship. These choices become more complicated in actual situations.

When a subordinate is in conflict with a superior, he or she must protect the superior's face to maintain interpersonal harmony requiring endurance. Opinions are expressed indirectly, and any personal goal must be achieved privately while pretending to obey the superior. When the conflict involves horizontal relationships among ingroup members, they may communicate directly and, to protect harmony, they may give face to each other through compromise. If, however, one insists on his or her personal goal in spite of the feelings of the other, this fight may continue for a long time. If both parties insist on their conflicting personal goals, they may treat the other as an outgroup member and confront that person directly, disregarding harmony and protecting their own face. A third party might be required to mediate this conflict, and it may result in destroying the relationship.

Hwang (1998) described the Confucian relationships of father/son, husband/wife, senior/junior brother, and superior/subordinate in a vertical structure emphasizing the value of harmony. "When one is conflicting with someone else within his or her social network, the first thing one has to learn is forbearance . . . . In its broadest sense, forbearance means to control and to suppress one's emotion, desire and psychological impulse" (p. 28). Therefore a subordinate must obey and endure the superior's demands, relying on indirect communication from some third party in their social network to communicate with the superior. Direct confrontation is described as when both parties "tear off their faces" and confront the other openly. When Chinese people are in direct conflict, third parties from their social network tend to intervene between them to reduce the escalation of violence. Confucian rules of politeness require both sides to "care about the other's face" at least superficially so conflict among family members may not be evident to outsiders. Members of the family take care of one another's face in front of outsiders to maintain superficial harmony by obeying publicly and defying privately.

One Pacific Islands model for maintaining conflict and managing conflict is through *ho'oponopono,* which means "setting to right" in the Hawaiian language. This traditional system is based on family systems, and variations of this model occur throughout the Pacific region. The traditional Hawaiian cultural context emphasizes working together, cooperation, and harmony (Shook, 1985). The extended family, or *ohana,* is the foundation of traditional Hawaiian society, with child-rearing practices fostering interdependence and contributions to the family's welfare emphasizing values of affiliation. "The successful maturation of a person in the Hawaiian culture thus requires that an individual cultivate an accurate ability to perceive and attend to other people's needs, often without being asked. These are attitudes and behaviors that help cement the relationship of the *ohana* and the community" (Shook, 1985, p. 6).

Unregulated conflict disrupts the balance and harmony, requires self-scrutiny, demands admission of wrong-doing, and requires asking forgiveness and restitution to restore harmony. Negative sanctions of illness and social pressure result from negative actions or feelings toward others. The traditional *ho'oponopono* approach to problem solving and conflict management was revived in the early 1970s by Pukui, Hartig, and Lee (1972) who, along with Panglinawan (1972), have increased an awareness of this traditional strategy. LeResche (1993) described this relationship-centered and agreement-centered process of peacemaking as "sacred" justice. Meyer (1994) described how peacemaking is unique.

> Peacemaking and mediation have two distinct vocabularies. Mediation terms like dispute and conflict become, in a peacemaking context: stubborn disagreement, having differences and, for Hawaiians, entanglement. Words like "punishment," "revenge," and "rights" in mediation become "restitution," "forgiveness," and "truth" in peacemaking. Clearly, in a philosophical way, mediation and peacemaking differ in both process and product. Peacemaking is not concerned with distributing justice, finding who is right, dispensing punishment, but rather strives for the maintenance of harmony between individuals and the exhibition of spiritual efficacy. Both peacemaking and mediation, however, strive for the ending of conflict. (p. 2)

Ho'oponopono includes prayer, identification of the problem, discussion, confession of wrongdoing, restitution when possible, forgiveness, and release. The *ho'oponopono* ceremony begins with prayer, or *pule*. Meyer (1994) described five conditions that must be met for *ho'oponopono* to occur.

1. Each member of the *'ohana* (family) must share a common commitment.
2. All members will share their words and deeds in an atmosphere of *'oia l'o,* or being truthful.
3. The *'ohana* will share a sense of *aloha* for one another which has been disrupted by conflict and be committed to reinstating that condition.
4. Everything said or done in *ho'oponopono* is kept confidential.
5. The *haku* (facilitator) or *kahuna* is accepted as fair and impartial.

The *ho'oponopono* ceremony begins with prayer or *pule,* asking God for assistance and placing the process in a cosmic or spiritual context. This is followed by identification, or *kululu kumuhana,* which means sharing strength to solve the family's problems by reaching out to the persons causing disruption to establish a favorable climate. The problem, or *hala,* is then described in a way that ties the person who was wronged and the wrongdoer together in an entanglement, or *hihia*. Then the many different dimensions of the problem entanglement are explored and clarified, one by one. As each aspect is identified through discussion, or *mahiki,* the layers or tangles of the problem are reorganized until family relationships are again in harmony. Individuals who have been wronged are encouraged to share their feelings and perceptions and honest open self-scrutiny is encouraged. If the group discussion is disrupted by emotional outbursts, the leader may declare a period of silence, or *ho'omalu,* for family members to regain harmony in their discussion. Following this is the sincere confession of wrongdoing, or *mihi,* during which the wrongdoer seeks forgiveness and agrees to restitution. Untangling the negative, or *kala,* then joins both the wronged and the wrongdoer in a mutual release and restores their cosmic and spiritual harmony together. A closing spiritual ceremony, or *pani,* reaffirms the family's strength and bond.

Mossman (1976) described the unique underlying philosophy and values that provide a favorable context for *ho'oponopono* to function effectively. The idea of *lokahi,* a natural and harmonious order in the universe, is the primary foundation for achieving harmony among God, nature, and the people. This idea depends on *akua*, which is reverence and respect for all humans and the importance of maintaining good relationships. *Ke ao nei* means a deep respect for nature or the natural environment surrounding people and the importance of maintaining harmony in that environment. *Mana* is a spiritual power possessed by special people and objects based on supernatural sources. *Aloha I ke ola* means a genuine positive appreciation for life and living to the fullest. *Hou'oli* describes the spontaneous ability to relax, enjoy life, and have a sense of humor. *Kapu* includes the laws to protect the rights of people and the environment with clearly defined penalties and immediate punishment. *Pau'a like* emphasizes the mutual responsibility of all people to protect these ideas.

Attempts to adapt *ho'oponopono* to Westernized contexts have applied those aspects of (a) recognizing the importance of conflict management in a spiritual context, (b) channeling the discussion with sanctions of silence should disruption occur, and (c) bringing the wrongdoer back into the community as a full member with complete restitution and forgiveness.

4. The Cultural Grid

The cultural grid described earlier in chapter 5 also has relevance in the context of constructive conflict management. The interpersonal cultural grid, demonstrated in Figure 5.7, describes the relationship between two people or groups by separating expectations from behaviors. The grid includes four quadrants. Each quadrant explains parts of a conflict between two individuals or groups, recognizing that the salience of each quadrant may change over time and across situations.

In the first quadrant, two individuals have similar behaviors and similar positive expectations. The relationship is congruent and harmonious, and there are positive shared expectations behind the behavior. Both persons are smiling (behavior), and both persons expect friendship (expectation). There is little conflict in this quadrant.

In the second quadrant, two individuals or groups have different behaviors but share the same positive expectations. There is a high level of agreement in that both persons expect trust and friendliness. However, each person or group is likely to incorrectly interpret the other's behavior as different and possibly/ probably hostile, when that behavior is interpreted out of context. This quadrant is characteristic of cultural conflict in which each person or group is applying a self-reference criterion to interpret the other person or group's behavior. The conditions described in the second quadrant are very unstable and, unless the shared positive expectations are quickly found and made explicit, the salience is likely to change toward the third quadrant. It is therefore important in cross-cultural conflict for at least one of the two persons to discover and identify the presence of shared positive expectations for trust, respect, fairness, and so on, which may be expressed through quite different behaviors.

In the third quadrant, the two persons have the same behaviors but now have different or negative expectations. The similar behaviors give the "appearance" of harmony and agreement through displaying the congruent or desired behaviors, but the hidden different or negative expectations will ultimately destroy the relationship. Although both persons are now in disagreement, this may not be obvious or apparent to others. One person may continue to expect trust and friendliness, whereas the other person is now negatively distrustful and unfriendly, even though they are both presenting the same smiling and glad-handing behaviors. If these two people can be guided to remember an earlier time when they shared positive expectations, they might be able to return to the second quadrant and reverse the escalating conflict between them. If the difference in expectations is ignored or undiscovered, the conflict will ultimately move to the fourth quadrant.

The fourth quadrant is where two people have different and/or negative expectations and they stop pretending to be congruent. The two persons are at war with one another and may not want to increase the harmony in their relationship any longer. They may just want to hurt one another. Both persons are in disagreement, and that disagreement is now obvious and apparent. This relationship is likely to result in hostile disengagement. It is very difficult to retrieve conflict from the fourth quadrant because one or both parties have stopped trying to find shared positive expectations. Unfortunately, most conflicts between people and groups remain undiscovered until the fourth quadrant is reached. An appropriate prevention strategy would be to identify the conflict in behaviors, as indicated in the second quadrant, early in the process when those differences in behaviors might be positive (as long as there is a context of shared positive expectations), allowing both parties to build on the common ground they share without forcing either party to lose integrity.

Therefore two people may both share the positive expectation of *trust* but one may be loud and the other quiet; they may share *respect* but one may be open and the other closed; they can both believe in *fairness* but one may be direct and the other indirect; they may value *efficiency* but one may be formal and the other informal; they may seek *effectiveness* but one may be close and the other distant; or they may want *safety* but one may be task oriented and the other relationship oriented. Only when each behavior is assessed and understood in its own context does that behavior become meaningful. Only when positive shared expectations can be identified will two individuals or groups be able to find common ground without sacrificing cultural integrity.

5. Constructive Conflict Management in the 21st Century

Cultural backgrounds shape people's ways of thinking, believing, and behaving by influencing their perceptions of themselves and others. The more cultural differences there are between people, the more difficulty they have communicating or understanding why they fail to communicate. Each culture expresses the same core values in different behaviors, increasing the likelihood of misunderstanding. Increased intercultural understanding will introduce new ideas, identify new values, and construct new sociopolitical structures at the macro- and microlevels to increase the quality of interpersonal and institutional interaction. Rabie (1994) observed:

> Diverse human interests and needs, largely incompatible religious social beliefs and competing individual and group goals cause conflict to arise and prevail. Moreover, different loyalties, cultural values, ideologies and geopolitical considerations provide a fertile ground for the planting and nurturing of conflict within and between states. Disparities in wealth, natural resources, technology and power among social classes and ethnic groups within and between states have also been a cause of increased grievances and conflict. (p. 2)

Research on the *contact hypothesis* suggests how different cultural groups can relate to one another successfully in a pluralistic society by creating "favorable" conditions for multicultural contact and avoiding "unfavorable" conditions (Amir, 1969; N. Miller & Brewer, 1984). Favorable conditions that tend to reduce intergroup conflict exist when (a) there is an equal-status contact between members, (b) the contact is between members of a majority group and the higher status members of a minority, (c) the social climate promotes favorable contact, (d) the contact is intimate rather than casual, (e) the contact is pleasant or rewarding, and (f) the members of both groups interact in functionally important activities while developing shared goals.

Unfavorable conditions that increase the likelihood of intergroup conflict occur when (a) contact produces competition, (b) contact is unpleasant and involuntary, (c) one's group's prestige is lowered as a result of the contact, (d) frustrations lead to scapegoating, and (e) moral or ethical standards are violated.

Spontaneous intergroup contact does not occur under favorable conditions but is much more likely to occur under unfavorable conditions, resulting in conflict between cultural groups. It is important to examine the balance of power for intergroup contact and to provide favorable conditions to promote a harmonious multicultural identity.

Sunoo (1990) provided seven guidelines for mediators of intercultural disputes:

1. Expect different expectations.
2. Do not assume that what you say is being understood.
3. Listen carefully.
4. Seek ways of getting both parties to validate the concerns of the other.
5. Be patient, be humble, and be willing to learn.
6. Apply win-win negotiating principles to the negotiation rather than traditional adversarial bargaining techniques.
7. Dare to do things differently.

These recommendations parallel Cohen's (1991) eight guidelines for the negotiator: study the opponent's culture and history, try to establish a warm personal relationship, do not assume that others understand what you mean, be alert to indirect communication, be sensitive to face/status issues, adapt your strategy to your opponent's cultural needs, be appropriately flexible and patient, and recognize that outward appearances are important.

Lund et al. (1994) concluded their review of research on disputing and culture beyond the "taxonomy trap" of lists and guidelines for each cultural group. Culture is complicated and dynamic, with considerable diversity within each cultural group. "The challenge is to develop a view of culture that delineates differences among individuals and subgroups within a culture and encompasses commonalities within that group without simplification, overgeneralization and stereotyping" (p. 24). The findings of that project provide guidelines for managing problems of intercultural understanding in the 21st century.

Dominant-culture methods of conflict resolution incorporate values and attitudes not shared by members of minority groups but are based on culture-bound assumptions. These culture-bound assumptions are implicit or explicit in the staged models of mediation and negotiation taught by the dominant culture.

First, conflicts are in essence communication problems. If effective communication can be facilitated, then the problem can be solved. In fact, the cultural context mediates all communications between groups so that good communication is only one of many factors in conflict management.

Second, there is a middle ground in which both parties can get some of what they want in any given conflict. In fact, the conflict may not fit a win-lose model, and compromising may be less effective than reframing the conflict so that both parties can get what they want without losing integrity.

Third, the optimal way to address conflict is to get the parties in the same room and facilitate an open, forthright discussion of the issues. In fact, open conflict in many cultural contexts may be destructive.

Fourth, parties in conflict emphasize their individual interests over collective values of family, community, or society. In fact, the collective interests may be more important than individual interests in the context of long-term solutions.

Fifth, a third-party intervener must be a neutral person with no connections to any of the parties. In fact, neutrality may be impossible or even undesirable when it requires going outside the group to find a third party.

Sixth, good intact procedures for conflict resolution should be standardized according to fair, reasonable, and rational formats and policies. In fact, the expectation of fairness, reasonableness, and rationality may be expressed quite differently by each culture.

Culture-based conflict between ethnocultural groups has become a serious problem in recent times and promises to be a major problem of the 21st century. By better understanding the positive contribution that a culture-centered approach to intercultural understanding provides, we might be better prepared to survive the problems of intercultural understanding in the 21st century.

6. Conclusion

By reframing conflict between people into cultural categories, it becomes possible for two persons to disagree without either of them being wrong, based on their different culturally learned assumptions. This chapter has described the advantages of reframing conflict into cultural categories for constructive conflict management. Until recently, the influence of cultural similarities and differences has been typically overlooked in the published literature about conflict management, applying a dominant culture, White, middle-class, urban, male, Euro-American model to the management of conflict across cultures and countries. With the increased influence of non-Western cultures and countries, a variety of different styles of conflict management have become more visible.

It is necessary to understand how conflict is understood and managed in non-Western cultures not only because those countries are increasingly involved in conflict with Western cultures but also because Western cultures can learn a great deal from non-Western cultures about constructive conflict management. Conflict is managed quite differently in a high-context culture than in a low-context culture, although each perspective has its advantages and disadvantages. The skilled conflict manager will need to understand both perspectives and know when either may be more appropriate.

Asian and Pacific cultures in particular offer a perspective for managing conflict in harmony, in which conflict between people is often described in a cosmic context with spiritual implications. The goal in Asian and Pacific cultures is often to prevent overt conflict from occurring at all, whereas the Western perspective is more often about resolving conflict once it has occurred. The Hawaiian practice of *ho'oponopono* provides an excellent example of conflict management.

A cultural grid is presented to demonstrate the importance of common ground and shared positive expectations in constructive conflict management. The dangers of interpreting behaviors outside the cultural context are demonstrated. A culture-centered perspective will identify shared positive expectations among persons in conflict and understand all parties' behavior in the context of those shared positive expectations. The same behavior might have a different meaning, and different behaviors might have the same meaning, when those behaviors are understood in context.

Constructive conflict management may become the first priority of counselors in the 21st century, especially when that conflict is between culturally different people. It will become important for counselors to understand interpersonal and intrapersonal conflict in the cultural context in which behaviors are learned and displayed.

EXERCISE: Public and Private Self

Professor Dean Barnlund from San Francisco State University developed a list of topics based on the work by Sidney Jourard. These topics may be public to some persons and private to others. Frequently, we assume that topics we consider public also will be considered public by others and unintentionally violate the other person's privacy. The list of items, available from Professor Barnlund, includes five items from each of the areas of attitudes and opinions, tastes and interests, work or studies, money, personality, and body. The trainer may wish to generate a new list appropriate to the specific training program. The more extensive original list of public and private items can be found in Sidney Jourard's book *The Transparent Self* (1964). Figure 8.1 shows Barnlund's modified list.

Ask each participant to review the list (in written or verbal form) and indicate whether the topic is private (e.g., comfortable to discuss only with self and intimate friends) or public (e.g., comfortable to discuss with casual friends, acquaintances, or strangers).

FIGURE 8.1

Categories of Public and Private Self-Disclosure

Objective

To compare different roles for public disclosure of private information appropriate to visitor and host culture residents.

Instructions

Please mark each of the following topics as:

Private: If it is comfortable to discuss only with self and intimates;

Public: If it is comfortable to discuss with casual friends, acquaintances, or strangers.

	PUBLIC	PRIVATE
ATTITUDES AND OPINIONS:		
1. What I think and feel about my religion (my personal religious views)	____	____
2. My views on Communism	____	____
3. My views on racial integration	____	____
4. My views on sexual morality	____	____
5. The things I regard as desirable for a person to be	____	____
TASTES AND INTERESTS		
1. My favorite foods; my food dislikes	____	____
2. My likes and dislikes in music	____	____
3. My favorite reading matter	____	____
4. The kinds of movies and TV programs I like best	____	____
5. The kind of party or social gathering I like best; the kind that bores me	____	____
WORK OR STUDIES		
1. What I feel are my shortcomings that prevent me from getting ahead	____	____
2. What I feel are my special strong points for work	____	____
3. My goals and ambitions in my work	____	____
4. How I feel about my career; whether I'm satisfied with it	____	____
5. How I feel about the people I work for or with	____	____

continued

FIGURE 8.1 *(continued)*
Categories of Public and Private Self-Disclosure

	PUBLIC	PRIVATE
MONEY		
1. How much money I make at work	_____	_____
2. Whether or not I owe money; if so, how much	_____	_____
3. My total financial work	_____	_____
4. My most pressing need for money right now	_____	_____
5. How I budget my money	_____	_____
PERSONALITY		
1. Aspects of my personality I dislike	_____	_____
2. Feelings I have trouble expressing or controlling	_____	_____
3. Facts of my present sex life	_____	_____
4. Things I feel ashamed or guilty about	_____	_____
5. Things that make me feel proud	_____	_____
BODY		
1. My feelings about my face	_____	_____
2. How I wish I looked	_____	_____
3. My feelings about parts of my body	_____	_____
4. My past illnesses and treatment	_____	_____
5. Feelings about my sexual adequacy	_____	_____
TOTAL PRIVATE TOPICS	_____	_____

Note. From personal communication with Dean Barnlund, San Francisco State University. Used with permission.

When everyone has identified the number of public items, tabulate the number of participants who had public items in six or more categories (30–25; 24–20; 19–15; 14–10; 9–5; 4–0). You will probably discover a bell-shaped distribution of scores on public and private levels among group members. You may then discuss the effect of respecting one another's privacy in working together even though that level may be different from your own.

PUBLIC AND PRIVATE SELF EXERCISE

Participant Objectives:
1. To demonstrate clearly learned and differentiated levels of privacy in a group.
2. To assess one's personal level of privacy relative to the group.
3. To examine the basis of public and private information in different cultures.

Learning Objective:
1. What is public for one person may be private for another.

CHAPTER 9

The Triad Training Model

Major objective:

1. To describe the Triad Training Model for training multicultural counselors.

Secondary objectives:

1. To examine the internal dialogues of culturally different counselors and clients in multicultural settings.
2. To describe variations of the Triad Training Model.
3. To review research on the Triad Training Model.
4. To describe strategies for using the Triad Training Model.
5. To present guidelines for using the Triad Training Model.

Our internal dialogues are perhaps the most meaningful indication of our culture as we think through the various aspects of where we fit in relation to the people around us, accepting some assumptions and challenging others in our mental conversations. In counseling, it is not enough for a good counselor to think and talk at the same time. A good counselor needs to have a good idea of what the client is thinking also. The more cultural differences there are between the client and counselor, the more difficult it will be for the counselor to have an "educated guess" about what that culturally different client is thinking. The Triad Training Model helps prepare counselors to be more accurate in their hypotheses about what a culturally different client is thinking but not saying.

Every counseling interview will include three simultaneous conversations. First, the client and counselor will have a verbal conversation that they can both hear. Second, the counselor will have her or his own internal dialogue exploring related or unrelated factors that the counselor can monitor but the client cannot hear. Third, the client will have her or his own internal dialogue exploring related or unrelated factors that the client can monitor but the counselor cannot hear. The counselor does not know what the client is thinking, but the counselor does know that some of the client's internal dialogue will be positive and some will be negative. The more cultural difference there is between the counselor and the client, the less likely that either one will accurately understand what the other is thinking but not saying. This chapter explores ways to train counselors to hear the self-talk of culturally different clients more accurately.

The recent emphasis on cognitive strategies in counseling and counselor training (Hirsch & Stone, 1983; Strong, 1995) has focused attention on how counselors conceptualize clients and develop strategies for processing information in counseling. At a symbolic level, the difference between the individual and the significant social context in which that individual lives is blurred (McCall & Simmons, 1991). Internal dialogue is not a new idea. Vygotsky's (1962) and Luria's (1961) work in Russia during the early 1930s on the connection between thought and behavior provided the basis for analyzing "private speech." The idea of an "inner forum" (Mead, 1934/1982), "self-talk" (Ellis, 1962), or internal dialogue (Meichenbaum, 1977) goes back at least as far as Plato, where thinking is described as a discourse the mind carries on with itself. While conceptualizing one's own self-talk is difficult, conceptualizing the self-talk of culturally different clients is even more so.

Being able to hear the self-talk of culturally different clients is important for three reasons:

1. There is considerable support for the importance of self-talk in the delivery of counseling services.
2. Counselors trained to increase their ability to monitor their own and the client's self-talk demonstrate more competence.
3. There are a variety of different methods for training counselors to hear the culturally different client's self-talk.

As mentioned in earlier chapters, a person's culture is like having a thousand people sitting in the person's seat whom the person has gathered throughout her or his lifetime to advise, support, argue, challenge, and guide her or him through life. The first step in gaining competence for working with culturally different clients is learning to hear the client's internal voices. When the client comes into your office and closes the door, you dare not assume that there are only two persons in that room. There are thousands of persons in that room, and as the counselor, you will only be competent when you are able to hear and understand the voices, both those surrounding yourself and those crowding around the client.

1. The Importance of Internal Dialogue

To the extent that thought is conducted in words, it may be characterized as talking to one's self, usually in terms of a two-sided or positive-versus-negative discussion. Cognitive behaviorists use the polarity to conceptualize cognitive features of pathology, such as rational versus irrational beliefs, positive versus negative appraisals, positive versus negative self-statements, and desirable versus negative life events (Swartz & Garamoni, 1989). Mead (1934/1982) called this continuous internal conversation an *inner forum*. This is not a simple dialogue. The individual is reacting to what is being said or thought as one is saying or thinking it. These internal voices are constant and continuous. By monitoring the internal dialogue constantly and continuously, one can discover all perspectives and contexts. It is this organization of multiple perspectives and contexts for reaction that is the "me" in Mead's terms, in which the "me" becomes the audience to a multiperson discussion. Each voice has a somewhat different reaction corresponding to each different perspective as members of this metaphorical audience strive to inform the "me" regarding their perspective.

One result of this cognitive trend is to focus more on the intrapersonal as the basis for understanding interpersonal processes of counseling. As counselors, we observe ourselves observing others, and from that we learn about the context in which counseling occurs. We continuously form a new sense of "us" that combines self and others. We recognize that we are more than one person. We are ourselves a multicultural group. People learn about their own emotions, attitudes, and internal states by observing their own behavior as they might evaluate the behavior of others (Montgomery & Haemmerlie, 1987). The need to investigate these internal cognitive processes might provide the key to skill generalization. We might come to a better understanding of how counselors and clients think during counseling. These schemas of cognitive structures facilitate top-down or conceptually driven processing as opposed to bottom-up or data-driven cognitive processing (Fiske & Taylor, 1991). Each schema comes from multiple sources as we actively construct reality. People continuously form a new sense of "us" relative to their perception of themselves in relation to each other (Shorter, 1987).

Facilitative self-talk leads to higher levels of reflection, confrontation, and empathy. The ability to consciously and intentionally listen to our own internal dialogue is positively correlated to counseling performance, and hearing this covert internal dialogue is important to counselor competency (Fiske & Taylor, 1991; Kimberlin & Friesen, 1980; Montgomery & Haemmerlie, 1987; Shorter, 1987).

Self-control, self-instruction, and mental imagery are all part of self-talk. Hypotheses formulation skills that occur through self-talk are positively related to facilitative performance (Morran, 1986). Self-talk has been used to reduce trainee anxiety. Self-talk mobilizes mental imagery and is expressed through beliefs and culturally learned assumptions (Kline, 1988). Competence

requires that we learn more about how our inner speech mediates our self-consciousness and inhibits our culturally encapsulated self-deception. Research
on self-talk suggests that it is the quality rather than the quantity of self-talk
that is most important (Kurpius, Benjamin, & Morran, 1985).

There are a number of ways that managing self-talk or internal dialogue
contributes to competency (Nutt-Williams & Hill, 1996):

1. Self-talk focuses attention on the task, self-evaluation, and perspective taking.
2. Self-talk leads to higher levels of self-awareness.
3. Self-talk permits the internalization of others' perspectives.
4. Self-talk contributes to self-observation in a continuous communication loop.
5. Guilt reactions are mediated by an internal thought process or "the voice" (Firestone, 1997a).
6. Emotions are what we tell ourselves more than what really happens.
7. By changing our self-talk, we can change feelings and actions.
8. Internal voices or "internal muzak" influences intrapersonal and interpersonal relationships.

Research on self-talk has indicated a number of ways that it influences the
therapy process (Nutt-Williams & Hill, 1996):

1. Self-talk is related to perceptions of therapy.
2. Therapists who think negatively about themselves are perceived as less helpful.
3. Self-talk changes the environment, finds meaning, and directs behavior.
4. Self-evaluation provides motivation.
5. Clients hide their true feelings through self-talk.
6. Therapists focus more on their own self-talk than the client's self-talk.
7. Therapists can use self-talk to manage anxiety and hear the client's internal dialogue.

Research has also focused on identity as a dialogical construct in which
self and society are not discrete conceptions. The dialogical self is constructed and reconstructed with input from others both within and outside
the self (Hermans & Kempen, 1993). The complexities of decision making
best demonstrate how our multivoiced selves interact in a sociocultural context. If self is a multiplicity of voices more than a unitary thought process,
then this polyphonic interpretation of self has more than one theme. Thought
is a discussion between what Sullivan (1953) called a "good me" and a "bad
me" as diversities of subpersonalities strive to express themselves and
become salient.

The counseling relationship is defined by an internalized complementarity of voices. The clients' perceptions are valid and powerful indicators of outcome. Over time, clients replace their perceptions of self with the counselors' perception of them in a working alliance requiring mutual trust and involvement. Clients are sensitive to changes of power influence by counselors. Counselors adjust their power influence to provide an envelope of safety for the clients to grow so that low-power clients require high-power counselors and vice versa. Good counselors adjust their power influence automatically. Automaticity requires minimal drain on the counselor's deliberate attention and frees the counselor's attentional capacity for higher level functioning.

Opposing ideas provide a dialogical basis for thinking. Optimal thinking will include both positive and negative ideas, although negative thoughts occur on a ratio of 1.7:1 for functional individuals in what has been called the "golden section proportion" (Swartz & Garamoni, 1989). Furthermore, research has revealed an asymmetry between positive and negative coping thoughts whereby negative thoughts have greater functional impact and are more likely to change as a result of therapy (Swartz, 1986, p. 591). The client's focus on negative aspects serves an important function, and the elimination of negative thinking is unlikely by itself to succeed. Counselors help clients monitor, manage, and modify their positive and negative thinking.

Firestone (1997a, 1997b) asserted that guilt reactions are mediated by an internal thought process he called "the voice." The inner voice of voice therapy acts to attack, punish, and destroy the individual in ways that go beyond negative self-image. The voice is an antiself, antithetical to the survival of the self-system by being critical, destructive, and punitive with the objective of preventing and destroying the individual's potential for intimate relationships. According to Firestone (1997b):

> Voice Therapy involves a process of individuation and separation from internalized parental introjects and addictive attachments. Separation as conceptualized here is very different from isolation, defense or retreat; rather it involves the maintenance of a strong identity and distinct boundaries at close quarters with others. Indeed, without a well-developed self-system or personal identity, people find it necessary to distort, lash out at, or withdraw from intimacy in interpersonal relationships. (p. 5)

Other research asserts that by changing self-talk, we can change feelings and actions (Zastrow, 1988), influence the self-concept (Phillips, 1990), and influence interpersonal relationships (Ledermann, 1996). Nutt-Williams and Hill (1996) demonstrated that when therapists think negatively about themselves, they evaluate themselves as less helpful and their clients as more negative. Self-talk provides a way to actively manipulate the environment, evaluate ourselves, find meaning, and direct our behavior accordingly. Counselors do not always accurately perceive their client's reactions, especially when those reactions are negative. This distortion may occur when the client hides his or her true reactions from the counselor. Another possibility is that counselors, particularly counselor trainees, focus on their own self-talk rather than their client's reactions. Counselor self-talk might interfere with the ability to accurately decode a client's reactions or to inflate the client's negative reactions. Counselors can use self-talk in counseling as a gauge for what is happening to the client as well as for recognizing and reorganizing their own perceptions and managing anxiety. "Adequate management of both quantity and quality of self-talk may be crucial in allowing [counselors] to maintain an appropriate focus on clients" (Nutt-Williams & Hill, 1996, p. 170).

There is also an expanding literature about self-talk as it relates to self-help and personal growth issues of clients. Siegrist (1995) reviewed the literature on inner speech as a cognitive process to mediate self-consciousness and inhibit self-deception by mediating self-consciousness. Ickes (1988) studied attributional styles and covert verbalizations of self-talk by patients with depression to suggest they have a tendency to interpret situations as evidence of their inadequacy even when that response might be inappropriate. By magnifying their failures and minimizing favorable outcomes in their self-appraisals and by making unfavorable social comparisons, the patients contribute to feelings of inferiority. Fuqua, Johnson, Anderson, and Newman (1984) pointed out that human cognition is a complex and elusive target for scientific assessment but that the increased tendency to test the role of cognition in counseling and training shows promise for the future.

2. Developing Competence in Monitoring Internal Dialogue

There is a teachable–learnable relationship between the trainee's thinking and behaving that we must capture in our attempts to develop competence (Richardson & Stone, 1981). Morran (1986) demonstrated "a positive relationship between higher quality clinical hypothesis formulation and higher levels of facilitative performance during counseling sessions" (p. 395). Traditional models of counselor training that focus on behavioral skills are expanded to accommodate the complex interrelationships between a counselor trainee's cognitive and behavioral processes. The techniques of self-control, self-instruction, and mental imagery are strategies to mobilize a trainee's self-talk. Moran (1986) researched the level of task-facilitative 'self-talk, the level of task-distractive self-talk, and the quality of clinical hypothesis formation, expecting that self-talk would relate to the level of facilitative performance. Surprisingly, the research found a positive zero-order correlation between task-facilitative and task-distractive measures but a consistent positive relationship between the counselor's hypothesis formulation skills and facilitative performance. "This suggests, as one might expect, that it is not how much one self-talks, but the quality of the self-talk that counts" (Moran, 1986, p. 394).

Kline (1988) reviewed the literature on counselor trainee anxiety as influenced by self-talk and increasing the counselor's focus on self-evaluative thinking. By increasing the trainee's concentration on client verbalization and self-talk as part of skill acquisition, it was presumed that trainee anxiety would be diminished. Neck, Stewart, Crag, and Manz (1995) also examined the application of cognitive processes in the organizational behavior literature applying thought self-leadership (TSL) to the performance appraisal process. TSL involves internal dialogue to gain purposive control of one's thoughts through self-talk, mental imagery, expressed beliefs, and assumptions. O'Quinn (1986) also studied the relationship between counselor's internal dialogue and counseling performance, emphasizing the importance of distracting versus facilitative self-talk. The importance of self-talk is being discovered from a variety of disciplinary perspectives as it relates to training.

> Covert cognitive activity, or self-talk, has long been recognized as an important aspect of therapist training programs. Although several researchers have investigated therapist self-talk . . . minimal empirical evidence exists in the counseling literature that describes the relationship between therapists' in session cognition and therapy process variables. (Nutt-Williams & Hill, 1996, p. 170)

Several researchers have used thought-listing procedures to measure counselor self-talk (Nutt-Williams & Hill, 1996). This involves listing the thoughts and having trained judges categorize or code the content of the self-talk. The most common global dimensions of self-talk measured in this way are *focus*, or the direction of counselors' thoughts to self or other, and *affect*, or the negative/positive salience of counselor self-talk. The early "think aloud" (Fuqua, Newman, Anderson, & Johnson, 1986) approaches to assessing internal dialogue were intrusive and time consuming. Other paper-and-pencil assessments of internal dialogue were also less than satisfactory. "Although popular cognitive–behavioral training strategies are being developed, their judicious application requires increased understanding. The principle and persisting barrier to understanding appears to be the lack of innovative and creative means for measuring internal dialogue" (Fuqua et al., 1986, pp. 170–171).

Most research has not correlated counselor self-talk to other process variables. Nutt-Williams and Hill (1996) found that trainee self-talk was related to perceptions of helpfulness and perceptions of client reactions. Presenting clients with observations contrary to the client's view of self, Strohmer, Moilapen, and Barry (1988) examined how individuals test hypotheses about themselves in counseling. Individuals process this information through self-talk guided by a more complicated sense of consistency and self-schema rather than simply personal hypothesis testing. Borders, Fong-Beyette, and Cron (1988) measured cognitive processes underlying skill acquisition and performance among counseling students, suggesting that beginning counseling students may have few intentional or self-instructive thoughts during a session and that research of the cognitive process requires a more complete contextual account through open-ended response formats rather than studying isolated cognitions out of their context.

Morin (1995) examined the characteristics of an effective internal dialogue for the mediation of self-awareness as a problem-solving task. Self-talk served to focus attention on the task, foster constant self-evaluation, and take the perspective of others. Morin (1993) suggested that two social mechanisms leading to self-awareness can be reproduced by self-talk. First, engaging in dialogues with oneself and fictitious persons permits the internalization of others' perspective, and addressing comments to oneself about oneself as others might do leads to the acquisition of self-information. Second, self-observation is possible only when there is a distance between the individual and any potentially observable self-aspect as through self-talk, which conveys self-information through words in a continuous communication loop.

Kendall, Howard, Dennis, and Hays (1989) studied self-referent speech and psychopathology related to positive and negative thinking. They used a self-statement inventory and discovered that introducing positive items made a significant difference in the self-talk of participants. Siegrist (1995) developed a questionnaire to measure the extent of inner speech about self and discovered a correlation between depression and public self-consciousness but that measures of depression did not correlate significantly with private self-consciousness, although there was a significant correlation between self-deception and depression. P. L. Hines, Stockton, and Morran (1995) studied self-talk among group therapists. While the difference in skill development from novice to experienced counselor is complicated, some of this difference seems to relate to self-talk. Thoughts about interpreting group processes and internal questions regarding members were found to account for 56% of the variance in counselor experience levels.

Kurpius et al. (1985) asked trainees to list all of the thoughts that had occurred to them immediately after each interview. Thought-listing results demonstrated an interaction between the type of training condition and the level of the trainee's expertise. Morran, Kurpius, Brack, and Brack (1995) incorporated cognitive skills training to sensitize trainees in their own thinking style, link cognitive to behavioral skills, promote critical self-examination of strategies, and provide systematic practice with new ways of thinking and responses. The specific components of cognitive skill included assessing necessary tasks in counseling, formulating specific counseling goals, rehearsing intervention plans, self-instruction on plans for action, evaluating interventions, providing positive self-reinforcement, and monitoring all these simultaneous processes.

Richardson and Stone (1981) developed a cognitive instructional approach to teach counselor trainees self-talk related to skills of predicting, planning, and problem solving. Their research compared behavioral and programmed learning approaches and found that facilitative self-talk skills led to higher levels of reflection, confrontation, and empathy. Meichenbaum (1974) and Mahoney and Arnkoff (1978) were among the first to apply the research about self-talk to counseling and clinical relationships. The research on self-talk grew naturally from research correlating internal dialogue to counseling performance, personality dimensions, and state/trait anxiety (Fuqua et al., 1986). Covert internal dialogue was described as important to counselor trainees. Counselor trainees were found to engage in internal dialogue, although it was unclear whether the nature of that internal dialogue resulted from training or from personality style.

A number of researchers and theorists in the counselor training and supervision field have recommended more emphasis on cognitive processes in counselor training. "However, a review of the counselor training literature indicates that no models currently exist that focus specifically on methods of facilitating trainee acquisition of cognitive skills" (Morran, Kurpius, Brack, & Brack, 1995, p. 384). Morran et al. described a cognitive skills model for counselor training emphasizing attending to and seeking information, forming hypotheses and conceptual models, and containing intervention planning for self-instruction. In a cognitive skills approach, the counselor learns to purposefully direct thoughts toward gathering information and filling in gaps as an active and creative process. New data are needed about both the counselor and the client's internal dialogue as they relate to the counseling process through a process of sorting out what is relevant from what is irrelevant. Studies of hypothesizing and conceptualizing skills have focused on hypothesis testing with less attention to how those hypotheses are formulated. According to Morran et al. (1995):

> The cognitive skills related to hypothesizing and conceptualizing include the self-instructional process of directing oneself to (a) consider the possible causal relationship between observed and reported client behaviors, inferred internal characteristics of the client and client environmental factors, (b) formulate multiple hypotheses to tentatively explain the relationship of these factors to each other, (c) formulate questions or strategies to test and evaluate each hypothesis, (d) discard or tentatively accept hypotheses on the basis of testing evidence, and (e) integrate viable hypotheses to form comprehensive conceptual models of the client. (p. 386)

3. The Triad Training Model

Although we cannot know exactly the client's internal dialogue, we can assume that some of these messages are negative or *anticounselor* in their orientation, whereas other messages are positive or *procounselor* in their orientation. The Triad Training Model is a training model for simulated cross-cultural interviews between a culturally different counselor and a culturally matched team, which includes a coached client, an anticounselor, and a procounselor (P. Pedersen, 1968, 1972, 1973, 1974, 1975, 1976, 1977, 1979, 2000). The anticounselor seeks to explicate the negative messages a client from that culture might be thinking but not saying, whereas a procounselor seeks to explicate the positive messages in the client's mind. While either an anticounselor or a procounselor may be used without the other, their combined influence is to hear the "hidden messages" behind the client's internal dialogue in both their positive and negative aspects. The procounselor and anticounselor provide continuous direct and immediate feedback to both the client and the counselor on the counseling process. Many of the sources of resistance to counseling across cultures consequently become explicit and articulate, even to a culturally different counselor.

The reader should be able to try out the model on the basis of the instructions in this chapter and P. Pedersen (1999b) to determine the model's usefulness in local settings. Local resource persons can be trained as client/anticounselor/procounselor teams to provide training resources without bringing in outside experts to the unit or agency. Additional data on the Triad Training Model are being collected to determine its specific strengths and weaknesses in a variety of settings.

The Triad Training Model simulates a force field of positive and negative factors from the client's viewpoint in the polarized roles of the procounselor and anticounselor, who make explicit the client's positive and negative internal dialogue. The Triad Training Model seems to work best when the following conditions apply:

1. There needs to be both positive and negative feedback to the counselor during the interview.
2. The simulated interview needs to reflect actual events in realistic ways.
3. The simulated interview needs to occur under conditions that the counselor considers "safe."
4. Procounselors and anticounselors need to be carefully trained to be effective.
5. The feedback to the counselor and client needs to be immediate and explicit during the actual interview.
6. The resource persons need to be articulate as well as authentic to the client's background.

7. The counselor needs to learn how to focus on the client while listening to the anticounselor and the procounselor at the same time.
8. The interview works best when it is spontaneous and not scripted.
9. The debriefing is much more effective if the interaction is videotaped for debriefing.
10. The actual simulated interview should be brief (8–10 minutes) to avoid overwhelming the counselor with information during or after the interview.

In the Triad Training Model, it is important to understand the role of the procounselor and the anticounselor. The anticounselor is deliberately subversive in attempting to exaggerate mistakes by the counselor during the interview. The anticounselor exaggerates the negative thoughts of the client toward counseling, emphasizing differences in behavior that drive the counselor farther apart from the client. The anticounselor does this using a variety of techniques, including building on positive aspects of a problem (which makes bad problems attractive) and the client's ambivalence, keeping the interaction superficial, obstructing communication, distracting or annoying the counselor and/or client, building a barrier of cultural differences, demanding immediate results from the counselor, using a foreign language or whispering private messages to the client, finding a scapegoat to blame for the problem, or requesting a more appropriate counselor. By involving the anticounselor, the counselor trainee is likely to gain insight in cultural self-awareness and explicit negative unspoken thoughts of the client, find opportunities for recovery skills in counseling, and learn to focus on client needs from the client's viewpoint.

The counselor and anticounselor are pulling in opposite directions, with the client judging which is "more right." There are several potential advantages of including an anticounselor in the simulation.

1. The anticounselor forces the counselor to be more aware of the client's perspective.
2. The anticounselor articulates the negative, embarrassing, and impolite comments, which a client might not otherwise say.
3. The anticounselor forces the counselor to examine her or his own defensiveness.
4. The anticounselor points out a counselor's inappropriate interventions immediately while the counselor still has time to recover.
5. The anticounselor's attempts to distract the counselor train the counselor to focus more intently on the client.

Conversely, the procounselor is a deliberately positive force that helps articulate the client's positive unspoken messages about counseling, emphasizing similarities of common-ground positive expectations between the counselor and the client and bringing the counselor and the client closer together.

The procounselor accomplishes this by restating messages in a positive framework; relating statements to regular cultural patterns; offering approval, reinforcement, or encouragement; reinforcing progress by the client; providing verbal and nonverbal encouragement; and helping the counselor focus accurately. The learning that results from the procounselor includes making cultural information explicit to the counselor, providing a team-mate or friend to support the counselor, reframing messages in a positive direction, and helping the counselor track the changing cultural salience in the interview.

The hidden messages of a client's negative internal dialogue are seldom addressed directly in counselor training. The Triad Training Model encourages the direct examination of these hidden negative messages, which a client, and especially a culturally different client, does not or might not otherwise know. This helps the counselor develop skills for dealing with those negative messages during the actual interview process.

The procounselor attempts to articulate the hidden positive messages, which might also be included in a client's internal dialogue. The culturally similar procounselor helps both counselor and client to utilize the counseling process as a potentially helpful activity. The procounselor functions as a facilitator for the counselor's effective responses. The culturally similar procounselor understands the client better than the culturally different counselor and is thus able to provide relevant background information to the counselor during the interview. The procounselor is not a cotherapist but an intermediate resource person who can guide the counselor through suggesting specific strategies and information that the client might otherwise be reluctant to volunteer. In these ways, the procounselor can reinforce the counselor's more successful strategies, both verbally and nonverbally.

There are several advantages contributed by the procounselor in the simulated counseling interview:

1. The procounselor is a resource person to consult when the counselor is confused or in need of support.
2. The procounselor makes explicit information about the client, which might facilitate the counselor's success.
3. The procounselor provides a partner for the counselor to work with on the problem, rather than the counselor having to work alone.
4. The procounselor helps the counselor stay on track and avoid sensitive issues in ways that might increase client resistance.
5. The procounselor provides beneficial feedback to the counselor to avoid mistakes and build on successful strategies.

The procounselor attempts to build on positive and constructive aspects of the counseling interview through encouragement and support to the counselor, who may feel under attack by the anticounselor. There are several ways the procounselor might provide that support:

1. The procounselor might restate or reframe what either the client or the counselor said in a positive fashion.
2. The procounselor might relate client or counselor statements to the basic underlying problem, keeping things on track.
3. The procounselor might offer approval or reinforcement to the client or the counselor when they are cooperating.
4. The procounselor might reinforce and emphasize important insights that need to be discussed and expanded.
5. The procounselor might reinforce client statements as the client becomes more cooperative in the interview.
6. The procounselor might suggest alternative strategies to the counselor when necessary.

4. Advantages of the Triad Training Model

The Triad Training Model lends itself to training classroom-sized groups. Each three-person resource team is matched with a counselor trainee or a small group of 8–10 trainees who share the role of counselor. A 10-minute simulated interview is followed by about 10 minutes of debriefing out of role with the counselor trainee and the resource persons. Then the resource team moves to another group and a different resource team takes over. The development of culture-centered counseling skill requires the ability to monitor both the client's positive and negative internal dialogue at the same time to better hear both the positive and negative hidden messages.

The Triad Training Model offers numerous advantages that complement other training models which, while not supported at this point with research evidence, suggest an accommodation of counseling technique and social psychological theory.

1. The role-play interaction provides an opportunity for persons from different ethnic or cultural groups to interact under controlled conditions for the accomplishment of limited training goals to their mutual advantage.
2. The role-play interaction provides an appropriate opportunity for persons from different cultural groups to teach one another about the implications of cultural values for counseling in a setting that will minimize the dangers of either party becoming overly defensive or threatened.
3. The application of social psychology research on triads to the role of the problem, counselor, and counselee in a balance of power and resistance provides a previously unexplored model for charting the counseling process.

4. Introducing the anticounselor and procounselor roles provides an opportunity for counselor trainees to empathize with the problem as more than a diffuse abstraction, resulting in a more articulate understanding of the client's problem in its cultural aspects.

5. Introducing the anticounselor and procounselor role provides an explicit modeling of negative feedback that serves to clarify specific sources of resistance in the verbal and nonverbal responses of the client.

6. Inappropriate counselor intervention is immediately and obviously apparent in the metaphorical contest among the counselor, procounselor, and anticounselor, particularly when a counselor's mistake damages the counseling relationship.

7. Videotaped simulations of the exchange among the counselor, procounselor, and anticounselor provide material that can be used in counselor education to illustrate specific ways in which cultural differences affect counseling.

8. Counselor trainees having been exposed to the effect of cultural differences in role play should be able to generalize from these experiences to increase their expertise for dealing with similar problems later as counselors.

9. A careful analysis of research data and transcripts of the interaction will identify implicit as well as explicit, inadvertent as well as deliberate, cultural bias in both the definition of problems and in the identification of specific problems in some cross-cultural situations.

10. The separation of individual differences from patterned or cultural difference can be taught as a skill necessary to cross-cultural counseling by analysis of the arguments and conflict in the three-way interaction of counselor/counselor trainee/client.

11. Counselor trainees will be able to rehearse the utilization of their most immediately available resource for learning about cross-cultural counseling by directly involving members of their own "target audience" such as potential counselees from other cultures rather than learning about them indirectly through abstract theories about those populations.

12. Cultural differences tend to exaggerate and magnify the likelihood of inappropriate counseling interventions. Providing immediate feedback to trainees regarding cultural differences and hidden messages of inadequacy that might otherwise be unnoticed creates opportunities for counselors to intervene more appropriately.

13. The simulation of coalition power relationships in counseling may stimulate experimental modes of viewing the counseling relationship as inevitably cross-cultural in the separation of culturally defined roles as "counselor" and as "counselee."

14. If videotaping the cross-cultural counseling interview proves effective as a mode of counselor training, it would provide a supplementary specialization to more traditional programs of counselor education.

15. The resources for rehearsing four-way interaction are readily available in every multicultural setting once the basic skills of the anticounselor and procounselor are learned through modeling demonstration videotapes and studying the transcripts.

16. The model provides for a "mutuality" in which potential clients from other cultures have a chance to educate the counselors who will be working among them in a balanced interview.

17. Making explicit the procounselor's positive and the anticounselor's negative hidden messages allows a counselor trainee to move more rapidly toward honest feedback, thereby accelerating the transition in early counseling sessions from rapport building to problem solving.

18. An experimental ratio of relationships is provided to suggest how changes in each of the four participant roles affect the other.

19. An experimental structure is provided to interpret the client's hidden messages in terms of appropriate interventions by the counselor, coordinated to the changing equilibrium of power in counseling.

20. The eclectic application of theoretical approaches is suggested for adjusting power influence to nurture a client–counselor coalition in the immediate context of changing counseling relationship without being tied to any one theoretical technique.

21. The effects of counseling practice toward an ultimate goal are described in a way that enables empirical instrumentation to evaluate the model's effectiveness to specific conditions.

22. The active and complex influence of problematic aspects in the environment are more clearly recognized in the ways they affect counseling.

23. Counseling goals can be behaviorally defined in terms of liberation or increased autonomy rather than merely accommodation.

24. The conceptual model lends itself to simulation as a training technique for cross-cultural counselor education.

25. The model incorporates anticounselor and procounselor roles as a counterbalance of hidden messages in counseling.

26. The environmental context is expressed in the interview with all its complex influences, in which rewards and punishments administered through the environment tend to reinforce appropriate or inappropriate client behaviors.

27. The problem is recognized as functioning as the dispenser of reinforcers much in the same way as the environment would in real-life situations.

Research on the Triad Training Model with multicultural groups has been supportive. Research with prepracticum counseling students at the University of Hawaii showed that those trained with the Triad Training Model achieved significantly higher scores on counselor effectiveness, had lower levels of discrepancy between real and ideal self-descriptions, and chose a greater number of positive adjectives in describing themselves as counselors (P. Pedersen, Holwill, & Shapiro, 1978). Bailey (1981) found that those trained in the Triad Training Model generally showed more gain than dyad-trained students on Carkhuff's measures of empathy, respect, and congruence; Gordon's scales on affective meaning; Ivey's Counselor Effectiveness scale; and the revised Budner Tolerance of Ambiguity scale. Niemeyer, Fukuyama, Bingham, Hall, and Mussenden (1986) found that the more confrontational anticounselor model, when used alone, was better suited to more advanced students who already have developed some confidence. D. W. Sue (1980) found the anticounselor model was more effective in achieving self-awareness, developing cultural sensitivity, and understanding political or social aspects of counseling, although students were more comfortable with the procounselor. Strous, Skuy, and Hickson (1993) trained family counselors in South Africa with the Triad Training Model and found a significant preference for the procounselor over the anticounselor and the anticounselor over conventional training models. Wade and Bernstein (1991) found that students trained with the Triad Training Model had higher ratings on expertness, trustworthiness, attractiveness, unconditional positive regard, satisfaction, and empathy. Chambers (1992) found the Triad Training Model increased the frequency of good verbal counseling responses and decreased the frequency of poor verbal counseling responses. Other research found students trained with the Triad Training Model increased self-awareness, reduced confusion or defensiveness (Irvin & Pedersen, 1996), and provided deeper exploration of presenting problems and more specific understanding of negative thoughts by culturally different clients.

In the training session with the Triad Training Model, each three-person resource team is matched with a counselor trainee or a small group of 8–10 trainees who share the role of counselor. A 10-minute simulated interview is followed by about 10 minutes of debriefing out of role with the counselor trainee and the resource persons. Then the resource team moves to another group and a different resource team takes over.

As an example of the resource teams at work, let us consider a situation in which a White American male counselor (CO) is working with a 24-year-old Japanese American female client (CL) who is troubled about whether or not to move out of her parents' home. The procounselor (PC) and anticounselor (AC) are also Japanese American women who articulate the positive or negative messages the client is thinking but not saying.

CL: What do you think I should do? I mean, what's correct? Do you think ...

PC: That's right, trust him. He wants to help you.

AC: He's White and he's male. How can anyone that different from us be any help?

CO: Well, I guess if you are going to play by your parents' rules staying home and suffering, I think ...

AC: See! He thinks you're suffering at home and that you should move out! Remember your parents and your obligations!

CL: Do you think I'm suffering at home?

PC: Something is certainly wrong and he is trying to help you find out what it is.

CO: Well, I think something brought you here to talk to me about the dilemma you're in about wanting to move out and being very uncomfortable ... having a rough time bringing it up to your folks in such a way that ... uh ... you can do that?

AC: Ask him when he moved out. When did he move out of his parents' home?

CL: Yeah, when did you move out of your parents' home?

PC: Keep the focus on yourself. Attacking him is not going to help you.

CO: I moved out of my folk's home when I was 16.

AC: Why did he move out so young? You know? He moved out at 16! After all that his parents did for him and everything! You know? He moved out at 16! Such disrespect!

CO: Well, I went away to school and it was important to live at school. The school was in another town.

PC: Keep the focus on your problem or he will never be able to help you. He wants to help you! Let him!

CL: Didn't your parents get mad that you went to another school?

PC: His family rules may be different, but they still loved one another. Focus on the positive part!

CO: No, they wanted me to go to school. Education was pretty important to them.

AC: See! He's saying that your parents don't think education is important! He is insulting your parents!

From this brief transcript, one can see the internal dialogue in action within the client's mind, focusing on positive common-ground expectations, but also aware of different and possibly negative behaviors at the same time. Culture-centered competency in counseling requires the ability to monitor both the client's positive and negative internal dialogue.

One characteristic of highly functioning counselors is the ability to take multiple perspectives: organizing a wide range of facts, factors, and interacting variables and then synthesizing these data in an integrated pattern to better understand the complex situation in which counseling occurs. As the counselor collects information about the client, analyzes alternative explanations, formulates viable hypotheses, and then selects appropriate intervention strategies, being able to take multiple perspectives becomes an important cognitive skill. While most of the counselor training literature emphasizes performance skills such as empathy, the research literature documents cognitive skills as equally if not more important in developing good counselors (Fuqua et al., 1984). Monitoring multiple perspectives is especially important in multicultural counseling interviews.

5. The Balance of Positive and Negative Thinking

Little is known about the cognitive process of self-awareness and self-consciousness. I have reviewed the literature on how inner speech mediates information about one's self and the external environment in ways that differ from external speech. Self-verbalization was formerly considered to be nonfunctional and a sign of immaturity, but with a better understanding of the link between inner speech and self-awareness, it is being given more importance.

> Self-awareness theory views conscious attention as dichotomous: attention is directed either towards the self or to the environment. High self-awareness means that for a relatively great part of the time a person focuses on aspects of the self. Not only the situation, but also personal disposition influences the focus of attention. (Siegrist, 1995, p. 259)

Inner speech mediates self-consciousness, but no one is sure how this is done. It appears that the same language that mediates social interaction in social relationships also mediates cognitive activity within individuals. This inner or private speech is typically in terms of a dialogue with two sides—identities or interactors participating, one typically in a positive role and the other typically in a negative role. The inner voices are not typically evenly or equally balanced in terms of the positive and negative messages.

More recent research on internal dialogue suggests that it is asymmetrical. According to Swartz (1986), "this research reveals an asymmetry between positive and negative coping thoughts, whereby negative thoughts have greater functional impact and are more likely to change as a result of therapy" (p. 591). Research on positive and negative internal dialogue suggests that they are characterized by a 1.7:1 ratio of (less) positive to (more) negative self-statements for individuals from functional groups and on a ratio of approximately 1:1 for individuals from mildly dysfunctional groups. Highly assertive participants had more positive than negative thoughts, whereas less assertive participants had about the same number of positive as negative thoughts (Swartz, 1986).

Swartz and Garamoni (1989) discussed what has been called the "golden section proportion," researched extensively by personal construct psychologists. The golden section is defined as the ratio that is obtained between positive and negative when the smaller is to the larger as the larger is to the whole in a relationship described as $a/b = b/(a + b)$.

> Specifically, the model proposes that functionally optimal states of mind consist of a precise balance of positive and negative cognitions and/or affects, closely approximating the gold section proportion of .618. Such asymmetrically balanced cognitive/affective structures render negative events and cognitions maximally salient and are therefore optimally suited for coping with stress. (Swartz & Garamoni, 1989, p. 272)

These asymmetrical patterns of positive and negative thinking have been confirmed by research using inventories, thought listing, talking aloud, and thought-sampling methods.

> In sum, it appears that negative events and cognitions are more salient and make a greater impact than positive ones—that negative thoughts and feelings, relative to positive, may be more central to adaptation. Perhaps psychology's focus on illness rather than health, or the well-known difficulties of defining health in ways other than the absence of illness, can be better understood in terms of this. (Swartz, 1986, p. 599)

Our internal dialogue is important to our psychological health. If opposing ideas provide a dialogical basis for thinking, then even optimal thinking will include both positive and negative ideas. The asymmetry of positive and negative thinking also suggests that focusing on negative or nonproductive thoughts by a client may be important and require more than merely building positive perspectives in therapy or training. The elimination of negative thinking by itself is no more likely to succeed than increasing positive thinking. The ideal relationship of positive and negative thinking is in this asymmetrical balance. According to Swartz (1986):

> In terms of treatment, it may be more critical to eliminate these negative thoughts than to establish positive ones, at least as the *final end point* of treatment. However, research on the process of therapeutic change over time that assesses both positive and negative cognitions may lead to the finding that a period of positive coping thought in the internal dialogue is necessary to facilitate short-term change until these newly acquired patterns of thinking, feeling and acting are integrated into new self structures. (p. 602)

Swartz and Garamoni (1989) discussed the importance of balancing the positive and negative sides of a person's internal dialogue in studying positive and negative states of mind, in research on the golden section hypothesis in information theory, in intrapersonal communication, and in cybernetic self-regulation. "Considering both positive and negative dimensions simultaneously and framing the polarity idea in terms of the *balance* between the opposing poles represents an integrative step with potential heuristic value" (p. 272).

The polarity of cognitive balance versus imbalance is a measurably appealing goal for counseling. Rather than focus only on increasing positive coping cognition or reducing negative dysfunctional cognitions, counselors can conceptualize counseling as striving toward a healthy balance of positive and negative thoughts, even though that balance is asymmetrical. Negative cognition is both necessary and inevitable, just as excessive positive cognition can be undesirable. The task of counselors is to help clients monitor and modify their own positive and negative thinking to achieve a balance between positive and negative elements in their lives.

> In assertiveness problems, for example, clients can conceptualize their problem along a bipolar dimension anchored by the extreme (undesirable) states of submissiveness and aggressiveness, with appropriate assertiveness representing the balanced mean. Similarly, problems of self-esteem can be viewed along a continuum anchored by the extremes of self-hatred and self-inflation, with true self esteem representing the balanced state. (Swartz & Garamoni, 1989, p. 292)

Counseling is the process of gradual oscillation between extremes until a balance is established in which clients can reduce dependence on their problem and experiment with alternative ways of thinking, feeling, and behaving.

6. Conclusion

Competence in culture-centered counseling is more than following a list of rules. Competence requires a more comprehensive change of perspective in the competent person and about the counseling process as a whole. Otherwise one can develop a high level of performance on skills in the classroom setting and fail to generalize that expertise to the outside world. Many of the most important elements of culture-centered counseling cannot be taught, but they can be learned. The primary teachers are inside ourselves, speaking to us if we will listen to them. We accumulate the best and the brightest talent we can discover throughout our lives and we add those voices to our collection. If and when we are competent, it is because those inside voices are guiding us toward competence.

In addition to hearing our own voices, as counselors we need to become more aware of the client's voices as well. Competence is measured by our ability to know what the client is thinking but not saying. To the extent that a client and a counselor are culturally different, the task of hearing the client's voices will be more difficult, but just as important. The Triad Training Model provides one way to hear what a culturally different client may be thinking but not saying, both positively and negatively. Feedback from an anticounselor and a procounselor helps counselors to break out of their culturally encapsulated self-reference criterion. This culture-centered foundation provides a basis for developing competence in counseling.

If we assume that our internal dialogue mediates our understanding or comprehension of the outside world, then the more similar the client and counselor are the more likely that each will be able to anticipate accurately the other's hidden messages through internal dialogue, and the more sociocultural differences there are the more difficult it will be to accurately anticipate what the culturally different client is thinking but not saying.

Although we know part of what the client is thinking is negative and part is positive, there are indications that a greater proportion of our thinking tends to be negative, resulting in an asymmetrical balance. There are several ways to train counselors to hear their culturally different clients. Interpersonal process recall (Kagan, 1975) is offered as a popular method, in which an inquirer debriefs the client and counselor after a videotaped interview to help them clarify their thoughts to one another. The Triad Training Model is another method, in which the immediate and continuous debriefing occurs during the role-play interview itself. The primary emphasis of this chapter focused on the Triad Training Model as a means of learning to hear what culturally different clients are thinking but not saying. Although the Triad Training Model is used exclusively in training and not in direct service, variations of that model for use in direct service are also available.

EXERCISE: Implicit and Explicit Cultural Messages

There are explicit and implicit levels of communication across cultures. Participants are matched into culturally similar two-person teams in which both members are likely to understand one another's point of view. Each team will contain one speaker and one "alter ego." The alter ego is instructed to say out loud what the speaker is thinking but not saying.

Two teams will work together to plan a script that contains two levels of the conversation between culturally different persons, one explicit and one implicit.

The four-person group will then present a role play to the larger group in which two persons from culturally different backgrounds carry on a discussion while, after each statement, the alter ego for the speaker says out loud what the speaker is probably thinking but not saying directly. The exercise is useful for learning to interpret the mixed messages we send and receive in multicultural communication and articulate the internal dialogue of culturally different clients.

IMPLICIT AND EXPLICIT CULTURAL MESSAGES EXERCISE

Participant Objectives:
1. To express accurately what someone from a similar culture is thinking but not saying.
2. To interpret the implicit messages accurately.
3. To incorporate both explicit and implicit messages in an appropriate response.

Learning Objective:
1. What someone says may be different from what he or she means.

CHAPTER 10

Multiculturalism as a Fourth Force

Major objective:

1. To describe how multiculturalism is becoming a "fourth force" or dimension in counseling.

Secondary objectives:

1. To review the support for multiculturalism as a fourth force.
2. To demonstrate the implications of Westernization for counseling and psychology.
3. To identify non-Westernized alternatives for multicultural counseling.
4. To present ways that counseling can become more multicultural on a global scale.

Until recently, the field of counseling psychology has been a monocultural science, even though it was born in Central Europe and has spread throughout much of both the Western and non-Western world. Gielen (1994) documented the trends suggesting that this monocultural emphasis in psychology is changing:

> Following a brief review of global society, it is argued that (a) at present American psychology routinely neglects perspectives and findings developed in other countries; (b) this is true even if foreign contributions appear in English; (c) this state of affairs differs from the situation prevailing in the hard sciences; and (d) in response to the multicultural movement and global developments, mainstream psychology in the United States and elsewhere will become less ethnocentric in the near future. (p. 26)

Part of this chapter is reprinted from P. Pedersen (1998), *Multiculturalism as a fourth force*, Philadelphia, PA: Bruner/Mazel. Reprinted with permission.

There are contemporary global changes that are having increased influence in psychology and counseling demonstrating the positive consequence of a culture-centered perspective. First, the ratio of non-American to American psychological and counseling researchers is gradually but steadily increasing (Rosensweig, 1992), suggesting that psychology and counseling are growing faster outside than inside the United States. Second, all fields are becoming more global in their focus as a result of technological innovations. Third, there is a multicultural movement particularly in the social sciences that has raised sensitivity to cultural variables. Fourth, the topic of cultural and multicultural issues is becoming more widely accepted in counseling and psychology. Fifth, there is a reexamination of cultural bias in counseling and psychology so that instead of assuming values and beliefs there is more emphasis on discovering each population's unique explanation of its behavior and meaning.

Thompson, Ellis, and Wildavsky (1990) described "cultural theory" as providing the basis for a new perspective, dimension, or "force" in psychology and counseling:

> Social science is steeped in dualism: culture and structure, change and stability, dynamics and statics, methodological individualism and collectivism, voluntarism and determinism, nature and nurture, macro and micro, materialism and idealism, facts and values, objectivity and subjectivity, rationality and irrationality, and so forth. Although sometimes useful as analytic distinctions, these dualisms often have the unfortunate result of obscuring extensive interdependencies between phenomena. Too often social scientists create needless controversies by seizing upon one side of a dualism and proclaiming it the more important. Cultural theory shows that there is no need to choose between, for instance, collectivism and individualism, values and social relations or change and stability. Indeed we argue there is a need not to. (p. 21)

The chapters in this book have attempted to demonstrate these positive consequences of a multicultural or culture-centered perspective (P. Pedersen, 1997b, 1997c).

1. A Review of the "Fourth-Force" Position

The previous chapters in this book have described the need for multiculturalism in counseling, the difficulties in establishing multicultural perspectives, and what has to happen before multiculturalism can claim to be a fourth force. These chapters can be reviewed in terms of separating what is known from what is not yet known about the role of culture in counseling.

First, we know that fundamental changes are taking place in the social sciences and particularly in the fields of counseling and psychology. Some sort of paradigm shift is occurring. We know that these patterns of change are more than a continuation of historical patterns and represent a significantly different set of rules or patterns. There is still a great deal of disagreement about the basis of these fundamental changes, but there is increased attention to the metaphor of "culture" or "multicultural" as the basis for understanding these changing rules. We do not know what impact the notion of culture or multiculturalism will have on traditional counseling and psychological theories. These changes do not eliminate the importance of psychodynamic, behavioral, or humanistic perspectives but rather allow them to become more relevant by making culture central rather than marginal.

Second, we know there is a necessary distinction between the processes of multicultural contact, including the behaviors, attitudes, perceptions, and feelings of participants, and the institutional structures that characterize, support, or hinder intercultural contact. We know that there is a multicultural process within particular culturally heterogeneous societies. We do not know whether multiculturalism can become a significantly global fourth force by also providing similar processes and structures across and among nations and societies. There is a danger in overstating the validity of multiculturalism as an international phenomenon, even though at the same time there is some hope and promise for multiculturalism to have a positive global impact in the future.

Third, we know that each society has had a different interpretation of "multiculturalism." In South Africa, for example, cultural relativism justified oppression, deemphasizing the importance of differences in the promotion of apartheid practices as legitimate. Multiculturalism meant that different cultures had different mental health needs, and dislocation was seen as a problem of cultural adjustment to the dominant culture. As a consequence, the term *multicultural* in postapartheid society is not ideologically neutral and must be redefined and reframed to emphasize potential positive consequences of a multicultural perspective.

Fourth, we know that multiculturalism is not yet a dominant force in counseling and psychology (as reflected in contemporary textbooks), even though it may be playing an increasingly important role in research and theory building. There is a tendency to overstate the importance of multiculturalism as an established fact rather than an aspiration for the future. There are many barriers to establishing multiculturalism as a fourth force that continue to have a powerful influence. It will be important to better understand these barriers before they can be removed and multiculturalism can become more central to counseling as a reality.

Fifth, we know that the dominant culture in a monocultural perspective, at least for the United States, has been grounded in the values of the North American majority culture. This perspective has emphasized the importance of individual autonomy, the attainment of individual goals, and the minimizing of cultural perspectives of more collectivist minorities, immigrants, or others who place more emphasis on relationships. We do not know what the counseling implications will be for either individualism or collectivism as coexisting cultural perspectives.

Sixth, we know that culture and multiculturalism, broadly defined, acknowledge both within-group and between-groups similarities and differences beyond nationality and ethnicity. Deafness may be one example of a "culture" that is outside the ethnographic categories but in which the deaf have their own language, perspective, sense of persecution, and many of the other cultural features that an ethnic group might also have. We know that members of the deaf community define themselves as a cultural and linguistic minority group rather than as a disability group. We know that the cultural deficit model is as hurtful when applied to people who are deaf or who are labeled according to any other affiliation as when it is applied to ethnic or national minority groups. We have not, however, fully explored the consequences of defining multiculturalism broadly in a more inclusive perspective.

Seventh, we know that cultural similarity among youths may be more salient across cultures than other obvious national and ethnic differences. We know that youths from many if not most cultures share with one another similar tasks of psychosocial development across various sociocultural, political, and historical conditions that separate them from previous generations. We know that these youth-culture influences have a profound impact on identity development. Theoretical frameworks for studying identity formation are based on monocultural or dominant culture assumptions, typically Western, and there is a need for an understanding of identity formation that is more sensitive to rapidly changing social conditions.

Eighth, we know that multiculturalism will not only change the content of our thinking but the very process of thinking itself. The notion of social homogeneity that has been emphasized in the past is giving way to a perspective of cultural heterogeneity. Instead of self-homogenization, a multicultural perspective will advocate self-heterogenization; instead of social homogeneity, the new perspective will advocate cross-cultural migration. This new way of thinking emphasizes both the complexity and the dynamism of multiculturalism as a fourth force.

Ninth, we know that a multicultural perspective enhances the meaningfulness of counseling by providing a context in which to accurately assess, understand, and recommend change. We know that all counseling in a multicultural context reflects the biases of both the provider and the consumer of counseling. A multicultural systems perspective, as might typically be used in family counseling, seems to be the most promising approach to manage the complex and dynamic context in which counseling occurs, although we have much to learn about multiculturally sensitive counseling.

This summary of what we have learned from reading the previous chapters in this book describe the beginning of a process for describing and anticipating the many changes in counseling in an increasingly multicultural global context. I now examine some of the changes occurring in counseling and psychology and the adequacy of multiculturalism as a metaphor to describe those changes.

2. The Search for Global Universals in Counseling and Psychology

Counseling and psychology have been "imported disciplines" for most of the world's cultures that have adopted and transferred Western theories and problems to a quite different cultural milieu. Kagitcibasi (1996) pointed out the limitations for counseling and psychology as imported disciplines:

> What is common in the ideographic, hermeneutic, emic, indigenous, relativist, cultural approaches is an emphasis on the uniqueness of concepts in each cultural context, because they derive their meanings from these contexts. There is also a stress on the variability and the uniqueness of the individual case (person, culture, etc.) that requires its study from within and in its own right, defying comparison. In contrast, the nomothetic, positivist, etic, universalist, cross-cultural approaches study the "typical" not the unique, which can be compared using a common standard or measure. The emphasis is on the underlying similarities that render comparison possible. There appears to be a basic conflict between the emic and the etic if accepted as exclusive orientations, because being stuck in one would negate the other. (p. 11)

The importance of cultural context is a continuing theme in much of contemporary counseling and psychological research in part because of the increased importance of cultural and cross-cultural counseling and psychology and in part because of the life span inclusive approach to understanding human development. Context is often conceptualized as culture as the organizer of meaning in each context. First, counselors are joining anthropologists in studying contextual issues. Second, there is more recognition of cultural bias and ethnocentric orientations in theory and research derived from Western cultural contexts. Third, collaboration between counselors from Western and non-Western cultural contexts is increasing. Finally, there is increased emphasis on within-group variables across cultures in counseling research. Western counseling and psychology have promoted the "separated self" as the healthy prototype across cultures, making counseling and psychology part of the problem—through an emphasis on selfishness and lack of commitment—rather than part of the solution (Kagitcibasi, 1996).

Sinha (1997) described a similar perspective as "indigenizing" psychology to emphasize that (a) psychological knowledge is not to be externally imposed, (b) psychology needs to address every-day activities outside experimentally contrived laboratories, (c) behavior is best understood from the local frame of reference, and (d) psychology must reflect the sociocultural reality of its social context. "The ultimate goal of indigenous psychology is the development of a universal psychology that incorporates all indigenous (including Western) psychologies . . . . It only asserts that panhuman psychological principles and theories cannot be taken for granted or assumed merely because they are developed in the West" (p. 160). It is therefore not destructive to challenge mainstream theories and principles of psychology and counseling, but indigenization may be a step toward discovering true universals in psychology and counseling.

The search for a universal psychology has been a continuing theme in the literature. A unified perspective requires cross-cultural coherence, generalizing findings across cultural boundaries in the search for both cultural similarities and cultural differences. The importance of national cultures has been widely accepted as a barrier to the discovery of universals emphasizing "objective" rather than subjective data. According to Eysenck (1995):

> There are many reasons why psychology has failed to become a unified science, and I have tried to indicate what some of the major problems are that face us in our attempts to reach this goal. I have also tried to indicate how we can best proceed in our endeavors to reduce the fissionable nature of psychology. Greater recourse to cross-cultural studies is certainly one of the most important ways of furthering this goal: science must be universal, and there cannot be a psychology for the United States, and another for India or Japan or Nigeria. We search for universal laws, and these must be tested in many different countries. (p. 11)

People are changing the environment even while being changed by it at the same time in a continuous feedback loop. The human impact and the impact on humans cannot be considered independently as we study global change, imposing a basic uncertainty principle to human predictability. Understanding global change requires a complex system. Mesarovic, McGinnis, and West (1995) wrote:

> In this regard, the notion of a complex system in the mathematical theory of general systems is relevant. The starting point is the notion of a system as a relation among items or objects. A complex system is then defined as a relation among the systems. Items which form a complex system through interaction (i.e. subsystems) have their own recognizable boundary and existence while their behavior (functioning) is conditioned by their being integrated in the overall system. The human body is an obvious example: its parts (i.e. organs) are recognizable as such but their functioning (and even existence) is conditioned by their being part of the total system, i.e., body. (p. 27)

Other approaches emphasize the importance of nonlinear processes especially in applications of chaos and complexity theory. According to Butz (1997):

> The message that this group of theories brings is that adaptation is a nonlinear process, and therefore so are most of the dynamics we find in nature. We too are part of nature, and it follows that we operate by similar intrinsic dynamics. Therefore change is a nonlinear, perhaps even a chaotic or complex process by which all life forms adapt . . . . What does this group of theories offer social scientists? Nothing less than validation. It offers social scientists validation in their attempts to describe and define phenomena of a previously ineffable nature. (p. xvii)

The importance of linear, mechanistic, logical, positivist assumptions in which therapists are sometimes considered the "police of mental life" are matched with a quite different holistic epistemology.

Butz (1997) contrasted the more exclusive conventional psychological and counseling perspective with a new and much more inclusive approach to coping with development, as well as long-lasting and meaningful change. This new framework will build on diversity as a positive vehicle for meaningful change.

> This process may be painful and even feel chaotic, but on the other side of it is a new adaptation. How is it possible that society can foster this kind of process and connotation of adaptation? Through acceptance. Because the models that emphasize prediction and control, rational thought, and a linear worldview center on rejecting that which they cannot explain. Acceptance seems to be the key. Stated another way, acceptance is tolerance, tolerance of the difficult process life is and always will be . . . . What is it that must be tolerated? Others—for each other's own frailties, for the bifurcations, complexities, and chaotic experiences that must be endured to allow this evolution. If tolerance and acceptance are some of the watchwords for this new myth, then diversity becomes a core issue in allowing the pattern to form. (Butz, 1997, p. 239)

Cross-cultural psychology and counseling have presumed general laws of human behavior, and the discovery of those laws is the goal. What is also clear is that cultural context has an essential role in the search for general laws.

> In general, what we observe in our analysis, above all, is an invigorated attempt to reintroduce some form of contextualism in a psychology that has long ignored the importance of the environment, broadly defined, as a constitutive component of human behavior. It is not clear that most current cross-cultural approaches, which seem to assign secondary status to the role of culture in psychological explanation, will be successful in this quest, but it is very encouraging to see that after a slow start cross-cultural psychology has found a voice that is heard beyond the borders of its own provinces. (Lonner & Adamopoulos, 1997, p. 77)

Kuhn (1970) expressed the belief that a major paradigm shift will occur when scientific theories cannot adequately account for ideas, concepts, or data and when some new competing perspective better accommodates these data. Elements of analytical reductionism in psychology and counseling seem to be giving way to a more holistic, culturally inclusive, and integrative approach that recognizes that people from all populations are both similar and different at the same time. In that regard, the dual emphasis on both the universal and the particular becomes complementary and necessarily joined in a combined explanation. Culture provides a metaphor for joining the universal and the particular at the same time. The culture models or schema are both public and private. Shore (1996) wrote:

> In this sense, cultural models are empirical analogues of culture understood as knowledge. As we shall see they are not analogues in any simple sense, since public models are not exactly the same thing as mental models. But approaching culture as a collection of models has the advantage of showing that making sense of culture as an aspect of mind requires that we both distinguish and relate these two notions of model. (p. 44)

Cultural boundaries are not static but dynamic reflections of accelerated change and interact through contact in bidirectional ways in which each party learns from the other.

> The psychological conception of culture is not the culture external to the individual, but the culture internalized as a result of enculturation within the individual. Introducing the concept of internalized culture opens the door to a new territory of thought. Interest is now focused on how culture is experienced and internalized by the individual. Thus the psychological conception gives full recognition to individual differences in cultural processes. (Ho, 1994, p. 13)

Increased attention in counseling and psychology is being given to the effect of contact among culturally different people or groups in multicultural settings. This new emphasis on culture at the cross-national and cross-ethnic level has resulted from "(1) the search for culturally sensitive assessments in diagnosis and treatment of psychopathology, (2) world wide voluntary and non-voluntary migrations of individuals and groups, and (3) problems resulting from acculturation and adaptation" (Tanaka-Matsumi & Draguns, 1997, pp. 468–469). Culture has become more of a dynamic and constructed concept. Triandis (1997) observed:

> Psychology has finally realized that culture has a major role to play in the way psychology is shaped. That is so because we humans are all ethnocentric. This is a fundamental reality, reflecting that we all group up in a specific culture (even when it is cosmopolitan and a mixture of other cultures) and learn to believe that the standards, principles, perspectives and expectations that we acquire from our culture are the way to look at the world. Unexamined assumptions are one of the central aspects of culture. When we construct psychological theories, the more the subject matter deviates from biological and physiological phenomena, the more our culture intrudes in the shaping of the theories that we construct. (p. ix)

3. The Multicultural Alternative

Multiculturalism has been described in this book as a "fourth force" or fourth dimension, but neither of these terms is completely adequate. The fourth force implies competition with humanism, behaviorism, and psychodynamism, which is not the intent. By comparing the fourth dimension of multiculturalism with the fourth dimension of time in three-dimensional space, then the complementary is indicated but other problems arise. "The very term dimension itself indicates the inadequacy assigned to the human role. One would not characterize the role of natural phenomena in analogous terms, e.g. by talking about the ocean dimension or atmosphere dimension of global change" (Mesarovic et al., 1995, p. 9). Cultures, like every other subsystem, are constituent parts of global systems. Multiculturalism is a means of coping with cultural and social diversity in society.

> In less than three decades multiculturalism has become a word immediately recognized by policy makers, social commentators, academics and the general public in Western industrial countries, if not elsewhere. The rapid adoption of the term multiculturalism has occurred in a situation where there is increasing international concern about the limitations of existing policies to address changing patterns of inter-ethnic relations. (Inglis, 1995, p. 15)

Multiculturalism, while popular, is used in a variety of ways. The demographic-descriptive usage refers to ethnic or racial diversity in a population. The programmatic-political usage refers to programs and policy initiatives in response to diversity. The ideological-normative usage is a slogan for political action by diverse groups in contemporary society.

Huntington (1993) pointed out the importance of multicultural and multiethnic factors in understanding the national and international relationships and managing the potential conflict between those diverse groups. According to Dana (1998):

> A multicultural perspective insists that we must not only be equal under the law, we must also be able to understand ourselves as the authors of the laws that bind us . . . . This issue is central to mental health problems, research, diagnosis and services. Ultimately, each multicultural group must provide the idiosyncratic perspective and cultural/racial idiom in which all providers become fluent. This is the meaning of culturally competent mental health services. (p. 13)

In this way, every experience can be seen as a multicultural experience. *Multiculturalism* refers to all educational and training practices, research, administration, or direct service in which issues of nationality, ethnicity, language, socioeconomic status, gender, lifestyle, age, religion, ability, or any other of the almost endless list of formal and informal affiliations are addressed.

S. Sue (1998) identified sources of resistance to the term *multicultural-ism* as a fourth force. First, some view multiculturalism as competing with already established theories of psychological explanation in ways that threaten the professions of counseling and psychology. Second, the terms *multiculturalism* and *diversity* are closely associated with *affirmative action, quotas, civil rights, discrimination, reverse discrimination, racism, sexism, political correctness,* and other emotional terms. Third, to the extent that multiculturalism is connected with postmodernism (as in multiple perspectives and belief systems), the arguments against postmodernism as a valid theory would also apply to multiculturalism. Fourth, those favoring a universalist perspective contend that the same practice of counseling and therapy apply equally to all populations without regard to cultural differences. Fifth, others contend that there are no accepted standards for describing multiculturalism as a theory in practice and that it is too loosely defined to be taken seriously. Sixth, there are no measurable competencies for multicultural applications of counseling or adequate standards of practice. Seventh, multiculturalism is too complicated and it would be unrealistic to expect counselors to attend to such a range of factors simultaneously. Eighth, more research is needed on multicultural competencies, standards, methods, and approaches. Ninth, multicultural standards cannot be incorporated into the counseling profession until all groups have been included. Tenth, multiculturalism represents reverse racism, quota, and is anti-White. In discussing these sources of resistance, S. Sue (1998) pointed out the tendency to misrepresent or misunderstand the notion of multiculturalism and the dangers of that misunderstanding.

Multiculturalism in the U.S. context has been misunderstood partly as an outcome of the controversy raised by D'Souza (1991), who equated multiculturalism with a "politically correct minority perspective" (pp. xii–xiv) which demanded intellectual conformity in the name of putative commitment to diversity. Given the gross oversimplification of issues in the arguments, both those who support and those who oppose the argument about "political correctness" are wrong.

Others have opposed multiculturalism for fear that it would heighten ethnic conflict, divisions, and tensions, although there is no supporting evidence for those fears.

This is because when combined, as it is in the case studies, with a strong emphasis on policies of social justice, it removes much of the basis for resistance among ethnic minority groups. The focus on social justice also counters criticisms that multiculturalism simply serves to continue the exploited powerlessness of these minority groups. (Inglis, 1995, p. 66)

However, in situations in which there has been extended and violent conflict or a history of ethnic hostility, any reconciliation will be problematic. Although the multicultural model's ability to turn around conflict is problematic, the lack of better alternatives leaves no other choice, as long as the potential for success is realistic and the difficulties are acknowledged.

4. Conclusion

In science, experiences are categorized according to their qualities, dimensions, or variables. These variables are related to one another in systematic relationships and lawful ways. Theories depend on this network of relationships or laws to predict the future. When these predictions are confirmed, the theory is supported (Triandis, 1977). This book has explored the possibility that we are moving toward a generic theory of multiculturalism as a "fourth force" or dimension, complementary to the other three forces of psychodynamic, behavioral, and humanistic explanations of human behavior. This perspective assumes that multiculturalism is relevant throughout counseling and psychology as a generic rather than an exotic perspective. Labels, such as *multiculturalism*, tend to oversimplify complicated relationships, and to that extent they are dangerous. This book has attempted to call attention to the ways in which a multicultural perspective is better able to address the complicated and dynamic cultural context in which counseling is practiced than the alternative monocultural models.

Gielen (1994) described specific ways that the field of counseling and psychology can appropriately respond to the multicultural imperative for positive change.

1. Textbook authors should be asked to provide examples from a variety of societies in order to encourage reflection on the strengths and limitations of existing theories and research.
2. Textbooks should introduce cross-cultural perspectives alongside other perspectives.
3. Psychological theories should be routinely contextualized within a cross-cultural framework regarding research design and theory construction.
4. Psychological theories must be consistently understood within historical frameworks as products of a specific cultural context.
5. Journals in the United States and elsewhere should invite foreign authors, editors referees, and authors to submit materials.
6. American journals should systematically encourage authors to cite relevant foreign literature.
7. Textbooks can be jointly authored by authors from different cultural backgrounds.

8. Institutional support and funding should be available for collaborative research and scholarship across cultural boundaries. If psychology fails to respond appropriately, then the field of psychology may be divided up among other related fields as a subspecialty.

Whether or not multiculturalism emerges as a fourth force in counseling and psychology at a level of magnitude equivalent to that of psychodynamic, behavioral, and humanistic theories, culture will continue to provide a valuable metaphor for understanding ourselves and others. It is no longer possible for counselors and psychologists to ignore their own cultural context or the cultural context of their clients. Until the multicultural perspective is understood as having positive consequences toward making counseling more rather than less relevant and increasing rather than decreasing the quality of counseling, little real change is likely to occur.

EXERCISE: Drawing a House

We are culturally conditioned to respond in predetermined ways to different situations. Ask participants to select a partner as culturally different from themselves as possible. Distribute one page of paper and one pen to every team of two persons. Ask each two-person team to hold on to the same pen or pencil and, with both persons holding the same pen at the same time, to draw a house on the paper. Instruct the teams partners *not to talk* with one another while doing the task.

After 2 or 3 minutes, ask them to stop and collect the house drawings. Show each drawing in turn to the group and encourage participants to talk about or present their "house" to the group, discussing any special problems or surprises that came up during the task. Then lead a discussion on how we are culturally conditioned to respond by emphasizing relationship (e.g., accommodating our partners) or task (e.g., drawing a "good" house). Likewise we may be culturally conditioned to favor the role of leader (who controlled the pencil?) or follower (who facilitated the leader?).

The cultural patterns of real-life responses are of course situationally specific for each cultural group, and in real life no single extreme (leader/follower, task/relationship) will apply uniformly to any one cultural group. The discussion should focus on examples of how two cultures might not share the same culturally conditioned expectations in the same situation. In some cases, cultural differences will be facilitative and preferred, as in a work team in which one member favors the leader role and the other favors the follower role. In other cases, cultural differences will present problems, as in a work team in which one member favors relationships and the other favors task accomplishment.

DRAWING A HOUSE EXERCISE

Participant Objectives:
1. To demonstrate situational leader–follower patterns.
2. To demonstrate situational relationship–task patterns.
3. To report patterns of personal culture.

Learning Objective:
1. Cultural differences are displayed in situational patterns of behavior.

REFERENCES

Adler, P. S. (1975). The transitional experience: An alternative view of culture shock. *Journal of Humanistic Psychology, 15*(4), 13.

Akbar, N. (1979). African roots of Black personality. In W. Smith, K. Burlew, M. Mosley, & W. Whitney (Eds.), *Reflections on Black psychology* (pp. 79–87). Washington, DC: University Press of America.

American Counseling Association. (1995). *Code of ethics and standards of practice.* Alexandria, VA: Author.

American Psychiatric Association. (1994). *Diagnostic and statistical manual of mental disorders* (4th ed.). Washington, DC: Author.

Amir, Y. (1969). Contact hypothesis in ethnic relations. *Psychological Bulletin, 71,* 319–342.

Arce, C. A. (1981). A reconsideration of Chicano culture and identity. *Daedalus, 110,* 177–192.

Arredondo, P., Toporek, R., Brown, S. P., Jones, J., Locke, D. C., Sanchez, J., & Stadler, H. (1996). Operationalization of the multicultural counseling competencies. *Journal of Multicultural Counseling and Development, 24,* 42–78.

Atkinson, D. R., Morten, G., & Sue, D. W. (1997) *Counseling American minorities: A cross-cultural perspective* (5th ed.). New York: McGraw-Hill Companies.

Atkinson, D. R., Morten, G., & Sue, D. W. . *Counseling American minorities* (5th ed.). Boston: McGraw-Hill.

Aubrey, R. F. (1977). Historical development of guidance and counseling and implications for the future. *Personnel and Guidance Journal, 55,* 288–295.

Augsburger, D. W. (1992). *Conflict mediation across cultures.* Louisville, KY: Westminister/John Knox Press.

Axelson, J. A. (1999). *Counseling and development in a multicultural society* (3rd ed.). Pacific Grove, CA: Brooks/Cole.

Bailey, F. M. (1981). *Cross-cultural counselor education: The impact of microcounseling paradigms and traditional classroom methods on counselor trainee effectiveness.* Unpublished doctoral dissertation, Department of Counselor Education, University of Hawaii.

Banks, J. A. (1981). The stages of ethnicity: Implications for curriculum reform. In J. A. Banks (Ed.), *Multi-ethnic education: Theory and practice* (pp. 129–139). Boston: Allyn & Bacon.

Barnes, B. (1991). *Mediation in the Pacific Pentangle (PCR) working paper.* Honolulu: University of Hawaii Press.

Basic Behavioral Science Task Force of the National Advisory Mental Health Council. (1996). Basic behavioral science research for mental health: Sociocultural and environmental processes. *American Psychologist, 51,* 722–731.

Benesch, K. F., & Ponterotto, J. G. (1989). East and West: Transpersonal psychology and cross cultural counseling. *Counseling and Values, 33,* 121–131.

Berry, J. W. (1980). Ecological analysis for cross-cultural psychology. In N. Warren (Ed.), *Studies in cross cultural psychology* (pp. 157–189). New York: Academic Press.

Berry, J. W., & Kim, U. (1988). Acculturation and mental health. In P. Dasen, J. W. Berry, & N. Sartorius (Eds.), *Cross-cultural psychology and health: Towards applications* (pp. 207–236). London: Sage.

Berry, J. W., Poortinga, Y. H., Segall, M. H., & Dasen, P. J. (1992). *Cross cultural psychology: Research and applications.* Cambridge, England: Cambridge University Press.

Bjorkqvist, K., & Fry, D. P. (1997). Conclusions: Alternatives to violence. In D. P. Fry & K. Bjorkqvist (Eds.), *Cultural variation in conflict resolution* (pp. 243–254). Mahwah, NJ: Erlbaum.

Bohr, N. (1950). On the notion of causality and complementarity. *Science, 11,* 51–54.

Bolman, W. (1968). Cross-cultural psychotherapy. *American Journal of Psychiatry, 124,* 1237–1244.

Bond-Claire, J., Pilner, P., & Stoker, S. C. (1998). An expert–novice approach to assessing implicit models of the self. In A. Colby & J. B. James (Eds.), *Competence and character through life* (pp. 113–137). Chicago: University of Chicago Press.

Borders, L. D., Fong-Beyette, M. L., & Cron, E. A. (1988). In-session cognitions of a counseling student: A case study. *Counselor Education and Supervision, 28,* 59–70.

Brewer, M. B. (1991). The social self: On being the same and different at the same time. *Personality and Social Psychology Bulletin, 17,* 475–482.

Brislin, R. S., Cushner, K., Cherrie, C., & Young, M. (1998). *Intercultural interactions: A practical guide.* Beverly Hills, CA: Sage.

Bruner, J. S. (1986). *Actual minds, possible worlds.* Cambridge, MA: Harvard University Press.

Bryne, R. H. (1977). *Guidance: A behavioral approach.* Englewood Cliffs, NJ: Prentice Hall.

Butz, M. R. (1997). *Chaos and complexity: Implications.* Washington, DC: Taylor & Francis.

Caplan, G. (1976). The family as support system. In G. Caplan & M. Killilea (Eds.), *Support systems and mutual help: Multidisciplinary explorations* (pp. 50–62). New York: Grune & Stratton.

Carter, R. (1991). Cultural values: A review of empirical research and implications for counseling. *Journal of Counseling and Development, 70,* 164–173.

Carter, R. T., & Helms, J. E. (1987). The relationship of Black value orientations to racial identity attitudes. *Measurement and Evaluation in Counseling and Development, 19,* 185–195.

Cayleff, S. E. (1986). Ethical issues in counseling gender, race and culturally distinct groups [Special issue: Professional ethics]. *Journal of Counseling and Development, 64*, 345–347.

Center for Applied Linguistics. (1982). *Providing effective orientation: A training guide.* Washington, DC: CAL Refugee Services Report.

Chambers, J. C. (1992). *Triad training: A method for teaching basic counseling skills to chemical dependency counselors.* Unpublished doctoral dissertation, Department of Educational Psychology and Counseling, University of South Dakota.

Cheung, F. M. C. (1986). Psychopathology among Chinese people. In M. H. Bond (Ed.), *The psychology of the Chinese people* (pp. 171–213). Hong Kong: Oxford University Press.

Christopher, J. C. (1992). *The role of individualism in psychological well-being: Exploring the interplay of ideology, culture and social science.* Unpublished doctoral dissertation, University of Texas at Austin.

Church A. T. (1982). Sojourner adjustment. *Psychological Bulletin, 91*, 540–572.

Cobb, S. (1976). Social support as a moderator of life stress. *Psychosomatic Medicine, 38*, 300–314.

Coffman, T. L., & Harris, M. C. (1984, August). *The U-curve of adjustment to adult life transitions.* Paper presented at the annual convention of the American Psychological Association, Toronto, Ontario, Canada.

Cohen, R. (1991). *Negotiating across cultures.* Washington, DC: U.S. Institute of Peace.

Corey, G., Corey, M., & Callanan, P. (1998). *Issues and ethics in the helping professions* (5th ed.). Pacific Grove, CA: Brooks/Cole.

Cortese, A. J. (1989). The interpersonal approach to morality: A gender and cultural analysis. *Journal of Social Psychology, 129*, 429–442.

Cross, W. E. (1971). The negro-to-Black conversion experience. *Black Worlds, 20*, 13–17.

Cross, W. (1991). *Shades of Black.* Philadelphia: Temple University Press.

Cruz, V., & Cooley, J. (1994). *White privilege: An adaptation of an essay by Peggy McIntosh "White privilege: Unpacking the invisible knapsack"* [Hungry Mind Review, Fall]. Birmingham, MI: Psychologists for Social Responsibility.

Dana, R. H. (1993). *Multicultural assessment perspectives for professional psychology.* Boston: Allyn & Bacon.

Dana, R. H. (1998). *Understanding cultural identity in intervention and assessment.* Thousand Oaks, CA: Sage.

D'Andrea, M., Daniels, J., & Heck, R. (1991). Exploring the different levels of multicultural counseling training in counselor education. *Journal of Counseling and Development, 70*, 143–150.

Delworth, U. (1989). Identity in the college years: Issues of gender and ethnicity. *Journal of National Association of Student Personnel Administrators, 26*, 162–166.

DeVoss, G. (1973). *Socialization for achievement: Essays on the cultural psychology of the Japanese.* Berkeley: University of California Press.

Dizzard, J. E. (1970). Black identity, social class, and Black power. *Journal of Social Issues, 26*, 195–207.

Draguns, J. G. (1989). Dilemmas and choices in cross-cultural counseling: The universal versus the culturally distinctive. In P. Pedersen, J. Draguns, W. Lonner, & J. Trimble (Eds.), *Counseling across cultures* (pp. 3–22). Honolulu: University of Hawaii Press.

Dreikurs, R. (1972, August). Equality: The life style of tomorrow. *The Futurist,* pp. 153–155.

D'Souza, D. (1991). *Illiberal education: The politics of race and sex on campus.* New York: Free Press.

Dubinskas, F. A. (1992). Culture and conflict: The cultural roots of discord. In D. M. Kolb & J. M. Bartuneck (Eds.), *Hidden conflict in organizations* (pp. 187–207). Newbury Park, CA: Sage.

DuBois, W. E. B. (1982). The Negro American family. In F. Erickson & J. Schultz (Eds.), *The counselor as gatekeeper: Social interaction in interviews.* New York: Academic Press. (Original work published 1908)

Duryea, M. L. B. (1992). *Conflict and culture: A literature review and bibliography.* Victoria, British Columbia, Canada: University of Victoria Institute for Dispute Resolution.

Ellis, A. (1962). *Reason and emotion in psychotherapy.* New York: Lyle Stuart.

Erikson, E. H. (1968). *Identity: Youth and crisis.* New York: Norton.

Eysenck, H. J. (1995). Cross-cultural psychology and the unification of psychology. *World Psychology, 1*(4), 11–30.

Firestone, R. W. (1997a). *Combating destructive thought processes: Voice therapy and separation theory.* Thousand Oaks, CA: Sage.

Firestone, R. W. (1997b). *Suicide and the inner voice: Risk, assessment, treatment and case management.* Thousand Oaks, CA: Sage.

Fiske, S. T., & Taylor, S. E. (1991). *Social cognition* (2nd ed.). New York: McGraw-Hill.

Fry, D., & Bjorkqvist, K. (1997). Culture and conflict-resolution models: Exploring alternatives to violence. In D. P. Fry & K. Bjorkqvist (Eds.), *Cultural variation in conflict resolution* (pp. 9–23). Mahwah, NJ: Erlbaum.

Fukuyama, M. A. (1990). Taking a universal approach to multicultural counseling. *Counselor Education and Supervision, 30,* 6–17.

Fuqua, D. R., Johnson, A. W., Anderson, M. W., & Newman, J. L. (1984, September). Cognitive methods in counselor training. *Counselor Education and Supervision, 24,* 85–95.

Fuqua, D. R., Newman, J. F., Anderson, M. W., & Johnson, A. W. (1986). *Psychological Reports, 58,* 163–172.

Furnham, A., & Bochner, S. (1986). *Culture shock: Psychological reactions to unfamiliar environment.* London: Methuen.

Furnham, A. (1988). The adjustment of sojourners. In Y. Y. Kim & W. B. Gudykunst (Eds.), *International and intercultural communication annual: Vol. XI. Cross cultural adaptation, current approaches* (pp. 42–61). Newbury Park, CA: Sage.

Gay, G. (1984). Implications of selected models of ethnic identity development for educators. *Journal of Negro Education, 54*(1), 43–52.

Geertz, C. (1973). *The interpretation of cultures.* New York: Basic Books.

Geertz, C. (1975). On the nature of anthropological understanding. *American Scientist, 63*, 329–338.

Gibbs, J. T. (1974). Patterns of adaptation among Black students at a predominantly White university: Selected case studies. *American Journal of Orthopsychiatry, 44*, 728–740.

Gielen, U. P. (1994). American mainstream psychology and its relationship to international and cross-cultural psychology. In A. L. Communian & U. P. Gielen (Eds.), *Advancing psychology and its applications: International perspectives* (pp. 26–40). Milan, Italy: Franco Angeli.

Gielen, U. P., & Markoulis, D. C. (1994). Preference for principled moral reasoning: A developmental and cross-cultural perspective. In L. L. Adler & U. P. Gielen (Eds.), *Cross-cultural topics in psychology* (pp. 73–88). Westport, CT: Greenwood.

Gilligan, C. (1982). *In a different voice.* Cambridge, MA: Harvard University Press.

Gilligan, C. (1987). Moral orientation and moral development. In E. F. Kittay & D. T. Meyers (Eds.), *Women and moral theory* (pp. 19–33). Totowa, NJ: Rowman & Littlefield.

Goldstein, A. (1981). *Psychological skill training: The structural learning technique.* New York: Pergamon.

Goodyear, R. K., & Sinnett, E. R. (1984). Current and emerging ethical issues for counseling psychology. *Counseling Psychologist, 12*, 87–98.

Gottlieb, B. H., & Hall, A. (1980). Social networks and the utilization of preventive mental health services. In R. H. Proce, R. F. Ketterer, B. C. Bader, & J. Monahan (Eds.), *Prevention in mental health: Research policy and practice* (pp. 167–194). Beverly Hills, CA: Sage.

Gudykunst, W. B., & Hammer, M. R. (1988). Strangers and hosts: An uncertainty reduction based theory of intercultural adaptation. In Y. Y. Kim & W. B. Gudykunst (Eds.), *Cross-cultural adaptation: Current approaches* (pp. 106–139). Newbury Park, CA: Sage.

Gudykunst, W., & Ting-Toomey, S. (1988). *Culture and interpersonal communication.* Newbury Park, CA: Sage.

Guthrie, R. (1976). *Even the rat was white: A historical view of psychology.* New York: Harper & Row.

Haas, L. J., & Malouf, J. L. (1995). *Keeping up the good work: A practitioner's guide to mental health ethics* (2nd ed.). Sarasota, FL: Professional Resource Press.

Hall, E. T. (1976). *Beyond culture.* Garden City, NY: Anchor.

Hardiman, R. (1982). *White identity development: A process oriented model for describing the racial consciousness of White Americans.* Unpublished doctoral dissertation, University of Massachusetts, Amherst.

Heilbronner, R. L. (1975). *An inquiry into the human prospect.* New York: Norton.

Helms, J. E. (1984). Toward a theoretical explanation of the effects of race on counseling: A Black and White model. *The Counseling Psychologist, 12*, 153–165.

Helms, J. E. (1985). Cultural identity in the treatment process. In P. Pedersen (Ed.), *Handbook of cross-cultural counseling and therapy* (pp. 239–245). Westport, CT: Greenwood Press.

Helms, J. (1990). *Black and White racial identity: Theory, research and practice*. New York: Greenwood Press.

Helms, J. E., & Cook, D. A. (1999). *Using race and culture in counseling and psychotherapy: Theory and process*. Needham Heights, MA: Allyn & Bacon.

Herlihy, B., & Corey, G. (1996). *ACA ethical standards casebook* (5th ed.). Alexandria, VA: American Counseling Association.

Herlihy, B., & Corey, G. (1997). *Boundary issues in counseling: Multiple roles and responsibilities*. Alexandria, VA: American Counseling Association.

Hermans, H. J. M., & Kempen, H. J. G. (1993). *The dialogical self: Meaning as movement*. New York: Academic Press.

Hermans, H. J. M., Kempen, H. J. G., & Van Loon, R. J. P. (1992). The dialogical self: Beyond individualism and rationalism. *American Psychologist, 47,* 23–33.

Herrnstein, R. J., & Murray, C. (1994). *The bell curve: Intelligence and class structure in American life*. New York: Free Press.

Hines, A., & Pedersen, P. (1980). The cultural grid: Matching social system variables and cultural perspectives. *Asian Pacific Training Development Journal, 1,* 5–11.

Hines, P. L., Stockton, R., & Morran, D. K. (1995). Self-talk of group therapists. *Journal of Counseling Psychology, 42,* 242–248.

Hirsch, P., & Stone, G. L. (1983). Cognitive strategies and the client conceptualization process. *Journal of Counseling Psychology, 30,* 566–572.

Ho, D. Y. E. (1994). Introduction to cross-cultural psychology. In L. Adler & U. P. Gielen (Eds.), *Cross-cultural topics in psychology* (pp. 3–13). Westport, CT: Praeger.

Hofstede, G. (1980). *Cultures consequences: International differences in work related values*. Beverly Hills, CA: Sage.

Hofstede, G. (1986). Cultural differences in teaching and learning. *International Journal of Intercultural Relations, 10,* 301–320.

Hofstede, G. (1991). *Cultures and organizations: Software of the mind*. London: McGraw-Hill.

Hofstede, G. J., & Pedersen, P. B. (in press). Synthetic national cultures: Intercultural learning through simulation games. *Journal of Simulation and Gaming*.

Hopkins, W. E. (1997). *Ethical dimensions of diversity*. Thousand Oaks, CA: Sage.

Horney, K. (1967). *Feminine psychology*. New York: Norton.

Howard, G. S. (1991). Culture tales: A narrative approach to thinking, cross-cultural psychology and psychotherapy. *American Psychologist, 46,* 187–197.

Hsu, F. L. K. (1985). The self in cross cultural perspective. In A. J. Marsella & F. L. K. Hsu (Eds.), *Culture and self: Asian and Western perspectives* (pp. 25–55). New York: Tavistock.

Hu, H. C. (1945). The Chinese concepts of face. *American Anthropologist, 46,* 45–64.

Huntington, S. P. (1993). The clash of civilizations. *Foreign Affairs, 72*(3), 22–49.

Hwang, K. K. (1998). *Guanxi* and *Mientze*: Conflict resolution in Chinese society. *Intercultural Communication Studies, 7*(1), 17–42.

Ibrahim, F. A. (1991). Contribution of cultural worldview to generic counseling and development. *Journal of Counseling and Development, 70,* 6–12.

Ickes, W. (1988). Attributional style and the self concept. In L. Y. Abramson (Ed.), *Social cognition and clinical psychology: A synthesis* (pp. 66–97). New York: Guilford Press.

Inglis, C. (1995). *Multiculturalism: New policy responses to diversity* (U.N. Policy Paper No. 4). New York: United Nations Publications.

International Association for Cross-Cultural Psychology. (1978, July). *Statement on ethics*. Bellingham, WA: Author.

Irvin, R., & Pedersen, P. (1996). The internal dialogue of culturally different clients: An application of the Triad Training Model. *Journal of Multicultural Counseling and Development, 23,* 4–11.

Ivey, A. E. (1987). The multicultural practice of therapy: Ethics, empathy and dialectics. *Journal of Social and Clinical Psychology, 5,* 195–204.

Ivey, A. E. (1988). *Intentional interviewing and counseling: Facilitating client development.* Pacific Grove, CA: Brooks/Cole.

Jackson, B. (1975). Black identity development. In L. Golubschick & B. Persky (Eds.), *Urban social and educational issues* (pp. 158–164). Dubuque, IA: Kendall-Hall.

Jahan, S. (1999). *Tenth annual United Nations human development report.* New York: United Nations Publications.

Jandt, F. E., & Pedersen, P. B. (1996). *Constructive conflict management: Asia-Pacific cases.* Thousand Oaks, CA: Sage.

Jensen, A. R. (1969). How much can we boost IQ and scholastic achievement? *Harvard Educational Review, 39,* 1–12.

Jones, E. E., & Korchin, S. J. (1982). *Minority mental health.* New York: Praeger.

Jordan, A. E., & Meara, N. M. (1990). Ethics and the professional practice of psychologists: The role of virtues and principles. *Professional Psychology: Research and Practice, 21,* 107–114.

Jourard, S. M. (1964). *The transparent self.* Princeton, NJ: Van Nostrand.

Kagan, N. (1975). Influencing human interaction: Eleven years with IPR. *Canadian Counselor, 9*(2), 74–95.

Kagitcibasi, C. (1996). *Family and human development across cultures.* Mahwah, NJ: Erlbaum.

Katz, J. H. (1978). *White awareness: Handbook for anti-racism training.* Norman: University of Oklahoma Press.

Katz, R. H. (1993). *The straight path: A story of healing and transformation in Fiji.* Reading, MA: Addison-Wesley.

Kealey, D. J. (1988). *Explaining and predicting cross-cultural adjustment and effectiveness: A study of Canadian technical advisors overseas.* Unpublished doctoral dissertation, Department of Psychology, Queens University, Kingston, Ontario, Canada.

Kendall, P., Howard, C., Dennis, L., & Hays, R. C. (1989). Self referent speech and psychopathology: The balance of positive and negative thinking. *Cognitive Therapy and Research, 18,* 588–590.

Kendler, H. H. (1993). Psychology and the ethics of social policy. *American Psychologist, 48,* 1046–1053.

Khatib, S. M., & Nobles, W. W. (1977). Historical foundations of African psychology and their philosophical consequences. *Journal of Black Psychology, 4,* 91–101.

Kim, B. C. (1981). *New urban immigrants: The Korean community in New York.* Princeton, NJ: Princeton University Press.

Kim, U., & Berry, J. W. (Eds.). (1993). *Indigenous psychologies: Research and experience in cultural context.* Newbury Park, CA: Sage.

Kim, U., Triandis, H. C., Kagitcibasi, C., Choi, S. C., & Yoon, G. (1994). *Individualism and collectivism.* Thousand Oaks, CA: Sage.

Kimberlin, C. L., & Friesen, D. D. (1980). Sex and conceptual level empathic responses to ambivalent affect. *Counselor Education and Supervision, 19,* 252–258.

Kiselica, M. S. (1999). *Confronting prejudices and racism during multicultural training.* Alexandria, VA: American Counseling Association.

Kitano, H. H. L. (1989). A model for counseling Asian Americans. In P. Pedersen, J. Draguns, W. Lonner, & J. Trimble (Eds.), *Counseling across cultures* (3rd ed., pp. 139–152). Honolulu: University of Hawaii Press.

Kitchner, K. S. (1984). Intuition, critical evaluation, and ethical principles: The foundation for ethical decisions in counseling psychology. *The Counseling Psychologist, 12,* 43–55.

Kitchner, K. S. (1986). Teaching applied ethics in counselor education: An integration of psychological processes and philosophical analysis. *Journal of Counseling and Development, 64,* 306–310.

Kline, W. B. (1988). Training counselor trainees to talk to themselves: A method of focusing attention. *Counselor Education and Supervision, 22,* 296–302.

Kluckhohn, F. R., & Strodtbeck, F. L. (1961). *Variations in value orientation* New York: Harper & Row.

Kohls, L. R. (1996). *Survival kit for overseas living for Americans planning to live and work abroad* (3rd ed.). Yarmouth, ME: Intercultural Press.

Kramer, R. A., & Messick, D. M. (1995). *Negotiation as a social process.* Thousand Oaks, CA: Sage.

Kruger, J. A. (1992). *Racial/ethnic intergroup disputing and dispute resolution in the United States: A bibliography and resource guide.* (Available from Judith A. Kruger, P.O. Box 3, Collingswood, NJ 08108)

Kuhn, T. S. (1970). *The structure of scientific revolutions* (2nd ed.). Chicago: University of Chicago Press.

Kurpius, D. J., Benjamin, D., & Morran, D. K. (1985). Effects of reaching a cognitive strategy on counselor trainee internal dialogue and clinical hypothesis formulation. *Journal of Counseling Psychology, 32,* 263–271.

LaFromboise, T. D., Coleman, H. L. K., & Hernandez, A. (1991). Development and factor structure of the Cross-Cultural Inventory–Revised. *Professional Psychology: Research and Practice, 22,* 380–388.

LaFromboise, T. D., & Foster, S. L. (1989). Ethics in multicultural counseling. In P. Pedersen, J. Draguns, W. Lonner, & J. Trimble (Eds.), *Counseling across cultures* (3rd ed., pp. 115–136). Honolulu: University of Hawaii Press.

LaFromboise, T. D., Foster, S., & James, A. (1996). Ethics in multicultural counseling. In P. Pedersen, J. Draguns, W. Lonner, & J. Trimble (Eds.), *Counseling across cultures* (4th ed., pp. 47–72). Thousand Oaks, CA: Sage.

Lakoff, G., & Johnson, M. (1980). *Metaphors we live by.* Chicago: University of Chicago Press.

Ledermann, L. C. (1996). Internal muzak: An examination of intrapersonal relationships. *Interaction and Identity: Information and Behavior, 5,* 197–214.

Lee, C. C. (1997). Promise and pitfalls of multicultural counseling. In C. C. Lee (Ed.), *Multicultural issues in counseling: New approaches to diversity* (2nd ed., pp. 3–13). Alexandria, VA: American Counseling Association.

Lee, W. M. I. (1999). *An introduction to multicultural counseling.* Philadelphia: Taylor & Francis.

LeResche, D. (Ed.). (1993, Summer). Native American perspectives on peacemaking. *Mediation Quarterly, 10*(4).

LeVine, R., & Padilla, A. (1980). *Crossing cultures in therapy: Pluralistic counseling for the Hispanic.* Monterey, CA: Brooks/Cole.

Lifton, R. (1986). *The Nazi doctors: Medical killing and the psychology of genocide.* New York: Basic Books.

Locke, D. C. (1990). A not so provincial view of multicultural counseling. *Counselor Education and Supervision, 30,* 18–25.

Lonner, W. J., & Adamopoulos, J. (1997). Culture as antecedent to behavior. In J. W. Berry, Y. H. Poortinga, & J. Pandey (Eds.), *Handbook of cross-cultural psychology* (Vol. I, pp. 43–83). Needham Heights, MA: Allyn & Bacon.

Lonner, W. J., & Ibrahim, F. A. (1989). Assessment in cross-cultural counseling. In P. Pedersen, J. Draguns, W. Lonner, & J. Trimble (Eds.), *Counseling across cultures* (3rd ed., pp. 229–334). Honolulu: University of Hawaii Press.

Lukes, S. (1973). *Individualism: Key concepts in the social sciences.* Oxford, England: Blackwell.

Lund, B., Morris, C., & LeBaron-Duryea, M. (1994). *Conflict and culture.* Vancouver, British Columbia, Canada: University of Victoria Institute for Dispute Resolution.

Luria, A. R. (1961). *The role of speech in the regulation of normal and abnormal behavior* (J. Tizard, Ed.). New York: Liveright.

Mahoney, M. J. (1988). Constructive metatheory: 1. Basic features and historical foundations. *International Journal of Personal Construct Psychology, 1,* 1–35.

Mahoney, M. J., & Arnkoff, D. B. (1978). Cognitive and self control therapies. In S. I. Garfield & A. E. Bergin (Eds.), *Handbook of psychotherapy and behavioral change: An empirical analysis* (2nd ed., pp. 689–722). New York: Wiley.

Mappes, D. C., Robb, G. P., & Engels, D. W. (1985). Conflicts between ethics and law in counseling and psychotherapy. *Journal of Counseling and Development, 64,* 246–252.

Marcia, J. E. (1980). Identity in adolescence. In J. Adelson (Ed.), *Handbook of adolescent psychology* (pp. 159–187). New York: Wiley.

Markus, H., & Kitayama, S. (1991). Culture and the self: Implications for cognition, emotion and motivation. *Psychological Review, 98,* 224–253.

Martinez, J. L., Jr. (1977). *Chicano psychology.* New York: Academic Press.

McCall, G. J., & Simmons, J. L. (1991). Levels of analysis: The individual, the dyad and the larger social group. In B. M. Montgomery & S. Duck (Eds.), *Studying interpersonal interaction* (pp. 56–81). New York: Guilford Press.

McGoldrick, M., Pearce, J., & Giordano, J. (1982). *Ethnicity and family therapy.* New York: Guilford Press.

McIntosh, P. (1989, July/August). White privilege: Unpacking the invisible knapsack. *Peace and Freedom,* pp. 8–10

McNamee, S., & Gergen, K. J. (1992). *Therapy as social construction*. Newbury Park, CA: Sage.

Mead, G. H. (1982). *The individual and the social self: Unpublished work of George Herbert Mead* (D. L. Miller, Ed.). Chicago: University of Chicago Press. (Original work published 1934)

Meichenbaum, D. (1974). *Cognitive–behavior modification*. Morristown, NJ: General Learning Press.

Meichenbaum, D. (1977). *Cognitive–behavior modification: An integrative approach*. New York: Plenum Press.

Mesarovic, M. D., McGinnis, D. L., & West, D. A. (1995). *Cybernetics of global change: Human dimension and managing of complexity* (United Nations MOST Policy Paper No. 3). New York: United Nations Publications.

Meyer, M. (1994). *"Ho'oponopono—To set right."* Unpublished manuscript, Harvard Graduate School of Education.

Micozzi, M. S. (1996). *Fundamentals of complementary and alternative medicine*. New York: Churchill Livingstone.

Miles, R. (1989). *Racism*. New York: Routledge.

Miller, J. (1994). Cultural diversity in the morality of caring: Individually oriented versus duty-based interpersonal moral codes. *Cross-Cultural Research, 28*(1), 3–39.

Miller, N., & Brewer, M. (1984). *Groups in contact: The psychology of desegregation*: New York: Academic Press.

Milliones, J. (1980). Construction of a Black consciousness measure: Psychotherapeutic implications. *Psychotherapy: Theory, Research and Practice, 17*, 175–182.

Montgomery, R. L., & Haemmerlie, F. M. (1987). Self-perception theory and hetersocial anxiety. In J. E. Maddux, C. D. Stoltenberg, & R. Rosenwein (Eds.), *Social process in clinical and counseling psychology* (pp. 139–152). New York: Springer Verlag.

Morin, A. (1993). Self talk and self awareness: On the nature of the relation. *Journal of Mind and Behavior, 14*, 223–234.

Morin, A. (1995). Characteristics of an effective internal dialogue in the acquisition of self information. *Imagination, Cognition and Personality, 15*(1), 45–48.

Morran, D. K. (1986). Relationship of counselor self-talk and hypothesis formulation to performance level. *Journal of Counseling Psychology, 33*, 395–400.

Morran, D. K., Kurpius, D. J., Brack, C. H. J., & Brack, G. (1995). A cognitive skills model for counselor training and supervision. *Journal of Counseling and Development, 73*, 384–389.

Mossman, M. (1976). *Kulia I ka lokahi i ke ola* [Strive for harmony in life]. Unpublished manuscript, Pikake Wahilani, Honolulu, Hawaii.

Nakamura, H. (1964). *Ways of thinking of Eastern peoples: India, China, Tibet, Japan*. Honolulu: University of Hawaii Press.

Neck, C. P., Steward, C., Crag, L., & Manz, C. C. (1995). Thought self leadership as a framework for enhancing the performance of performance appraisers. *Journal of Applied Behavioral Science, 31*, 270–302.

Nelkin, D. (1984). *Science as intellectual property*. New York: MacMillan.

Niemeyer, G. J. (1993). *Constructivist assessment: A casebook*. Newbury Park, CA: Sage.

Niemeyer, G. J., Fukuyama, M. A., Bingham, R. P., Hall, L. E., & Mussenden, M. E. (1986). Training cross-cultural counselors: A comparison of the pro and anticounselor triad models. *Journal of Counseling and Development, 64*, 437–439.

Nutt-Williams, E., & Hill, C. E. (1996). The relationship between self-talk and therapy process variables for novice therapists. *Journal of Counseling Psychology, 43*, 170–177.

Oberg, K. (1958). *Culture shock and the problem of adjustment to new cultural environments.* Washington, DC: U.S. Department of State.

O'Connor, A. (1999). *The multi-city study of urban inequality* [Report]. Washington, DC: Russell Sage Foundation.

Oetting, E. R., & Beauvais, R. (1991). Orthogonal cultural identification theory: The cultural identification of minority adolescents. *International Journal of the Addictions, 25*, 655–685.

Opotow, S. (1990). Moral exclusion and injustice: An introduction. *Journal of Social Issues, 46,* 1–20.

O'Quinn, G. M. (1986). A study of the relationship between counselor internal dialogue and counseling performance. *Dissertation Abstracts International, 47*, 180.

Panglinawan, L. (1972). *Ho'oponopono Project II.* Honolulu: Cultural Committee, Queen Liliuokaloni Children's Center.

Parham, T. A., & Helms, J. E. (1981). The influence of Black students' racial identity attitudes on preference for counselors' race. *Journal of Counseling Psychology, 28*, 250–257.

Patterson, C. H. (1978). Cross-cultural or intercultural psychotherapy. *International Journal for the Advancement of Counseling, 1*, 231–248.

Patterson, C. H. (1996). Multicultural counseling: From diversity to universality. *Journal of Counseling and Supervision, 74,* 227–231.

Pearce, W. B. (1983, Summer). *International Communication Association Newsletter, 11*(3).

Pearson, R. E. (1990). *Counseling and social support: Perspectives and practice.* Newbury Park, CA: Sage.

Pedersen, A., & Pedersen, P. (1985). The cultural grid: A personal cultural orientation. In L. Samovar & R. Porter (Eds.), *Intercultural communication: A reader* (pp. 50–62). Belmont, CA: Wadsworth.

Pedersen, P. (1968). A proposal: That counseling be viewed as an instance of coalition. *Journal of Pastoral Care, 11,* 43–54.

Pedersen, P. (1972, September). *Simulating the problem role in cross-cultural counseling.* Paper presented at the annual convention of the American Psychological Association, Honolulu, HI.

Pedersen, P. (1973, September). *A cross-cultural coalition training model for educating mental health professionals to function in multicultural populations.* Paper presented at the Ninth International Congress of Ethnological Sciences, Chicago.

Pedersen, P. (1974). Cross-cultural communications training for mental health professionals. *International and Intercultural Communication Annual, 1,* 53–64.

Pedersen, P. (1975). Counseling clients from other cultures: Two training designs. In D. Hoopes (Ed.), *Readings in intercultural communication* (pp. 47–53). Pittsburgh, PA: Intercultural Communication Network.

Pedersen, P. (1976). A model for training mental health workers in cross-cultural counseling. In J. Westermeyer & B. Maday (Eds.), *Culture and mental health* (pp. 83–99). The Hague, The Netherlands: Mouton.

Pedersen, P. (1977). The Triad Model of cross-cultural counselor training. *Personnel and Guidance Journal, 56,* 94–100.

Pedersen, P. (1979). Cross-cultural Triad Training Model: The case of the counselor. In M. Asante & E. Newmark (Eds.), *Handbook of intercultural communication* (pp. 403–420). Buffalo: State University of New York Press.

Pedersen, P. (1981). *Developing interculturally skilled counselors* (Final Report, NIMH Grant 1-724-MH-1552). Honolulu, HI: Institute of Behavioral Science.

Pedersen, P. (1983a). Asian theories of personality. In R. Corsini & A. Marsella (Eds.), *Contemporary theories of personality* (Rev. ed., pp. 537–582). Itasca, IL: Peacock.

Pedersen, P. (1983b). The transfer of intercultural training skills. *Interventional Journal of Psychology, 18,* 333–345.

Pedersen, P. (1984). The cultural complexity of mental health. In P. Pedersen, N. Sartorius, & A. J. Marsella (Eds.), *Mental health services* (pp. 13–27). Beverly Hills, CA: Sage.

Pedersen, P. (1986). Developing interculturally skilled counselors: A training program. In H. Lefley & P. Pedersen (Eds.), *Cross-cultural training of mental health professionals* (pp. 73–88). Springfield, IL: Charles C Thomas.

Pedersen, P. (1988). *Handbook for developing multicultural awareness.* Alexandria, VA: American Counseling Association.

Pedersen, P. (1989). Developing multicultural ethical guidelines for psychology. *International Journal of Psychology, 24,* 643-652.

Pedersen, P. (1991a). Counseling international students. *The Counseling Psychologist, 19,* 10–58.

Pedersen, P. (Ed.). (1991b). Multiculturalism as a fourth force in counseling [Special issue]. *Journal of Counseling and Development, 70*(Whole issue).

Pedersen, P. (1991c). Multiculturalism as a generic approach to counseling. *Journal of Counseling and Development, 70,* 6–12.

Pedersen, P. (1993). The multicultural dilemma of the White cross-cultural researcher. *The Counseling Psychologist, 21,* 229–232.

Pedersen, P. (1994). *Handbook for developing multicultural awareness* (2nd ed.). Alexandria, VA: American Counseling Association.

Pedersen, P. (1995a). Culture-centered ethical guidelines for counselors. In J. Ponterotto, J. M. Casas, L. A. Suzuki, & C. M. Alexander (Eds.), *Handbook of multicultural counseling and therapy* (pp. 34–49). Thousand Oaks, CA: Sage.

Pedersen, P. (1995b). *The five stages of culture shock: Critical incidents around the world.* Westport, CT: Greenwood Press.

Pedersen, P. (1997a). The cultural context of the American Counseling Association Code of Ethics. *Journal of Counseling and Development, 76,* 23–29.

Pedersen, P. (1997b). *Culture-centered counseling interventions.* Thousand Oaks, CA: Sage.

Pedersen, P. (1997c). Doing the right thing: A question of ethics. In K. Cushner & R. Brislin (Eds.), *Improving intercultural interactions: Vol. II. Models for cross-cultural training programs* (pp. 149–165). Thousand Oaks, CA: Sage.

Pedersen, P. (1997d). Recent trends in cultural theories. *Applied and Preventive Psychology, 6,* 221–231.

Pedersen, P. (1998). *Multiculturalism as a fourth force.* Philadelphia, PA: Brunner/Mazel.

Pedersen, P. (1999a). Confronting racism through increased awareness, knowledge, and skill as a culture-centered primary prevention strategy. In M. Kiselica (Ed.), *Confronting prejudice and racism during multicultural training* (pp. 107–122). Alexandria, VA: American Counseling Association.

Pedersen, P. (1999b). Intercultural understanding: Finding common ground without losing integrity. In D. Christie, D. Wagner, & D. Winter (Eds.), *Peace, conflict and violence: Peace psychology for the 21st century.* Englewood Cliffs, NJ: Prentice Hall.

Pedersen, P. (2000). *Hidden messages in culture-centered counseling.* Thousand Oaks, CA: Sage.

Pedersen, P., Carter, R. T., & Ponterotto, J. G. (1996). The cultural context of psychology: Questions for accurate research and appropriate practice. *Cultural Diversity and Mental Health, 2,* 205–216.

Pedersen, P., Draguns, J., Lonner, W., & Trimble, J. (1996). *Counseling across cultures* (4th ed.). Thousand Oaks, CA: Sage.

Pedersen, P., Holwill, F., & Shapiro, J. (1978). A cross cultural training procedure for classes in counselor education. *Journal of Counselor Education and Supervision, 17,* 233–237.

Pedersen, P., & Ivey, A. (1993). *Culture-centered counseling skills.* Westport, CT: Greenwood Press.

Pedersen, P., & Jandt, F. E. (1996). Cultural contextual models for creative conflict management. In F. E. Jandt & P. B. Pedersen (Eds.), *Constructive conflict management: Asia-Pacific cases* (pp. 3–26). Thousand Oaks, CA: Sage.

Phillips, A. A. (1990). Inner voices, inner selves: A study of internal conversation in narrative. *Dissertation Abstracts International, 50,* 3677.

Phinney, J. S. (1990). Ethnic identity in adolescents and adults. *Psychological Bulletin, 108,* 499–514.

Pike, R. (1966). *Language in relation to a united theory of the structure of human behavior.* The Hague, The Netherlands: Mouton.

Ponterotto, J. G. (1988). Racial/ethnic minority research: A content analysis and methodological critique. *Journal of Counseling Psychology, 3,* 410–418.

Ponterotto, J. G., & Casas, J. M. (1991). *Handbook of racial/ethnic minority counseling research.* Springfield, IL: Charles C Thomas.

Ponterotto, J. G., Casas, J. M., Suzuki, L. A., & Alexander, C. M. (1995). *Handbook of multicultural counseling.* Thousand Oaks, CA: Sage.

Ponterotto, J. G., & Pedersen, P. B. (1993). *Prejudice prevention: A developmental counseling perspective.* Beverly Hills, CA: Sage.

Ponterotto, J. G., Rieger, B. P., Barrett, A., & Sparks, R. (1994). Assessing multicultural counseling competence: A review of instrumentation. *Journal of Counseling and Development, 72,* 316–322.

Pope-Davis, D., & Coleman, H. (1997). *Multicultural counseling competencies.* Thousand Oaks, CA: Sage.

Pope-Davis, D. B., & Dings, J. G. (1995). The assessment of multicultural counseling competencies. In J. G. Ponterotto, J. M. Casas, L. A. Suzuki, & C. M. Alexander (Eds.), *Handbook of multicultural counseling* (pp. 287–311). Thousand Oaks, CA: Sage.

Pukui, M. K., Hartig, E. W., & Lee, C. A. (1972). *Nana I Ke Kumu* [Look to the source]. Honolulu, HI: Queen Lili'uokalani Children's Center.

Rabie, M. (1994). *Conflict resolution and ethnicity*. Westport, CT: Praeger.

Rest, J. R., & Narvaez, D. (1994). *Moral development in the professions: Psychology and applied ethics*. Hillsdale, NJ: Erlbaum.

Reynolds, D. K. (1980). *The quiet therapies: Japanese pathways to personal growth*. Honolulu: University of Hawaii Press.

Richardson, B., & Stone, G. L. (1981). Effects of a cognitive adjunct procedure within a microtraining situation. *Journal of Counseling Psychology, 28,* 168–175.

Ridley, C. (1989). Racism in counseling as an aversive behavioral process. In P. Pedersen, J. Draguns, W. Lonner, & J. Trimble (Eds.), *Counseling across cultures* (3rd ed., pp. 55–79). Honolulu: University of Hawaii Press.

Ridley, C. R. (1995). *Overcoming unintentional racism in counseling: A practitioner's guide to intentional intervention*. Thousand Oaks, CA: Sage.

Rosensweig, M. R. (1992). Psychological science around the world. *American Psychologist, 39,* 877–884.

Rothenberg, A. (1979). Einstein's creative thinking and the general theory of relativity: A documented report. *American Journal of Psychiatry, 136,* 38–43.

Rothenberg, A. (1983). Psychopathology and creative cognition. *Archives of General Psychiatry, 40,* 937–942.

Ruben, B. D., & Kealey, D. J. (1970). Behavioral assessment of communication competency and the prediction of cross-cultural adaptation. *International Journal of Intercultural Relations, 3*(1), 15–47.

Rubin, J. Z., Pruitt, D. G., & Kim, S. H. (1994). *Social conflict: Escalation, stalemate and settlement* (2nd ed.). New York: McGraw Hill.

Sarbin, T. R. (1986). The narrative as a root metaphor for psychology. In T. R. Sarbin (Ed.), *Narrative psychology: The storied nature of human conduct* (pp. 3–21). New York: Praeger.

Sartorius, N., Pedersen, P. B., & Marsella, A. J. (1984). Mental health services across cultures: Some concluding thoughts. In P. Pedersen, N. Sartorius, & A. Marsella (Eds.), *Mental health services: The cross-cultural context* (pp. 281–286). Beverly Hills, CA: Sage.

Sedlacek, W. E., & Brooks, J. C. (1976). *Racism in American education: A model for change*. Chicago: Nelson Hall.

Segall, M. H., Dasen, P. R., Berry, J. W., & Poortinga, Y. H. (1990). *Human behavior in global perspective: An introduction to cross-cultural psychology*. New York: Pergamon Press.

Shaw, G. B. (1919). *Man and superman: A comedy and a philosophy*. New York: Brentanos.

Sheikh, A., & Sheikh, K. S. (1989). *Eastern and Western approaches to healing: Ancient wisdom and modern knowledge*. New York: Wiley.

Sheikh, A. A., & Sheik, K. S. (1996). *Healing East and West: Ancient wisdom and modern psychology.* New York: Wiley.

Shook, E. V. (1985). *Ho'oponopono.* Honolulu: University of Hawaii Press.

Shore, B. (1996). *Culture in mind: Cognition, culture and the problem of meaning.* New York: Oxford University Press.

Shorter, J. (1987). The social construction of an "us": Problems of accountability and narratology. In R. Burnett, P. McGhee, & D. Clarke (Eds.), *Accounting for relationships* (pp. 225–247). New York: Methuen.

Shweder, R. A., Mahapatra, M., & Miller, J. A. (1990). Culture and moral development. In *Cultural psychology: Essays on comparative human development* (pp. 130–204). New York: Cambridge University Press.

Siegrist, M. (1995). Inner speech as a cognitive process mediating self consciousness and inhibiting self deception. *Psychological Reports, 76,* 259–265.

Sinha, D. (1997). Indigenizing psychology. In J. W. Berry, Y. H. Poortinga, & J. Pandey (Eds.), *Handbook of cross-cultural psychology* (Vol. I, pp. 129–170). Needham Heights, MA: Allyn & Bacon.

Smith, E. (1991). Ethnic identity development: Toward the development of a theory within the context of majority/minority status. *Journal of Counseling and Development, 70,* 181–188.

Smith, J. A., Harre, R., & Van Langenhove, L. (1995). *Rethinking psychology.* London: Sage.

Snarey, J. R. (1985). Cross-cultural universality of social–moral development: A critical review of Kohlbergian research. *Psychological Bulletin, 97,* 202–232.

Sodowsky, G. R., Taffe, R. C., Gutkin, T. B., & Wise, L. I. (1994). Development of the Multicultural Counseling Inventory: A self-report measure of multicultural competencies. *Journal of Counseling Psychology, 41,* 137–148.

Spengler, P. M., Strohmer, D. C., Dixon, D. N., & Shivy, V. A. (1995). A scientist–practitioner model of psychological assessment: Implications for training, practice and research. *The Counseling Psychologist, 23,* 506–537.

Steenbarger, B. N. (1991). All the world is not a stage: Emerging contextualist themes in counseling and development. *Journal of Counseling and Development, 70,* 288–296.

Stephen, C. W., & Stephen, W. G. (1992). Reducing intercultural anxiety through intercultural contact. *International Journal of Intercultural Relations, 16,* 89–106.

Stewart, E. C. (1972). *American cultural patterns: A cross-cultural perspective.* Yarmouth, ME: Intercultural Press.

Stigler, J. W., Shweder, R. A., & Herdt, G. (1990). *Cultural psychology: Essays on comparative human development.* New York: Cambridge University Press.

Strohmer, D. C., Moilapen, D. L., & Barry, L. J. (1988). Personal hypothesis testing: The role of consistency and self-schema. *Journal of Counseling Psychology, 33,* 56–65.

Strong, S. (1995). From social psychology: What? *The Counseling Psychologist, 23,* 686–690.

Strous, M., Skuy, M., & Hickson, J. (1993). Perception of the Triad Model's efficacy in training family counselors for diverse South African groups. *International Journal for the Advancement of Counseling, 16,* 307–318.

Sue, D. W. (1977). Barriers to effective cross-cultural counseling. *Journal of Counseling Psychology, 24,* 420–429.

Sue, D. W. (1980). *Evaluation report from DISC: 1978–79.* Honolulu, HI: East West Center.

Sue, D. W. (1981). *Counseling the culturally different.* New York: Wiley Interscience.

Sue, D. W., Arrredondo, P., & McDavis, R. J. (1992). Multicultural counseling competencies and standards: A call to the profession. *Journal of Counseling and Development, 70,* 477–486.

Sue, D. W., Berneir, J. E., Durran, A., Feinberg, L., Pedersen, P., Smith, C. J., & Vasquez-Nuttall, G. (1982). Cross-cultural counseling competencies. *The Counseling Psychologist, 19*(2), 45–52.

Sue, D. W., Carter, R. T., Casas, J. M., Fouad, N. A., Ivey, A. E., Jensen, M., LaFromboise, T., Manese, J. E., Ponterotto, J. G., & Vasquez-Nutall, E. (1998). *Multicultural counseling competencies.* Thousand Oaks, CA: Sage.

Sue, D. W., & Sue, D. (1972). Counseling Chinese Americans. *Personnel and Guidance Journal, 50,* 637–645.

Sue, D. W., & Sue, D. (1990). *Counseling the culturally different: Theory and practice* (2nd ed.). New York: Wiley.

Sue, D. W., & Sue, D. (1999). *Counseling the culturally different: Theory and practice* (3rd ed.). New York: Wiley.

Sue, S. (1998). In search of cultural competencies in psychology and counseling. *American Psychologist, 53,* 440–448.

Sullivan, H. S. (1953). *The interpersonal theory of psychiatry.* New York: Norton.

Sunoo, J. J. M. (1990, October). Some guidelines for mediators of intercultural disputes. *Negotiation Journal,* 383–389.

Suzuki, L., Meller, P., & Ponterotto, J. (1996). *Handbook of multicultural assessment.* San Francisco: Jossey-Bass.

Swartz, R. M. (1986). The internal dialogue: On the asymmetry between positive and negative coping thoughts. *Cognitive Therapy and Research, 10,* 591–605.

Swartz, R. M., & Garamoni, G. L. (1989). Cognitive balance and psychopathology: Evaluation of an information processing model of positive and negative states of mind. *General Psychology Review, 9,* 271–294.

Szapocznik, J., Kurtines, W. M., & Fernandez, T. (1980). Bicultural involvement and adjustment in Hispanic-American youths. *International Journal of Intercultural Relations, 4,* 353–365.

Taft, R. (1977). Comments on the 1974 Tapp Report on the ethics of cross cultural research. *IACCP Cross Cultural Psychology Newsletter, 11*(4), 2–8.

Tajfel, H. (Ed.). (1978). *Differentiation between social groups.* London: Academic Press.

Tanaka-Matsumi, J., & Draguns, J. G. (1997). Culture and psychopathology. In J. W. Berry, M. H. Segall, & C. Kagitcibasi (Eds.), *Handbook of cross-cultural psychology* (Vol. 3, pp. 449–491). Boston: Allyn & Bacon.

Tapp, J. L., Kelman, H., Triandis, H., Wrightman, L., & Coelho, G. (1974). Continuing concerns in cross cultural ethics: A report. *International Journal of Psychology, 9,* 231–349.

Tart, C. T. (1975). Some assumptions of orthodox, Western psychology. In C. T. Tart (Ed.), *Transpersonal psychologies* (pp. 59–112). New York: Harper & Row.

Thomas, C. (1971). *Boys no more.* Beverly Hills, CA: Glencoe Press.

Thompson, M., Ellis, R., & Wildavsky, A. (1990). *Cultural theory.* San Francisco: Westview Press.

Ting-Toomey, S. (1985). Toward a theory of conflict and culture. In W. Gudykunst, L. P. Stewart, & S. Ting-Tommey (Eds.), *Communication, culture and organizational processes* (pp. 71–86). Beverly Hills, CA: Sage.

Ting-Toomey, S., & Cole, M. (1990). Intergroup diplomatic communication: A face-negotiation perspective. In F. Korsenny & S. Ting-Toomey (Eds.), *Communicating for peace: Diplomacy and negotiation* (pp. 77–95). Newbury Park, CA: Sage.

Toldson, I., & Pasteur, A. (1975). Developmental stages of Black self-discovery: Implications for using Black art forms in group interaction. *Journal of Negro Education, 44,* 130–138.

Tong, B. (1971). The ghetto of the mind: Notes on the historical psychology of Chinese Americans. *Amerasian Journal, I,* 28.

Triandis, H. C. (1972). *The analysis of subjective culture.* New York: Wiley.

Triandis, H. C. (1975). Cultural training, cognitive complexity and interpersonal attitudes. In R. Brislin, S. Bochner, & W. Lonner (Eds.), *Cross-cultural perspectives on learning* (pp. 39–78). New York: Wiley.

Triandis, H. C. (1977). *Interpersonal behavior.* Monterey, CA: Brooks/Cole.

Triandis, H. C. (1980). Values, attitudes and interpersonal behavior. In H. Howe & M. Page (Eds.), *Nebraska symposium on motivation, 1979* (Vol. 27, pp. 195–260). Lincoln: University of Nebraska Press.

Triandis, H. C. (1997). Forward. In J. W. Berry, P. R. Dasen, & T. S. Saraswathi (Eds.), *Handbook of cross-cultural psychology* (Vol. 2, pp. ix–x). Boston: Allyn & Bacon.

Triandis, H. C., Bontempo, R., Leung, K., & Hui, C. H. (1990). A method for determining cultural, demographic and person constructs. *Journal of Cross-Cultural Psychology, 21,* 302–318.

Trimble, J. E. (1976). Value differences among American Indians: Concerns for the concerned counselor. In P. Pedersen, W. J. Lonner, & J. G. Draguns (Eds.), *Counseling across cultures* (pp. 65–81). Honolulu: University of Hawaii Press.

Vontress, C. E. (1971). *Counseling Negroes.* Boston: Houghton Mifflin.

Vygotsky, L. S. (1962). *Thought and language* (E. Hanfmann & G. Vakar, Eds. & Trans.). Cambridge, MA: MIT Press.

Wade, P., & Bernstein, B. L. (1991). Culture sensitivity training and counselor's race: Effects on Black female client's perceptions and attrition. *Journal of Counseling Psychology, 38,* 9–15.

Watson-Gegeo, K., & White, G. (Eds.). (1990). *The discourse of disentangling: Conflict discourse in Pacific societies.* Palo Alto, CA: Stanford University Press.

Watt, A. W. (1961). *Psychotherapy East and West.* New York: Mentor Press.

Watts, A. (1963). *The two hands of God: The myths of polarity.* New York: Braziller.

Weidman, H. (1975). Concepts as strategies for change. *Psychiatric Annals, 5,* 312–314.

White, J. L. (1984). *The psychology of Blacks: An Afro-American perspective.* Englewood Cliffs, NJ: Prentice Hall.

Williams, L. N. (1978). *Black psychology: Compelling issues and views* (2nd ed.). Washington, DC: University Press of America.

Wrenn, C. G. (1962). The culturally encapsulated counselor. *Harvard Educational Review, 32,* 444–449.

Wrenn, C. G. (1985). Afterward: The culturally encapsulated counselor revisited. In P. Pedersen (Ed.), *Handbook of cross-cultural counseling and therapy* (pp. 323–329). Westport, CT: Greenwood Press.

Yankelovitch, D. (1972). *Supermoney.* New York: Random House.

Zastrow, C. (1988). What really causes psychotherapy change? *Journal of Independent Social Work, 2*(3), 5–16.

INDEX